Rough Guide to Sustainability

2nd edition

by Brian Edwards

RIBA Enterprises

© Brian Edwards, 2005
Second Edition
First Edition published in 2002

Published by RIBA Enterprises Ltd, 15 Bonhill Street, London EC2P 2EA

ISBN 1 85946 174 3

Stock Code 3675

British Library Cataloguing in Publications Data
A catalogue record for this book is available from the British Library.

Publisher: Steven Cross
Commissioning Editor: Matthew Thompson
Project Editor: Anna Walters
Editor: Alasdair Deas
Designed and typeset by Philip Handley
Printed and bound by Cambridge Printing, Cambridge

Contents

Acknowledgements | *Page* v

| 1 | **The Environmental, Educational and Professional Context** | Environmental Stress | 3 |

The Challenge of Sustainability | 7

Nature as Design Guide | 11

Is it Oil or Water that Matters? | 16

Towards a Cross-cultural Understanding of Sustainability | 17

The Aesthetics of Sustainability: New Visual Paradigms | 18

What is Sustainable Development? | 19

Johannesburg World Summit on Sustainable Development | 20

The Impact of Buildings | 22

Buildings as Wealth Creation | 23

The Idea of 'Capital' | 24

The Concept of 'Natural and Cultural Capital' | 25

Monitoring Progress Towards Sustainable Development | 27

Education for Sustainability: from School to University | 28

Advisory Panels on Education for Sustainable Development | 31

Ecology, Consumption and Architecture | 32

Architecture, Floods and Agriculture | 34

A Brief History of Architectural Education for Sustainability | 36

A Review of Education for Sustainability in the Construction Professions | 47

2 Resources

Energy Use and Global Warming | 55

EU Energy Directive | 58

Changes to UK Energy Policy | 58

Climate Change | 62

How Does Global Warming Work? | 66

The Importance of Energy | 67

Climate Instability and Building Design | 68

Renewable Energy | 69

Renewable Energy and Taxation | 71

Main Types of Renewable Energy | 72

Other Renewable Energy Sources | 84

Strategies for Energy Efficiency | 89

Integrating the Three 'E's: Energy, Environment and Ecology | 90

Contents

2 Resources *continued*

Importance of Indicators 94
Water: Tomorrow's Oil? 97
Water: Poverty and Health 98
Domestic Water Collection 103
Reducing Water Demand 104
Recycling of Water 106
The Need for Integration of All Resources 107

3 **Sustainable Design and
   Construction**

Life-cycle Assessment 113
A Working Definition of LCA 116
Other Environmental Management Tools 117
Specific Building Type Environmental Assessment Tools 120
Measuring the Environmental Impact of Materials Used in Construction ... 121
Waste 126
Complexities of Designing for Waste Reduction 127
Which is the Greener: Steel or Concrete? 131
The Four 'R's – Reduce, Reuse, Recycle and Recover 134
Buildings, Health and Construction Materials 141
Comfort 141
Being Pollution-free 142
Responsive and Stimulating Environments 144
Windcatchers 146
Window Design 149
Healthy Materials 149

4 **Design Solutions**

Space, Time and Sustainability 157
Sustainability as a Key Quality Indicator 159
Action for Sustainable Design 160
Lessons from Vernacular Architecture 162
Design Approaches for Key Building Types 166
City Form for the 21st Century 209

Acknowledgements

The author wishes to thank Spon Press, Architectural Press, Earthscan and John Wiley & Sons Ltd for permission to adapt parts of earlier books and journal articles by the author for use in this edition. This includes the section on school design from *Green Buildings Pay* (Spon Press: Edwards, 2003), sections on waste, materials and pollution from *Sustainable Architecture* (Architectural Press: Edwards, 1999), sections on sustainability and nature from *Green Architecture* (AD/Academy: Edwards, 2001) and the chapter by the author on professional education from *The Sustainability Curriculum* edited by John Blewitt and Cedric Cullingford (Earthscan, 2004). It also includes an article from the journal *Sustainable Development* published by John Wiley & Sons Ltd.

The author wishes to thank the many architects who have provided illustrations used to support the argument of this book.

The cover illustration uses a plan drawing of the Eden Project, designed by Grimshaw and reproduced with their permission.

The Environmental, Educational and Professional Context

1

1 The Environmental, Educational and Professional Context

Fifty per cent of all resources consumed across the planet are used in construction, making it one of the least sustainable industries in the world. However, our daily lives are carried out in and on constructions of one sort or another: we live in houses, we travel on roads, we work in offices and we socialise in bars and pubs. Contemporary human civilisation depends on buildings for its continued shelter and existence, and yet our planet cannot support the current level of resource consumption. Clearly, something has to change, and architects, as building designers, have an important role to play in that change.

What does it mean to be sustainable? As we shall see, the definition of sustainability has grown out of a number of important world congresses, and encompasses not just construction but all the resources needed to support human activity. For the architect, sustainability is a complex concept. A large part of designing sustainably is to do with addressing global warming through energy conservation and using techniques such as life-cycle assessment to maintain a balance between capital cost and long-term asset value. However, designing sustainably is also about creating spaces that are healthy, economically viable and sensitive to social needs. It is concerned with respecting natural systems and learning from ecological processes.

Origins of sustainability

Nature as support	Nature as inspiration	Ecological systems	Environmental protection
■ food ■ clean air ■ water	■ Ruskin ■ Lethaby ■ Wright	■ habitats ■ rainforests ■ biodiversity	■ global warming ■ waste and pollution ■ resource depletion

Environmental Stress

The World Health Organization estimated in 2003 that global warming was causing 150,000 deaths a year. This was largely the result of sea-level changes affecting agricultural production, lack of rainfall and the evaporation of drinking water supplies. In addition to the 50 per cent contribution that the burning of fossil fuels for heating, lighting and ventilating buildings makes to global warming, transport is another major contributor (about 25 per cent worldwide): hence the importance of the interaction between building design, urban design and town planning. Also, because of the long life of a typical building, it is important to think in the long term and be willing to pay today for green technologies whose benefits will flow in the future.

Shades of green design

Light green	Mid green	Dark green
Affordable now with financial payback in 8–10 years	Provision made for green technology which is not affordable today but will be necessary during lifetime of building to maintain comfort levels and resource availability, e.g. ■ photovoltaics and local wind-generated electricity ■ rainwater harvesting ■ grey water recycling ■ waste digestion or conversion to energy	Buildings which are independent of grid supplies (energy and water) and, over their lifetime, generate more power and resources than they consume. Such buildings can also be carbon neutral in their selection of construction materials.

Environmental damage resulting from current construction practices will be manifested first in our cities. It is here that the stresses will be felt first – rising temperatures, health problems caused by air pollution or contaminated water, food shortages and energy scarcity. Individual buildings may still function adequately but the collective landscape of cities and their relationship to the global ecosystem will begin to fail. This is because cities are a cocktail of impacts – the waste chain is long, deep and pervasive. Cities are also increasing their footprints and becoming more densely inhabited. Half of all humans now live in urban areas; about one-quarter of those live in cities with over a million inhabitants, and one-half of them live in megacities of over eight million people. These megacities are where global environmental stress will be felt first – in the big conurbations like Tokyo, Mexico City and São Paulo.

Fig 1.1
Half of the human population now live in cities
of over 1 million people. Sydney, Australia.

Doomsday scenario for the year 2050

- Air –
  unbreathable
- Water –
  undrinkable
- Waste –
  unmanageable
- Fossil fuels –
  exhausted
- Planet –
  unliveable

Addressing environmental stress can only be achieved by the use of more intelligent technologies, greater respect for natural resources and a shift from non-renewal resource exploitation to self-sustaining renewable practices. The city has a key role to play in the quest to establish a more symbiotic relationship between buildings, land and nature. As one of the units of the city, the design of buildings, moderated by life-cycle assessments, can make an important contribution to sustainability. Buildings can produce their own energy, capture and recycle their own water, employ recycled materials, encourage the reuse of waste, and balance CO_2 (carbon dioxide) released during construction and building work against CO_2 converted back into oxygen by planting trees elsewhere.

The advantage of looking at buildings rather than major urban areas is their relative simplicity. Buildings have predictable performance characteristics, with readily measured inputs and outputs. If society accepts the idea of sustainable design in buildings, then the sustainable development of cities will follow. In fact, it is sustainable construction that informs sustainable design, which, in turn, influences sustainable development, not vice versa. The complexity of the development of sustainable cities is a barrier to action, whereas in buildings the simplicity of the resource impacts can be exploited to allow the new generation of green architecture to shine as a beacon for change. Increasingly, this is the agenda adopted by some of our most highly respected practitioners – Norman Foster, Nicholas Grimshaw, Richard Rogers and Michael Hopkins.

Carbon dioxide production is essentially an urban consequence, but the level of emissions depends on many factors: climate, land use patterns, density and lifestyle. Action to limit CO_2 production can be taken on many fronts. Microclimates can be modified to enhance human comfort levels, thereby using less energy. Cold northern cities can benefit by improving shelter and harvesting solar radiation, both relatively simple and cost-effective solutions. In hot climates,

Fig 1.2
Mixing land uses reduces the need for transport and hence lessens the consumption of fossil fuels.
Source: LDDC

Fig 1.3
Low-density cities, such as Milton Keynes, depend upon high levels of energy use. They are unsustainable in the long term.
Source: MKDC

trees and buildings can be grouped to create shade and channel natural air currents, thereby reducing the need for air-conditioning.

Land use patterns, too, have a big impact on carbon emissions. The dispersed, single land use city generates a great deal more CO_2 than the traditional mixed-use neighbourhood. The extra consumption of fossil fuels, and the accompanying increased CO_2 emissions, is the result of private modes of transport and energy-inefficient detached buildings. Population density is a significant issue: public transport only becomes economically viable in compact cities. Dense urban patterns with a diversity of land uses achieve significantly lower CO_2 generation than typical modern suburban cities. This is why carbon dioxide production per head of population varies between countries. It is the pattern of living that is the key.

CO_2 emissions by head of population per country

USA	5.85 tonnes	Japan	2.35 tonnes	China	0.65 tonnes
UK	2.92 tonnes	EU	2.31 tonnes	India	0.23 tonnes

Source: Adapted from Peter Smith, *Options for a Flexible Planet*, Sustainable Building Network, Sheffield University, 1996, p. 38.

Lifestyle is clearly a related issue. As we become more prosperous, we desire and consume more. Consumption carries a corresponding burden of resource use, waste generation and, ultimately, CO_2 production. Buildings which are necessary to support life and consumption, could, through better design, reduce adverse ecological impacts. The great irony is that the world's most advanced nations are also its greatest polluters. Industrialisation sows the seeds of its own destruction by generating high levels of carbon emissions, leading directly to global warming. Architecture alone cannot solve global environmental problems but it can make a significant contribution to the creation of more sustainable human habitats.

The environmental think tank The Rocky Mountain Institute predicts that society can achieve a fourfold improvement in productivity without consuming further resources. This *factor four* concept is based on the assumption that leaner technologies, greater use of recycling and better management and design will allow mankind to grow without further ecological damage. Underpinning this idea is the notion of 'natural capital' — a kind of global accounting system for all

Fig 1.4
Rapid industrialisation in China and India is
further stressing planet Earth.
Source: HKPD

ecological resources. Ecological resources will come to resemble stocks and shares from the world's financial markets. Ecology will be traded: as ecological richness becomes scarce its value will increase, thereby ensuring its survival. It is an attractive idea but has, at its root, the concept of free market economies, except that under this system the market will be encouraged to conserve natural resources rather than exploit them. The *factor four* concept contains many lessons for those who design, engineer and commission buildings. The Rocky Mountain Institute is against greater environmental regulation, believing that it is in the best interests of companies to conserve resources since they will acquire a competitive edge by so doing. It is a position which runs counter to that of the EU, with its emphasis on environmental law and precaution, highlighting the political difference between Europe and the USA on this issue.

Architecture is inevitably influenced by the socio-political context. The market-led ethos that supports individualism prevails at the expense of community values. Sustainability as a series of ideals is a concept grounded in the ethics of environmental responsibility. The techniques and technologies of green design are now generally understood – what is still lacking is an architecture profession which gives priority to ecological issues and a construction industry which puts sustainability at the heart of its operations. Buildability and cost effectiveness are, in themselves, of little value unless what the construction industry creates is a new breed of resourceful, robust and spiritually uplifting buildings. The tragedy of initiatives such as the Latham and Egan Reports is the almost total absence of an environmental dimension.

The Challenge of Sustainability [1]

The evidence that global warming exists appears to be increasingly overwhelming. Climate science has established the likely correlation between burning fossil fuels, planetary warming and weather instability. However, other human activities are also accelerating the rise in global temperatures, such as the destruction of rainforests (often to supply the world's construction industry), the creation of landfill waste and the associated release of methane gases, and the use of ozone-thinning chemicals. Global warming is an uncomfortable fact for politicians (some of whom remain in denial), building designers, the construction industry and the human race. It is also an uncomfortable reality for many other global species,

Fig 1.5
Global warming is leading to the expansion of
deserts, putting many poor nations under stress.
Sub-Saharan Morocco.

whose habitats are threatened by sea-level rise and desertification. Global
warming not only places our species under threat, but also stresses the whole
ecosystem upon which farming and fishing depend.

Major global environmental agreements

1972	Stockholm Conference on the Human Environment (UK)
1979	Geneva Convention on Air Pollution (UN)
1980	World Conservation Strategy (IUCN)
1983	Helsinki Protocol on Air Quality (UN)
1983	World Commission on Environment and Development (UN)
1987	Montreal Protocol on Ozone Layer (UN)
1987	Our Common Future (Brundtland Commission) (UN)
1990	Green Paper on the Urban Environment (EU)
1992	Earth Summit (Rio) (UN)
1996	Habitat Conference (UN)
1997	Kyoto Conference on Global Warming (UN)
2000	The Hague Conference on Climate Change (UN)
2002	Johannesburg Summit on Sustainable Development (UN)

The drift to cities by the human population puts pressure on housing land, water
and energy supplies, and sewage and waste capacity. The year 2000 marked the
first time in human history that the urban population exceeded the rural one. Of a
global population of 6.2 billion, a greater number of people now live in cities than
in the countryside. This not only entails an intensification of urban problems
(pollution, space, crowding and resource stress) but urban living also raises
expectations of an enhanced lifestyle. The personal goals of air-conditioning, cars
and energy-consuming gadgets of various kinds (including over a quarter of a
billion mobile phones discarded each year) require resources whose supplies
seem increasingly finite.

As the human species becomes more urbanised we consume more, waste more
and pollute more. This, as Richard Rogers pointed out in his Reith lectures in
1996, shifts the emphasis from single buildings to urban design, from simple
choices (such as energy) to complex ones (such as sustainability) and from a

Fig 1.6
Urbanisation leads to increased consumption of
scarce resources. Yokohama, Japan.

> ### UK Cabinet Office policies for sustainable development in field of building design
>
> - CO_2 abatement and climate change: 10–15 per cent reduction in carbon emissions over 10–15 years.
> - Impact of buildings on environment: more efficient use of raw materials, waste minimisation and recycling.
> - Competitiveness: enhanced productivity through better design, especially of the internal working environment.
> - Construction industry efficiency: aim to achieve 30 per cent efficiency improvement over 10 years.

profit-driven agenda to an ethical one. The environment is increasingly stressed by our economic success and population growth. By 2050 it is anticipated that the human race will have four times the environmental impact it had in 2000 (based on a 2 per cent annual economic growth and a global population of 10 billion).

The stresses imposed by such growth touch upon resources, the waste chain and how the conflict between economic, environmental and social sustainability is to be resolved. The big question facing ecologists is whether human success as a species will be constrained by resource scarcity or by the scale of human-generated pollution. Will waste succeed in limiting growth more effectively than the inability to secure an ever-increasing supply of resources? These tensions will be felt primarily in cities and will lead to stressing of existing infrastructure to the same degree as they will demand a fresh approach to designing buildings. Architecture will need to address the resource and waste equation, exploiting waste as a potential source of energy or future construction material.

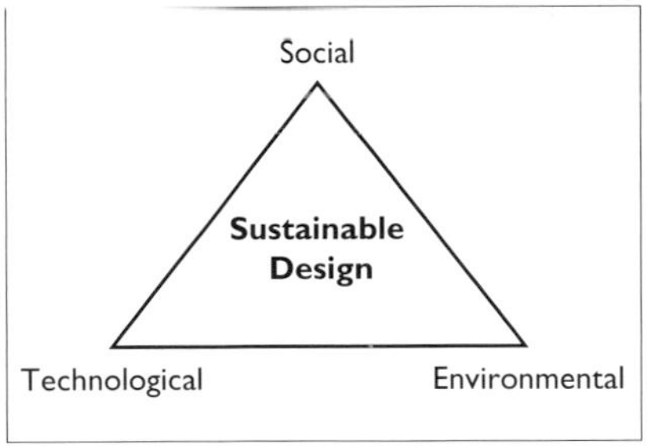

We have moved, over the past decade, from a position of narrowly focused concern for global warming with its associated international agreements (Rio, Kyoto, Johannesburg) to a wider concern for the state of cities, the global environment, resource shortages and ecological health. This shift is central to the notion of sustainable development. Sustainability is intellectually more interesting, professionally more challenging and, in design terms, more exacting than any other agenda. It has emerged as the new cutting edge in science, the basis for

Fig 1.7
The tripartite agenda of sustainable design.

innovative technologies and design approaches, the fresh paradigm for social equity, and the lens through which businesses increasingly plot their future. However, what is often ignored in architectural circles is the way 'Sustainable Development' as a concept bridges the two central agendas of modernism – technological innovation and social provision. Many recent movements in architecture have addressed only one side of the equation. High tech was high architecture with scant social justification.

Community architecture often ignored the power of design and technology to solve human problems. But sustainability brings the two camps together: it not only reinvigorates architecture, it gives fresh moral validity to the creation of human settlements, provides a new ethical basis for the architectural profession, and ultimately refashions the aesthetic/cultural landscape.

It is time to take stock of where green architecture is going. Early eco-designers emphasised the energy dimension of sustainability. It remains a primary concern due to the accelerating levels of global carbon dioxide emissions. But does low-energy design on its own produce great architecture? There is little evidence to

Fig 1.8
Three perspectives on sustainable design: social, technological and environmental.

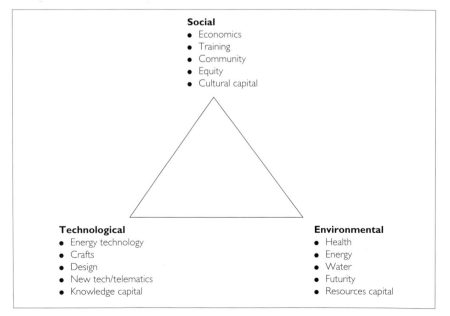

Social
- Economics
- Training
- Community
- Equity
- Cultural capital

Technological
- Energy technology
- Crafts
- Design
- New tech/telematics
- Knowledge capital

Environmental
- Health
- Energy
- Water
- Futurity
- Resources capital

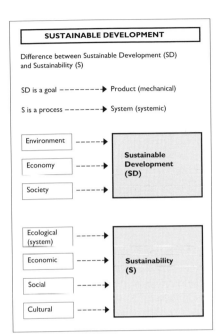

Fig 1.9
Difference between sustainable development and sustainability.

Benefits of environmentalism to the construction industry

- Cost savings
- Ensured legislative compliance
- Anticipation of future legislation
- Reducing environmental risk
- Improved relations with regulators
- Improved public image
- Increased market opportunities
- Enhanced employee productivity

link high aesthetics to energy conservation – in fact the contrary is often the case. It is only when the full picture of ecological design is addressed that a rich, complex and beautiful architecture emerges.

The work of the offices of Grimshaw and Feilden Clegg Bradley in the UK, Piano's in Italy and Ken Yeang's in Malaysia are landmarks to sustainable design, not just low-energy design. Their buildings address human need, both physical and psychological, as well as the demands of energy efficiency.

The search for a responsive environment is driven as much by human appetite for aesthetic uplift as by the need for technological fixes. Social, ecological, cultural and technological sustainability will be the measures employed to judge tomorrow's buildings. However, there are many tensions which need to be resolved, which necessarily lead to variety in the solutions adopted to solve the environmental problems ahead.

Nature as Design Guide

Globally, 'nature' is used as the guiding light of sustainability in quite distinct ways. Different designers have learnt to employ nature's order in their own fashion, from Grimshaw's breathing walls and water cooling to Yeang's adoption of termite structure principles of natural ventilation in office buildings. Nature, however, is not without problems as a design framework: it lacks a technological base and its outputs are rarely cross-species benign. However, by blending

Sustainable architecture: creative tensions

- Sustainable development versus sustainability
- Energy conservation versus personal health
- Global versus local
- Holistic versus analytical
- Systemic versus linear
- 'Them' versus 'Us'
- Human time versus ecological time
- Incremental change versus radical change
- Ecological design versus low-energy design
- Natural capital versus cultural capital
- High tech versus low tech
- Conflict between environmental sustainability and economic sustainability

technology and ecology it is possible to design a fresh generation of buildings which have reduced environmental impact across a wide front. Nature not only recycles, its systems move upwards towards even greater complexity and beauty as the scale increases. As such, it seems to have an in-built motor of diversity. It shuns repetition, cloning and the mindless search for perfect duplication. In this, natural ecology offers a model for designers to employ.

Learning from nature entails using ecological principles in quite distinct ways. Nature, however, is not neutral – it has its own laws and methods of working. Darwin helped to discover the keys to the evolution of species and their interdependence within habitats. Others have unravelled the genetic code to life itself. The human race is master of this knowledge but too rarely brings the fundamental laws of nature to bear upon architectural design. The linear thinking of prefabrication and factory perfection is preferred to organic design. Our buildings are increasingly cloned one on another. As for major cities, these are dying just like the coral reefs – pollution, global warming, mindless repetition and waste ultimately destroy all that which is delicate and beautiful.

Nature can be a useful guide to building design in four quite distinctive ways [2].

(a) **Learning from nature:** This was Ian McHarg's clarion call in his remarkable book of 1970 entitled *Design with Nature*. Nature employs patterns and orders which can be used in the design of buildings. Ecological design is an attempt to put these systems into the linear, functional equations normally employed by architects. Life-cycle assessment allows the building to take on the characteristics of natural systems. An analogy can be drawn between buildings (species) and cities (habitats). Learning from nature encourages an appreciation of the interaction in resource terms of energy, water and materials going in, waste, pollution and contamination coming out. In effect, we have an architectural ecosystem with its own potential recycling path and waste chain. Here we have a lesson from nature.

(b) **Using nature's models to inform:** Ecological structures are thoroughly tested, often in hostile environments. The shapes, compositions, configurations and materials used in nature are enduring and sustainable. Foster's famous gherkin-shaped Swiss Re tower in London is an obvious example of bio-mimicry. His debating hall for the GLA which resembles a section through a lung is another. In both cases, nature's tried and tested

Fig 1.10
The ICI Visitor Centre, Runcorn, designed by AMEC Design brings nature and architecture together.
Source: AMEC Design and Engineering

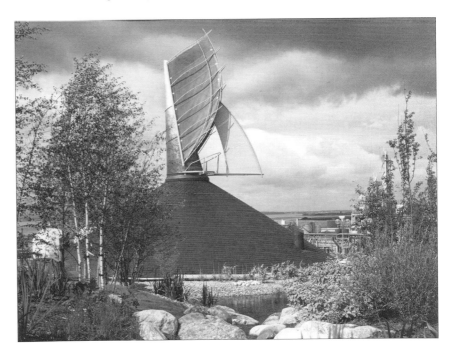

Fig 1.11
Ecolonia in Holland uses natural systems to deal with domestic waste water.
Source: Novem

models are adapted to provide a responsive, breathing architecture. Rogers' citing of the chameleon as a model for a potential building whose skin changes according to weather and light is another. Others, from Future Systems to Santiago Calatrava, draw upon a repertoire of forms found in nature, and the effect is to produce elegant rather than ugly design.

(c) **Making nature explicit:** Here, architectural design brings nature into the equation, either inside or out, or directly in the construction materials employed. Nature is a source of tactile, visual and aural pleasure. Welcomed into buildings, nature serves both a practical purpose (to cleanse the air) and a spiritual one (to uplift the spirit and reduce stress). The growth in atria within buildings has been accompanied by a corresponding increase in the practice of bringing nature indoors. Like the Victorian palm house, nature is now a commodity in commercial premises and almost a pet in the home. This has led some to speculate that our buildings are joined to us as another species – a kind of living entity which shares our life as a dynamic organism. Nature gives buildings their 'anima' and, hence, in Jungian terms, they are transcended from inanimate to living things.

Fig 1.12
Nature influences the design of the Wetlands Centre at Slimbridge, from site planning to construction details.

(d) **Using nature for ecological accounting:** All environmental assessment systems have an ecological basis although, due to the pressure of global warming, energy is normally the dominant theme. BREEAM in the UK, Quantum-auditing in The Netherlands, and LEED in the USA employ an auditing system which treats the building as a habitat. Each subject, be it water, materials or energy, is a resource whose value is weighted according to scarcity or damaging impact. The idea of nature-based accounting leads to the identification of 'indicators' which relieve designers of the task of assessing everything. These indicators are guides to good practice – they cast light on the health of the building.

Nature's language	Architects/organisation	Example
Learning from nature	Feilden Clegg Bradley ECD Thomas Herzog Lucien Kroll	BRE Offices, Watford Slimbridge Visitor Centre German Pavilion, Hanover Expo Ecolonia, Aalphen, Holland
Using nature's models to inform design	Norman Foster Future Systems Santiago Calatrava Ken Yeang Chetwood Associates	Swiss Re Building, London Media Centre, Lord's Cricket Ground Bilbao Airport Shanghai Armoury Tower, Pudong Sainsburys, Greenwich
Using nature as a tool	Richard Rogers Nicholas Grimshaw Michael Hopkins Ted Cullinan	Madrid Airport Eden Centre Jubilee Campus, Nottingham Hooke Park, Dorset
Using nature for ecological accounting	Novem (The Netherlands) BRE (UK) DETR Kyoto Protocol Green Buildings Council (USA)	Eco-auditing system BREEAM, SEAM 'Opportunities for Change' Carbon trading LEED

Fig 1.13
Bringing nature indoors. The author's house in
Scotland.

Green aesthetics

- Ecological accounting informs design
- Making nature visible
- Design with nature
- Learn from nature's structures
- Everybody is a designer
- Solutions grow from place

Is it Oil or Water that Matters?

The different regional perspectives on sustainability are well illustrated by the
distinctive nature of 'sink limits' (the ability to deal with pollution and waste)
between different parts of the world. In rapidly industrialised cities, air pollution is
becoming a major constraint on development. The EU estimates that air pollution
from traffic is the second biggest killer in Europe, leading to 60,000 deaths a year
from bronchitis, asthma and heart disease (source: European Environment
Agency website, 2001) [3]. In Africa, on the other hand, water pollution is the
killer. Here, unsafe drinking water kills more people than AIDS, and only one-third
of Africa's population, according to the UN, has adequate drinking water. So
whereas the strategy for sustainable development in the West focuses on energy
conservation (and hence less air pollution and less damage in terms of global
warming) that in much of Africa and Asia revolves around water supply issues and
the related problem of domestic waste. And herein lies one of the roots to the
diversity of practice in the field of sustainable development: energy and the
corresponding equation of global warming is abstract, scientific and mechanistic
whereas water is wedded to the land and connects not with the rational but with
the spiritual world. Water is tactile, visible and related, in Africa and India
especially, directly with health and agricultural productivity. Their world connects
with water not oil, and hence with the aesthetic and spiritual realm. No wonder
water is increasingly seen as tomorrow's oil. Those of us in the West can learn
about environmental conservation by studying water use in Africa and Asia – its
collection, consumption and recycling.

Different approaches to sustainable development

Western	Eastern
■ mechanistic	■ mystical
■ scientific	■ spiritual
■ high-technology	■ low-technology
■ energy-based	■ water-based

Towards a Cross-cultural Understanding of Sustainability

Oil and water practices help us to understand the differences in sustainability ideologies in various regions of the world. The mechanistic strength of the West and the spiritual depth of the East can be combined around the global challenge of ecological design. Even if society does not perceive itself limited by resource constraint (as in the USA), the sink limit (how we deal with waste and pollution) will drive design towards a more holistic agenda: holistic in the sense of combining the priorities of energy and water conservation, of adopting life-cycle assessment as a measure of robustness in the choice of all materials, and in the integration of the rational and spiritual dimension. And herein lies one of the seeds of architecture's renaissance. By relieving building design of its obsessive abstraction and material consumption, architecture can explore solutions which draw on the three great traditions of cultural thought – Christianity, Buddhism and Islam. Then there will be greater connection between the abstract and largely modern notions of sustainable development and the indigenous knowledge and skills held by the different peoples of the world. Then sustainability will be seen less as a Western importation and more as a continuation of local practices.

Global resources used in buildings

Resource	Building use (%)
Energy	50
Water	50
Materials (by bulk)	50
Agricultural land loss	80
Coral reef destruction	50 (indirect)

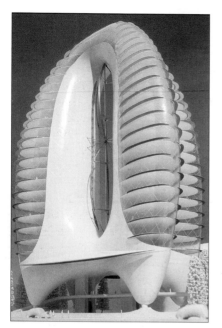

Fig 1.14
Project ZED – a low-energy office design by
Future Systems points to a new eco-aesthetic.
Source: Future Systems

Global pollution

Pollution	Building related (%)
Air quality (cities)	24
Global warming gases	50
Drinking water pollution	40
Landfill waste	20
CFCs/HCFCs	50

The Aesthetics of Sustainability: New Visual Paradigms

The aesthetics of sustainability is a poorly understood concept, lacking in theoretical underpinning and rarely articulated through practice. What this book seeks to develop is a body of knowledge around green design practices and, hence, green aesthetics. The argument is based on the premise that society will more readily accept the discipline of ecological design if it is also beautiful. Not beautiful in the sense that architects on their own make it so, but by the way in which architects, engineers and landscape designers can portray sustainable design in all its visual richness and spatial diversity through a collective approach to architecture.

Design and ecology are not normally discussed from the point of view of cultural politics, so it is difficult to develop a constructive cultural dialogue beneficial to both. Theories of public art, taking the art–ecology axis into cities, squares and parks, carry the possibility, however, of connecting sustainability with the social, economic and technological worlds. Art and architecture inspired by nature have the power to challenge the supremacy of other socio-cultural orders. In this, 'sustainable design' can present an alternative vision allowing eco-aesthetics to gradually emerge as a new style or movement in architecture. As such, 'green' can become a powerful cultural force beyond its technological and social assumptions. The challenge for the architect is to create more beauty with less intervention: to do, in fact, what nature does in our own backyard. This is why this book refers frequently to ecological design as well as low-energy design, and puts sustainability into a cultural context as well as a technological one.

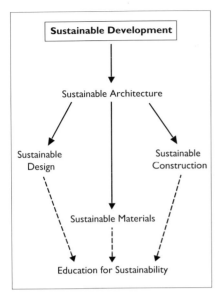

Fig 1.15
The concept of sustainable development spawns several sub-definitions relevant to building design.

What is Sustainable Development?

The Brundtland definition of sustainable development is increasingly seen as a virtuous but imprecise concept, open to various and often conflicting interpretations, although it remains the global standard. Coined in 1987 by the UN Environment Commission under Gro Harlem Brundtland, it addresses the needs of both the present and future generations in terms of environmental resources. The definition Brundtland coined may well be the single biggest imperative for global development in the 21st century. The consequences have been enormous.

The Brundtland Commission (1987) defined sustainable development as *development that meets the needs of the present without compromising the ability of future generations to meet their own needs.* This definition has spawned a series of sub-definitions to meet particular sector needs. Typical of these is that used by the practice of Foster and Partners. It defines sustainable design as creating *buildings which are energy-efficient, healthy, comfortable, flexible in use and designed for long life.* The Building Services Research and Information Association (BSRIA) has defined sustainable construction as the *creation and management of healthy buildings based upon resource efficient and ecological principles.* These definitions show the value of coining terms of reference for specific topics — be they building types, services provided or levels of development. The Brundtland definition outlines a philosophy which benefits from a degree of imprecision. There is a general understanding and set of principles which allow useful sub-definitions to be framed within its broad embrace.

The old emphasis on environmental resources, especially energy conservation, has been superseded by a wider resource framework. The Brundtland Commission argued that economic and social systems could not be divorced from the carrying capacity of the environment. The idea of growth and social welfare has to be balanced by the conservation of environmental resources by the present generation for the benefit of future generations. Hence the term 'sustainable development' has wide ramifications for those such as architects who carry out the 'development'. However, in the context of sustainable growth the question is whether environmental and economic sustainability are truly reconcilable. Are architects fooling themselves into thinking that 'development' can ever be sustainable?

Fig 1.16
The Johannesburg World Summit on Sustainable Development stimulated investment in clean energy technologies such as photovoltaic cells.

Key definitions

- **Sustainable development** is 'development that meets the needs of the present without compromising the ability of future generations to meet their own needs' (Brundtland, 1987).
- **Sustainable design** is the 'creation of buildings which are energy-efficient, healthy, comfortable, flexible in use and designed for long life' (Foster and Partners, 1999).
- **Sustainable construction** is the 'creation and management of healthy buildings based upon resource efficient and ecological principles' (BSRIA, 1996).
- **Sustainable materials** are 'materials and construction products which are healthy, durable, resource efficient and manufactured with regard to minimising environmental impact and maximising recycling' (Edwards, 2004).

Sustainable development: key issues

- Environment – all resources
- Futurity – our collective future
- Equity – sharing across generations
- Development – what architects do

Johannesburg World Summit on Sustainable Development

The Johannesburg World Summit on Sustainable Development held in 2002 introduced the concept of 'sustainable consumption and production' leading to a number of international agreements. The key principle was to establish a link between productivity, resource use and levels of pollution. Specifically, the agreement is about:
- ensuring that economic growth does not cause environmental pollution at a global and regional level;
- improving efficiency in resource use;
- examining the whole life cycle of a product;
- giving consumers more information on products and services;
- exploiting taxation and regulation to stimulate innovation in clean technologies.

Although the Johannesburg World Summit has an economic bias, the ramifications are likely to be felt by architects and the wider construction industry over the next decade. The agreements will, for instance, stimulate investment in new energy technologies and in new ways of recycling or reusing waste. It provides an international framework to develop taxes and laws needed to deliver the UK government's commitment to cut CO_2 emissions by 60 per cent by 2050, to keep water use within the limits of replenishment and to reduce biodegradable waste by 65 per cent by 2020. Since more information is to be made available to consumers, designers will benefit both from the environmental credentials now to be displayed on products and from the pressure for more green solutions which will flow from better informed clients.

By giving the concept of sustainable development such a high profile in the world economic order, there has been an inevitable rebalancing of national priorities. Not all nations however have accepted the new imperative, especially the USA, which has resisted international agreements such as those signed at Kyoto in 1997 and, more recently, The Hague Conference on Climate Change (2000). The USA's intransigence is a particular problem for global ecological health. It is the world's

Fig 1.17 *(right)*
The American model of urbanism is a threat to both the global environment and personal safety. San Francisco.

Fig 1.18 *(far right)*
The European model of urbanism favours streets for people and low-energy design. City of London.

biggest consumer nation and, if all of the Earth's population used energy at the rate that the USA does, the world would run out of fossil fuels within ten years.

Likely action as a result of the Johannesburg World Summit, 2002

1. Architectural practice will need to develop environmental management systems
2. Expansion of best practice programmes (with grant aid)
3. Innovation in eco-design
4. Development of cleaner, leaner architectural technologies
5. Increased product information on environmental impact
6. Increased reporting on environmental performance of buildings and architectural services

The Impact of Buildings

The role of buildings and cities is fundamental to the realisation of sustainable development. Buildings are long-lived, and cities have even longer lives: they stretch into the future realm which the Brundtland Commission addressed, a future of unknown resources, pollution and unstable climate. The typical lives of different aspects of construction are listed below:

- building finishes   10   years
- building services   20   years
- buildings   50+ years
- infrastructure (roads, railways)   100+ years
- cities   500+ years

Buildings are also big users of raw materials. The environmental capital locked in them is enormous, as is the waste footprint:

- **Materials:** 60 per cent of all resources globally go into construction (roads, buildings, etc.).
- **Energy:** nearly 50 per cent of energy generated is used to heat, light and ventilate buildings and a further 3 per cent to construct them.
- **Water:** 50 per cent of water used globally is for sanitation and other uses in buildings.

Fig 1.19
Buildings are a form of wealth creation. This design of the Halifax Bank headquarters by Aedas Architects attractively blends economic and ecological criteria.
Source: Aedas

- **Land:** 80 per cent of prime agricultural land lost to farming is used for building purposes and much of the remainder has been lost through flooding due to global warming.
- **Timber:** 60 per cent of global timber products end up in building construction and nearly 90 per cent of hardwoods.

Buildings as Wealth Creation

Architects design buildings, which in turn create wealth. Half of all fixed capital formation annually is vested in buildings, which, taken together with the inherited assets of buildings, represents about 75 per cent of all UK wealth [4]. It is therefore prudent, with this perspective in mind, that environmental issues are addressed at the outset; otherwise our created wealth will be undermined. The long-term asset value of a building depends on its ability to satisfy user needs, changing environmental conditions and evolving expectations of design quality. Naturally lit and ventilated buildings, those which utilise alternative energy sources and those which are attractive to consumers are more likely to be sound wealth investments than those which are over-dependent on fossil fuels or which ignore the fundamental human need for a healthy and wholesome lifestyle.

Ratio of costs of building over 50-year period

Cost of design and construction	1
Operating costs	5
Staff costs	150

Fig 1.20 (right)
Tibetan school designed by Arup Associates creates social capital for the future.
Source: Arup Associates

Fig 1.21 (far right)
The Reuters Building in London, designed by the Richard Rogers Partnership, helps create economic capital with a reduced environmental footprint.

Fig 1.22
Integer House designed by Cole Thompson
explores new sustainable technologies.

The Idea of 'Capital'

The Brundtland Report devised other concepts that are beginning to bed themselves into the consciousness of the 21st century. The first is the notion of 'capital' – sources of global resource which need to be husbanded. There are three main types of 'capital', each based on the triple bottom line of social sustainability, economic sustainability and environmental sustainability:

- social capital;
- economic capital;
- environmental capital.

As a concept, **social capital** has been well understood for some time, but in the context of sustainable development it allows us to relate skills and education to the agenda of environmental resource use. We need a society trained and equipped to understand the new agenda. We need architects, engineers and builders who can create useful social products (buildings) using the minimum of resources, so that future generations can have their share. To achieve this requires a new approach to education in the construction industry and new values to be adopted by society (including building clients). It also requires a recognition that society is a resource, and that the good design of cities helps to achieve social cohesion. Cultural value, social value and design skill are interconnected in social sustainability.

Economic capital is the clearly understood concept of financial resources and has been at the political heart of world order for at least the past 100 years. Businesses use their share value, an indicator of their economic capital, as a measure of success, while governments can make certain adjustments to the performance of the economy by controlling interest rates. The amount of economic capital depends on resource exploitation (land, people, resources) and so, of course, the concept of sustainable development challenges its foundations. However, economic systems work well – they are relatively transparent and comprehensible. What is needed is a way of joining up the measures of economic capital with the imperatives of other 'capitals', especially environmental and ecological.

Technological capital is the knowledge and design base that allows us to turn raw materials and other resources into useful human products (cars, buildings, etc.). It therefore has much in common with economic capital and is a form of capital

Fig 1.23
The skills of architectural design are a form of cultural capital. GLA Building, London.
Source: Foster and Partners

with a strong basis in science and in design. In fact, the two (science and design) are essential to the realisation of technological capital in an architectural sense. However, as our natural resources diminish, our design and scientific skills need to expand. Technology is never static, especially at a time of environmental stress. New skills and technologies are required for sustainable development. And those technologies not only need to be lean and smart, they must also be environmentally benign and socially acceptable. How architects are to employ technology and help the construction industry to develop new sustainable technologies is the challenge ahead.

Environmental capital is the term used to quantify all the resources of the Earth. It embraces fossil fuels, water, land and minerals, as well as a series of potentials or capacities, for example agriculture, fisheries, forestry and renewable energy. The term also covers negative values such as pollution, contamination and desertification. Brundtland brought the idea of environmental capital to political attention, especially in the context of future, rather than present, needs. Ecological capital is a branch of environmental capital and includes habitats, species and ecosystems. It has tended to be outside the terms of reference of other capital measuring systems or annexed to environmental capital. Yet ecological or natural capital is the basic life system to which the human species is intimately attached and upon which we all depend. The UN Earth Summit at Rio in 1992 brought biodiversity to political attention, paving the way for the introduction of the concept of ecological capital. Today, ecological capital remains the most fragile of the systems listed and is ignored by governments, companies and individuals alike. The arguments surrounding the genetic modification of crops are, however, a symptom of a growing awareness of ecological capital.

The Concept of 'Natural and Cultural Capital'

Sustainable development touches on many understandings of the concept of 'capital'. The normal measure of capital is that of economic capital expressed as stocks and shares, as gold and as currency. This is the measure used by government, by companies and by individuals to assess their wealth and economic performance. Unfortunately, it makes little allowance for other forms of capital such as natural capital or cultural capital or of the interactions of one form of capital on another.

Natural capital is a form of accounting which recognises the value of all environmental and ecological systems. It seeks to quantify the worth of forests, natural ecosystems, land, oceans, water and air. Natural capital is a technique developed to measure and assign value to biodiversity and natural wealth, just as stocks and shares give value to companies. The basis of natural capital is that of production from nature expressed in the form of harvests (on land and from oceans), of clean air and water, of renewable energy such as the sun and wind, and of the power of nature to renew damaged ecosystems. The currency of natural capital is divided into four categories – natural resources, habitats, species and genetic diversity. Hence, what natural capital seeks is a balancing of the human construct of economic capital by the carrying capacity of natural systems. It allows the impact of the world industrial economy to be set against that of global ecology and natural resources, using a form of accountancy employed in economics.

Cultural capital is a form of capital which recognises the knowledge, skills and creativity locked into socio-cultural systems. It embraces a wide range of capital on which the modern world depends – the state of knowledge expressed in the various sciences, creativity and design skills, technology, the arts and humanities. Education has a key role to play in handing on the skills across generations, research into expanding the knowledge base, the arts in expressing contemporary life in all its complexity, and the professions in serving society with skill and integrity. Cultural capital is in some way what the profession of architecture stands for. It is also what bodies such as the Architects Registration Board (ARB) seek as their overarching mandate – i.e. the assurance that an architect will be up to date in knowledge, skilled in design and management, and ultimately answerable to society at large.

The main forms of capital are part of a trilogy of interactions necessary to achieve a sustainable future. They mirror the three dimensions of sustainable development – environmental, social and economic – but differ in their emphasis on the cultural role of design and, in particular, architecture. The concept of 'capital' is a useful means of understanding the architect's role and especially the importance of buildings and cities as inter-generational assets.

Monitoring Progress Towards Sustainable Development

In 2002, the UK government reinforced its commitment to sustainable development by strengthening the four themes identified in the earlier report *Achieving a Better Quality of Life: a Strategy for Sustainable Development in the UK* (DETR, 1999). The 2002 review [5] highlighted that, although the UK construction industry accounts for 7 per cent of GDP, it operates with small profit margins and has high levels of internal instability. Both facts militate against investment in sustainable design and construction. The review also brings attention to the interrelationship between development and pollution, both at the site and in the manufacturing/disposal process. Too little is known of the third-party effect of pollution. In terms of encouraging social sustainability, there has been a marked increase in investment in social housing, schools and hospitals (many based on Public Finance Initiative (PFI) procurement methods). This investment, aimed at 'improving the quality of life', also provides the opportunity to test whether the goal of sustainable design and construction is being implemented in specific projects.

In order to monitor its own targets, the UK government published a progress report in 2003 showing the trends for a number of indicators in its sustainability policy [6] following independent reports which had suggested that targets in key areas, such as renewable energy and waste recycling, were unlikely to be met [7]. Part of the reason given was the conflict between the four themes and the particular crisis facing UK housing at the turn of the last century (unfit homes, greenfield site development, construction waste). Another reason cited was the lack of demand from end-users for sustainable design and the inadequate levels of financial support from government. Although there was a great deal of knowledge and rhetoric, there was little action by way either of PFI projects or of other government initiatives on the ground. Part of this was attributed to the reluctance of government either to fund demonstration projects or to use its own powers as a client to set an example. Governments need to realise that legislation alone is unlikely to bring about the wider cultural change required of sustainability.

The Egan Report *Rethinking Construction* sought to encourage the transfer of lean manufacturing concepts from the car industry to UK building construction [8]. At its heart, the concept of lean manufacturing is about achieving more with less and is, hence, similar to the concept of sustainable design. The elimination of waste, the recognition of differential performance benefits over time (life-cycle costing),

Fig 1.24
The challenge ahead is to balance the demands of prefabrication with that of sustainability. Greenwich Millennium Village.

the need to respond quickly to changing resources and human need are all characteristics of green design [9]. However, in spite of the structural similarities between new construction processes and sustainability paradigms there is little evidence on building sites that 'green' is winning the ideological battle. Elsewhere in Europe (especially in Germany, Sweden and Holland) action is more evident because here government rhetoric is matched by specific incentives in the form of energy grants and funding for demonstration projects [10].

Comparison of the impact of building construction and buildings in use

Impact	Building construction	Building use
Energy resources	Medium	High
Water resources	Medium	High
Mineral resources	High	Low
Transport	Medium	High
Air pollution	Low	Medium
Water pollution	High	Low
Noise pollution	High	Low
Visual impact	High	Medium
Wildlife impact/biodiversity	High	Low
Solid waste	Medium	High
Health	High	Medium

Education for Sustainability: from School to University

Although the city is our oldest work of art it is also our common living room [11]. The city has been given to us by our ancestors and we, briefly, are its custodians. The concept of sustainable development has been coined to ensure that we hand it over to our children and grandchildren in a healthy state. A great deal of attention has been paid to shaping the principles of sustainable development but little to how the concept can be bedded into society's values. The key is education from primary school to post-graduate degree level. The professions have a key role to play through the course accreditation process but so too do local education authorities, national curriculum bodies and, of course, schools of architecture.

MONITORING, DISTRIBUTION AND FEEDBACK

	Mapping green design onto UK government policy for sustainable development	
Theory	Sustainability	
	■ Economic: Maintaining capital stock ■ Environmental: Maintaining environmental functions ■ Social: Maintaining social welfare and cohesion	
Strategy	Sustainable development framework	
	■ Social progress which recognises the needs of everyone ■ Effective protection of the environment ■ Prudent use of natural resources ■ Maintenance of high, stable levels of economic growth and employment	
Indicators	National	Local
	■ Maintaining a stable economy ■ Building sustainable communities ■ Managing the environment and resources ■ Sending the right signals	■ Prudent use of resources ■ Protection of the environment ■ Better health and education ■ Access to services and travel ■ Shaping our surroundings ■ Sustainable local economy ■ Social/community enterprises
Design	Central government funded projects	Local green projects
	■ Demonstration projects ■ Own buildings for occupation	■ Green social housing ■ Green transport ■ Sustainable schools ■ Sustainable hospitals

Source: After Ekins and Russell, 2000

MONITORING, DISSEMINATION AND FEEDBACK

Since education is compulsory, it is in a unique position to provide the mechanism to foster sustainable development alongside other values. Education is the primary tool for raising awareness of environmental issues, reinforced later by professional training – the whole system being underpinned by exemplar buildings and projects which visibly demonstrate green principles. The starting point for awareness change is the chilling UNESCO (United Nations Educational, Scientific and Cultural Organisation) warning that if we want this Earth to provide for the needs of inhabitants of the future, human society must undergo a fundamental transformation. Education is a powerful instrument of change, and environmental education in particular can introduce schoolchildren to the interdisciplinary nature of sustainability. This is achieved by a combination of lessons in school, trips to sites outside school (such as, in the UK, Millennium Projects) and the use of the school itself as a physical resource of learning. The latter is promoted by the Eco Schools initiative, [12] which seeks specifically to introduce children to concepts of energy efficiency, recycling and biodiversity through the design of school buildings and use of their grounds.

The UN, through UNESCO, which was active in helping to coin the concept of sustainable development in the 1980s, is now concerned more with promoting its dissemination. A recent key report entitled 'Action Plan for the Human Environment' [13] has sought to influence governments by establishing an international programme in environmental education, encompassing all levels and all major stakeholders. The plan is based on the following key principles:
- sustainable development should be an integrated part of the development process;
- the needs of future generations must be respected;
- human beings are at the centre of concerns for sustainable development;
- the creativity, ideals and courage of youth should be forged in a global sustainable development partnership [14].

The plan recognises that whilst education is critical, both formal and non-formal means are needed to fully promote the concept of sustainable development. The plan also recognises that, although sustainable development has evolved in the West, it is a global concern which cuts across political, ethnic and cultural divides. It also promotes the idea that sustainable development is basically multi-disciplinary, and should, as a consequence, occur as a theme in a number of subject areas.

The linkage of ideas, concepts, approaches and values in education for sustainable development results in learning which is often project-based. Whether in primary school or at university level, education for sustainable development cuts across old subject boundaries. It also promotes creativity and independence in learning, and respect for other disciplines, methods and procedures. Hence the call for placing the concept of sustainable development into primary and secondary education has potential benefits beyond that of environmental understanding. The life-long and transferable skills of project-based education benefits individuals beyond the acquisition of new knowledge.

Global education for sustainable development involves not just schools, universities and the professions but clients, governments and NGOs [15]. There remains a considerable lack of awareness of the interrelated nature of human impacts on the environment. The involvement of users at the design stage in a project helps to ensure that green issues are addressed before economics takes a grip. Similarly, adjusting the *RIBA Plan of Work* to include sustainable development principles in the early briefing stage of a project ensures that the environmental agenda is an integrated element. Education strikes at core values; it is not sufficient to see a body such as the RIBA or ARB addressing educational standards alone. Changes in professional codes of conduct and in the ethics of practice are needed to ensure that environmental connections and commitments are made [16].

Advisory Panels on Education for Sustainable Development

In order to offer advice and raise awareness of sustainable development, the UK government established the following three bodies in the 1990s:
- The Government Panel on Sustainable Development, to bring together representation of the main sectors and education groups;
- Citizens' Environment Initiative, to carry the message at grass roots level;
- Sustainable Development Education Panel, to influence all levels of education.

These bodies seek to increase awareness of the part that personal choices play in delivering sustainable solutions. After all, decisions taken by people today on the design of buildings may have an impact on the environment a century later. To help raise awareness, especially in the important area of education and training, the government-funded Sustainable Development Education Panel was established in 1998 to promote three key principles:

Fig 1.25 *(right)*
The design of schools can do much to promote an understanding of sustainable design. Swanlea School, Whitechapel, London, designed by Percy Thomas Architects.
Source: Percy Thomas Architects

Fig 1.26 *(far right)*
Universities can do much to raise awareness of energy issues through the approach to estate design. Solar residences at the University of Strathclyde.

- sustainable development is the responsibility of everyone;
- education for sustainable development needs to influence every aspect of life;
- the UK's prosperity depends on our capacity to learn about sustainable development [17].

As a priority, the panel advised that sustainable development be represented in the National Curriculum and made a subject in the inspection framework of Ofsted visits. Although UK schools are now required to specifically teach sustainable development (under the UN Decade of Education for Sustainable Development), and some have endeavoured to make the school itself a vehicle for relaying the message of sustainable development, Ofsted is yet to address the subject in a systematic fashion. The latter is disappointing since, while children represent just 20 per cent of our population, they are 100 per cent of our future.

Key factors in achieving sustainable development

- Education
- Legislation
- Taxation
- Practice efficiency and business advantage
- Image and reputation

Ecology, Consumption and Architecture

During the past 50 years, average life expectancy around the world has risen from 46 to 64 years and the difference in longevity between people in the developed

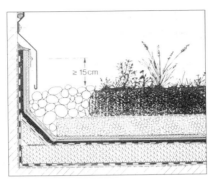

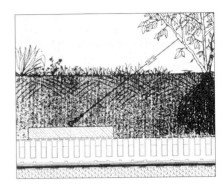

Fig 1.27
Details for planted roofs.
Source: Erisco Bauder

and developing worlds has shrunk from 26 to 12 years. As we live longer, we consume more, and in old age our dependency on heat, light and transportation increases. Improvements in living conditions, aided by the ever-increasing average rate of energy use per person globally (from 0.6 kW in 1900 to 2.3 kW in 2000), have led to an increase in human numbers and life expectancy. Food production has more than doubled over the past century from a diminishing area of productive agricultural land. Land has been lost to urban expansion, to desertification and to pollution, but thanks to new technologies (particularly irrigation) and greater energy input, total agricultural productivity has increased. In achieving this, biodiversity has suffered, and Rachel Carson's prediction of a 'Silent Spring' has become a reality in places like East Anglia. Carson writes about a landscape without birdsong – places which are productive but devoid of beauty or ecological richness.

The habitats that architects create have their place in satisfying the needs both of humans and of other species. Biodiversity is everybody's responsibility: designers, engineers, farmers, politicians and so on. Architects can play their part in three ways:

- they can design natural habitats as part of the development process – these could include ponds or wetlands, tree planting, turf roofs, creeper-clad walls, natural grasslands (flower-rich and left uncut);
- they can source construction materials from an ecological point of view, helping to maintain local or regional biodiversity by the choice of products or materials employed;
- they can bring nature into closer contact with people's lives. This can entail interior as well as exterior planting and the exploitation of views to enhance

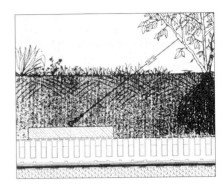

Fig 1.28
Example of ivy-clad wall in Paris, which gives the apartments behind greater climatic protection on an exposed gable.

the perception or visibility of the natural world. Here, the objective is both perceptual and spiritual, to ensure that the human species is not disconnected from the natural world. Just as television has done much to bring an appreciation of wildlife and an understanding of ecology, buildings can play their part in providing a window on biodiversity.

According to the World Wide Fund for Nature (WWF), forests the size of Greece are lost each year to serve the construction industry, resulting in the extinction of thousands of species a year (most before they have been discovered) [18]. In addition, it is estimated that each of us carries several hundred synthetic chemicals in our bodies that were not present in our grandparents. As the global construction industry is responsible for much of the forest clearing (to create timber products used in buildings) and for putting the new chemicals into people by way of the materials they specify, architects share some of the responsibility. Having witnessed generations of ruthless resource exploitation, the 'century of the environment', which is the predicted focus for the 21st century, will inevitably change design practices.

Fig 1.29
Bath stone used in new office designed by Bennetts Associates.

Architecture, Floods and Agriculture

The interaction between architecture and agriculture is highlighted by an increasing rate of severe flooding as witnessed in the UK, Italy, Cambodia, Vietnam and India in the period 2000–2004. The combined effect of urban expansion and agricultural intensification has exceeded the carrying capacity of the land to absorb exceptional levels of rainfall. With global warming, rainfall has become more intensive, concentrated and erratic. The design of buildings and landscapes has a role to play in absorbing the new rainfall peaks and thereby reducing stress on drains and river systems. Hard surfaces should be replaced by those which act as a sponge to soak up moisture and release it gradually. Paving around buildings is frequently impervious, with rainwater taken quickly to land drains via concrete drainage channels. A better solution is to allow the moisture to replenish groundwater supplies by, for example, bedding paving on a sand mix, by using soakaways as opposed to storm drainage, and by using ponds to catch excess water run-off. These are quite different from most water engineering solutions adopted today. Even when buildings are constructed on flood plains, they rarely adopt natural solutions for absorbing rainfall peaks, such as reedbeds,

Fig 1.30
The visibility of nature from British Gas offices in Leeds designed by Peter Foggo Associates.
Source: Peter Foggo Associates

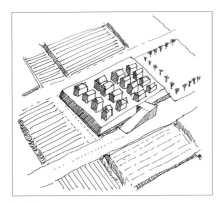

Fig 1.31
Example of new settlement on flood plain. Ajiki, Japan.

Fig 1.32
New settlement of 6,000 people designed ecologically by Feilden Clegg Bradley at the disused Shipton Quarry, Oxford.
Source: Feilden Clegg Bradley

meandering watercourses, irregular river banks, riverside tree planting and overflow areas. Instead, design solutions are predominantly concrete, contained, sealed and engineered in a protective rather than responsive manner.

The farming landscape is less able to absorb water than in the past. Agricultural land that surrounds cities is over-farmed and over-grazed, with the result that the rainwater quickly runs off all surfaces. For example, the sheep population in the UK is 40 million (four sheep for every six humans), and fields not grazed are ploughed for winter cereal production. Under this kind of intensive regime, rainwater cannot percolate through to ground aquifers and instead runs off to flood the valleys where buildings are concentrated. River speeds increase, eroding banks and flooding the houses, shops and industrial premises which make up our urban landscape. Every doubling of a river's velocity increases its destructive power fourfold [19]. The relationship between global warming, land use and architecture is one which society needs to understand quickly. The old idea of separate urban and rural ecologies is no longer valid, although it is the basis for

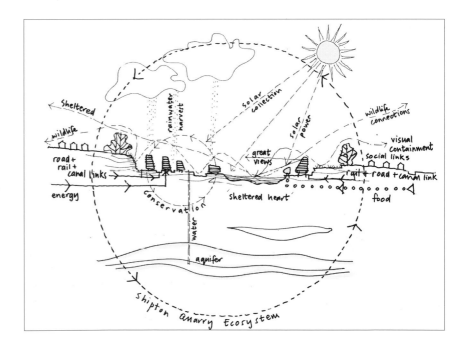

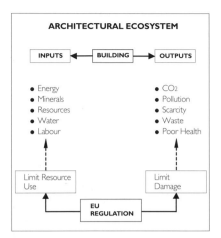

Fig 1.33
Architectural ecosystem and the role of EU regulation.

much official thinking, implied, for example, in the term 'town and country planning'. Designers can play their part by rethinking the choice of surfaces around buildings, by introducing more bioengineering methods of flood control (such as SUDS – sustainable urban drainage systems), by questioning the validity of green belts, and by avoiding development on flood plains.

A Brief History of Architectural Education for Sustainability [20]

Environmental design became a coherent theme of architectural education only in the 1970s. Inevitably, then, education in schools of architecture was preoccupied with energy rather than the broader concerns of sustainable development. Conceptually, however, the environmental tradition existed in texts which are the very bedrock of architecture and design. In Vitruvius, for instance, comfort and climate are integrated into the tri-partite model of 'utility, beauty and commodity'. Vitruvius declared that the site of cities, the layout of streets and the orientation of buildings should be determined by environmental factors [21]. He suggested as early as the first century BC that the very nature of building design was the primary agent in the mediation between internal comfort and the external environment. For Vitruvius, architecture had a part to play in affording shelter which exploited the resources of nature (sun and wind) rather than excluding them.

The Vitruvian model is still promulgated in the curricular division between design, technology and social studies which occurs in many schools of architecture. It too is to be found in the dialogue between science and art which underpins much of the studio culture in schools of architecture. The idea of sustainability, therefore, draws upon a foundation which is deeply embedded in classical and Renaissance thought. However, the concept of bioclimatic design is more recent and owes much to visionaries from the 1960s such as Buckminster Fuller and Reyner Banham. Fuller took the Vitruvian challenge of the environmental design of cities to the limit by suggesting enclosing urban activities in a huge glass envelope. Beneath a sheltering glazed embrace, food would be grown, waste recycled as compost, energy demands reduced and social interactions enhanced. His utopianism has left a mark on today's practitioners in the form of the Great Court at the British Museum by Lord Foster or the Eden Centre in Cornwall by Sir Nicholas Grimshaw.

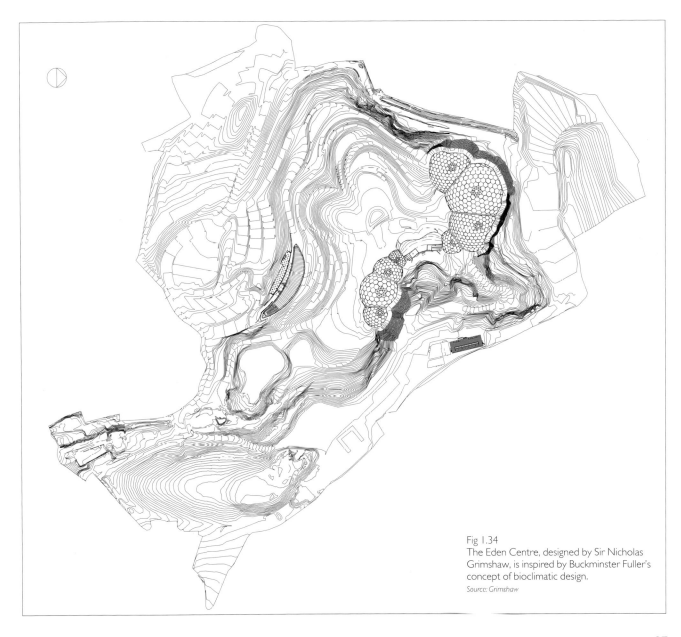

Fig 1.34
The Eden Centre, designed by Sir Nicholas
Grimshaw, is inspired by Buckminster Fuller's
concept of bioclimatic design.
Source: Grimshaw

The Search for a Well-Tempered Environment

Reyner Banham was more a theorist than a practitioner. His book *The Architecture of the Well-Tempered Environment* published in 1969 presented historical perspectives on the environmental function of modern buildings. To Banham the technology of environmental control held the key to an alternative understanding of the history of modern architecture. He openly challenged the thesis promulgated by Nikolaus Pevsner that structure and construction were the primary agents in giving form to architecture, not environmental design. Until Banham voiced his concerns, the relationship between energy use and building design was a subject for specialists with their own ethics, values and professional bodies rather than architects. A typical student of architecture in the 1960s (like the author of this guide) was encouraged to believe that heat, light, comfort and sound were design problems to be handed 'over to the emerging profession of mechanical and electrical consultants'. Banham argued that environmental technologies were as important as the emergence of reinforced concrete or steel-framed construction in giving shape to 20th century architecture [22].

The Oxford Conference of 1958

Banham's ideas gave impetus to a movement whose origins lay in the Oxford Conference on Architectural Education sponsored by the Royal Institute of British Architects in 1958. The RIBA sought to ensure that architectural education was located in universities and with it went a preoccupation with rational design methods underpinned by research. The former art college tradition and office-based system of pupillage was replaced by one where acquiring technical knowledge was as important as drawing and professional know-how. With this shift in emphasis went a recognition that the environmental agenda was crucial to architectural design and the assessment of building performance. Building science emerged as a discipline almost as important as architecture itself. The aesthetics of design were absorbed within a wider lexicon of environmental concerns, a movement which gained momentum with the energy crisis of the 1970s.

Schools of architecture responded in different ways. Some, such as at Strathclyde and Liverpool Universities, became schools of architecture and building or engineering science; others adopted the title of centres for building engineering, where architecture existed alongside the portfolio of new disciplines. The ambiguity of nomenclature allowed research and teaching to embrace the concept of architects becoming scientists and scientists becoming architects. The

Fig 1.35
Section through the Eden Foundation Building.
Source: Grimshaw

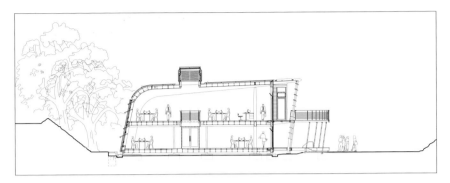

outcome was a mushrooming of interest in the measurable world of climatic responsive design and ultimately of sustainability.

Modernist educators became the new heads of schools of architecture formed in the wake of the Oxford Conference. The change in the culture of architecture, into a scientific as opposed to an artistic discipline, benefited the teaching of environmental science. The former Beaux-Arts tradition had a coherent and consistent approach to design which largely denied the presence of the environmental agenda. Low-energy design existed only in the orientation of buildings to afford sun-traps or to cast powerful shadow patterns onto classical facades. What the post-Oxford Conference schools of architecture offered was a system of university education with an emphasis on scientific methods.

Another significant development was the election in 1970 of a president of the RIBA sympathetic to the environmental cause. Alex Gordon had earlier served on the RIBA council and, since 1960, had helped to steer the post-Oxford reforms. He had made his name in public service, mainly as chief architect for Birmingham City Council, and approached building design from the angle of social reform. Gordon combined his utopianism within a deep sense of environmental awareness. He is remembered today mainly for coining the mantra 'long life, loose fit, low energy' as the basis for architectural design. It is a legacy which combined elements of thinking from the Archigram Group, Buckminster Fuller and E.F. Schumacher, whose *Small is Beautiful* was published in the UK during Gordon's tenure in Portland Place.

Fig 1.36
Four student projects testing the understanding
of technology and environment.
Left to right: Leigh Brown, Keith Dillon,
Opposite page: Michael Heath, Martin Bates.

Curricular Reforms and the Layton Report

Although the Oxford Conference had little to say about the detailed content of
the curriculum, this was addressed by the Layton Report of 1962 [23]. This report
introduced the notion that architectural education should be diversified by the
introduction of technical specialisms such as building services design. The latter
was one of eight 'scientific' specialisms which were intended to ensure that
graduating architects had a good general knowledge of the integration of
structure, services and construction. So, whereas the Oxford Conference
introduced the quasi-scientific approach, the report of 1962 reinforced this by
requiring the teaching of technology-based specialisms. As each was intended to
be underpinned by research and tested through studio-based projects, the effect
was to give further weight to the emergence of environmental design as an
important element in the design of buildings.

The Concept of an Environmental Duty of Care

The RIBA and, more recently, the ARB have adopted standards of professional
behaviour which place an environmental duty of care upon practitioners.
Inevitably, this has been adopted also in curriculum revisions since the late 1990s.
Unlike the impetus for environmental understanding following the Oxford
Conference and Layton Report, the origins of which were quasi-scientific, the
code of professional conduct changes have at their core an ethical basis.
Environmental ethics have emerged now to stand alongside the wider
professional responsibilities adopted by architects.

Ethics and the concept of environmental duty of care have a long taproot in
professional perceptions. The ethical basis for architectural practice in the 20th
century evolved from a duty of care to the client, through a responsibility to

society as a whole, to one where the architect has to consider the environmental impact of the decisions taken. In 1962, Sir Robert Matthew in his presidential address to the RIBA declared that 'architecture today ... is a service to the client and the community' [24]. Until then the interests of the client were uppermost, and this sometimes ran counter to wider social or environmental interests. Matthew was the first president to voice the legitimate interests of society as a whole. To Matthew, the ethical function of architecture was to help articulate a shared ethos – a compact between the client who commissions and pays for building work and the community at large which uses the building. It was a foundation of sufficient breadth to allow the absorption of subsequent environmental concerns. After all, 'a strict professional ethic, even if self-regarding in origin and imprecisely formulated, inevitably tends to generate an ideal of social service' [25]. This view, when applied to sustainability, allowed the UK government-sponsored Sustainable Development Education Panel to suggest in 2000 that 'acting in accordance with sustainability principles is a defining characteristic of being a professional' [26].

The European Dimension

As ethical codes evolved, a parallel impetus appeared in the mid-1980s, not from the RIBA but from the European Union. The Architects' Directive 85/384/EEC required consistent standards of education, professional standards and codes of conduct to ensure the free movement of architects across Europe. The Single European Act of 1986 introduced a number of minimum standards to ensure harmonisation of architectural services across the diverse professional landscape of Europe. The impact was felt particularly acutely in terms of architectural education. A harmonised system of education for architects across Europe, implemented in 1987, required students to master 11 areas of study. Two specifically refer to environmental awareness: students are required to have an 'understanding of the relationship between people, comfort and buildings, and between buildings and the environment' [27]. This field of understanding suggests a tri-partite synthesis of people, buildings and environment with Vitruvian overtones. Later in the Directive, students have to acquire an 'adequate knowledge of physical problems and technologies ... so as to provide ... internal conditions of comfort and protection against climate'. These clauses substantially increased the level of environmental teaching in schools of architecture and required the joint visiting boards of the RIBA and ARB (the latter body given specific responsibility to ensure that the Directive was implemented in the UK) to vet standards in architecture schools. The wording of the two environmental clauses had the effect of broadening the perception of the environment to embrace interests beyond low-energy design. Questions of climate-responsive design, comfort, global warming and the bigger agenda of sustainable development now crept into the curriculum.

Wider Environmental Concerns

The year 1992 was important in other respects, too. The UN Earth Summit held in that year in Rio de Janeiro alerted world governments to the looming environmental and ecological problems associated with urban development. Across the world 182 governments signed up to a series of declarations, aimed not only at reducing adverse environmental impacts but also at adopting measures such as Agenda 21 initiatives to take positive action. The impetus from the declaration influenced the construction industry professions in the UK, some of which subsequently adopted new codes and standards. The RIBA took the lead, instituting a new committee to steer action. Known originally as the Energy Committee (from 1992), then the Energy and Environment Committee (from 1994), it became the Sustainable Futures Committee in 1998. The changing title reflected the altering perception of environmental problems. Traditionally, the construction industry had concerned itself with low-energy design, supported enthusiastically by quasi-governmental bodies such as the Building Research Establishment (BRE). However, after the Earth Summit, the emphasis shifted towards wider ecological concerns such as rainforest destruction and biodiversity. Initially, the design professions were slow to reorientate their environmental focus, but with government moves towards adopting the broad agenda of sustainable development, the professions and construction industry after 1995 saw the benefit to their members.

One resource which gained in professional attention was water. Although many understood that heating, lighting and ventilation of buildings was responsible for about 50 per cent of UK fossil fuel energy use, few realised that about 50 per cent of all water consumption was building related. With growing stress on water reserves, a series of droughts in the late 1990s and increasing water utility bills following industry privatisation, architects and engineers began to design for water conservation. In parallel, the need to examine the source of hardwood timbers employed in building meant that the building industry woke up to its central position in helping to address sustainability. The idea that local design decisions had an impact on global problems began to be absorbed within higher education and the professions.

The Earth Summit provided a framework for development which has been adopted in many curriculum revisions, especially for those degree courses in sustainable design or sustainable architecture. Four main areas were addressed at the summit – energy conservation, rainforest conservation and associated ecological management, biodiversity, and action plans for environmental recovery. The latter, known as Agenda 21 (action for the 21st century) led to initiatives from central and local government, the professions, grass roots organisations and universities.

The adoption of the Maastricht Treaty in 1992 added further weight to the environmental argument. Various articles of the Treaty strengthened laws on the environment, such as article 130v, which introduced policies for 'preserving, improving and protecting the quality of the physical environment, protecting human health and encouraging the prudent use of natural resources' [28]. Architects and educators in the built environment became increasingly aware of their environmental responsibilities and the impact of buildings on the quality of life, health and resource consumption.

The Maastricht Treaty also introduced four important principles which span sectoral interests but which had serious implications for the way buildings are designed and architects educated. The first was an obligation to use best environmental knowledge – to incorporate the benefits of environmental innovation into building design. The second was to follow the 'precautionary principle' with the implication that risks should be assessed and caution exercised in the use of new materials and construction processes. The third was an obligation to rectify environmental damage at source rather than disperse pollutants into air or water. This meant that the polluter paid for the clean-up operation. Since many buildings pollute, the principle questioned the gas-guzzling technologies of modern air-conditioned development and, in theory at least, exposed the architect to potential litigation. The final principle was the need to consider all ecological impacts and to incorporate consistent environmental practice across Europe into local laws and codes of practice. This led to a revision of the Architect's *Code of Conduct* in 1997.

Key environmental principles of EU law

- Polluter pays
- If uncertain take precautionary action
- Consider all ecological impacts
- Use best scientific information

Within UK higher education itself, the Toyne Report of 1992 was an important milestone [29]. This report, under the chairmanship of Peter Toyne, vice chancellor of Liverpool John Moores University, advocated a range of measures including the greening of courses which traditionally had ignored environmental issues. Cross-curricular greening, whereby undergraduates experience sustainability best practice from other courses, proved an important avenue for the broadening of environmental understanding in schools of architecture. Toyne also suggested the use of the university campus itself as the test bed for environmental innovation. As a consequence, a generation of green buildings was constructed, some for built environment faculties, which were used in teaching and research (a good example being the School of Engineering building at De Montfort University built in 1995). By the 1990s, therefore, there was pressure to incorporate sustainability into architectural education from three important quarters – changes to the code of conduct governing architectural services, European legislative reforms, and pressure from the university sector itself via the Toyne Report. The latter gained further impetus when the UN General Assembly adopted the World Summit on Sustainable Development's recommendation that 2005 should mark the beginning of a 'decade of education for sustainable development'. Ratified by the UK Prime Minister, higher education authorities are now drawing up plans to take the green agenda forward, in terms of action both on the campus and in the curriculum.

Fig 1.37
Fig 1.37
The masterplan for Shanghai by the Richard
Rogers Partnership, an example of sustainable
urban design which could provide a model for
the university campus of the future.
Source: RRP

It is necessary at this point to review the current framework of legislation and
codes under which architects operate. Although these are specific to the
architectural profession, similar provisions exist for other professions such as the
Institution of Civil Engineers, The Royal Institution of Chartered Surveyors and the
Construction Industry Council. The Union of International Architects (UIA), the
umbrella group which coordinates architectural institutes across the world, has
adopted principles intended to form the framework for action at national level.
Principle 2 states that 'architects have obligations to the public ... and should
thoughtfully consider the social and environmental impact of their professional
activities'. Principle 3 goes further: architects, it states 'shall strive to improve the
environment and the quality of the life and habitat within it in a sustainable
manner'. In 1999, the ARB of the UK amended its code with regard to the
environment. The new code of conduct stated that while 'architects' primary
responsibility is to their clients, they should nevertheless have due regard to their
wider responsibility to conserve and enhance the quality of the environment and
its natural resources'.

Fig 1.38
The widening influence of sustainability.

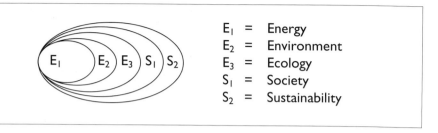

E₁ = Energy
E₂ = Environment
E₃ = Ecology
S₁ = Society
S₂ = Sustainability

These code revisions have wide implications for architectural education since, whereas ARB regulates through the prescription process 36 schools of architecture in the UK, the RIBA helps to validate these and a further 70 worldwide. As a consequence, the RIBA influences the ethos and curriculum of around 25 per cent of architectural training globally. One repercussion is that sustainability now assumes subject importance in its own right rather than being taught as an aspect of technology. Ecological design has almost moved to centre stage in design projects. The latter is important since about half of credits awarded in a typical school of architecture are design based, and unless sustainability engages with the studio culture, it fails to address the core of design education.

The Special Contribution of Richard Rogers

The contribution to the design culture of sustainability from the architect Richard Rogers (Lord Rogers of Riverside) should not be underestimated. His chairmanship of the UK's Urban Task Force (1999) was influential in redirecting government attention towards urban sites and the value of sustainable design. One valuable principle set out in the subsequent report is that 'social well-being and environmental responsibility' are fundamental to 'design excellence' [30]. His Reith lectures of 1998, his books such as Cities for a Small Planet (with Philip Gumuchdjian) published in 1997, and the example of his buildings, have ensured that by the beginning of the 21st century sustainable development had begun to have a significant impact on professional perceptions.

To a large extent the views of early pioneers of green design have become mainstream. Within a generation authors like Ian McHarg, whose book Design with Nature was almost underground reading in the early 1970s, find their principles now underpinning architectural education. The broadcaster and journalist Jonathan Dimbleby, giving the first RIBA Annual Lecture in May 2002, went even further. He suggested that architects should refuse to undertake unsustainable jobs, arguing that the ethical basis of the profession was undermined by commissions which did not place sustainable design to the fore [31]. Dimbleby called for a new awareness of the 'broad picture of sustainability' where 'ecological concerns, economic development and community identity' were brought together.

The history of architectural training in the 20th century is one of growing technological and environmental awareness – of a shift from art to science as the basis for design education. Although the early years of the 21st century see the re-emergence of art architects (Frank Gehry, Zaha Hadid), the agenda of sustainability will in time embrace both camps. Then sustainable design will become a cultural movement which unites art, science and nature.

A Review of Education for Sustainability in the Construction Professions

Outside of architecture schools, the construction industry as a whole has had to grapple with course changes to accommodate the rapidly evolving educational demands made by the adoption of the concept of sustainable development.

However, action across the industry as a whole has been hampered by a number of institutional and cultural impediments. These may be summarised as follows.

1. There is a wide interpretation of the term 'sustainability' across the various higher education built environment courses in the UK. Although Brundtland is cited in much course material as a unifying definition and set of values, in reality the interpretation is distinctive to disciplines rather than universal. As a result, different priorities tend to be promoted, with the risk that students lack either a common language of terms or a shared perception of solutions.

2. The professional bodies have a big impact on the priority awarded to sustainability in the higher education curriculum. With various professional bodies involved (RIBA, ARB, ICE, RICS, CIBSE, CIOB, RTPI) comes an inevitable diversity of approach within the courses that they validate. If the professional bodies were to agree a set of core values, environmental

Date	Milestone publication	RIBA/ARB syllabus response
58 bc	Vitruvius (environmental triangulation of comfort, climate and design)	
1860	John Ruskin (nature as guide)	
1880	William Morris (small, sustainable communities)	
1910	Patrick Geddes (ecology of cities)	
1930	Frank Lloyd Wright (nature as inspiration)	
1948	Lewis Mumford (environment of cities)	
1965	Richard Buckminster Fuller (bioclimatic cities)	Building services incorporated into syllabus after Oxford Conference of 1958
1970	Ian McHarg (*Design with Nature*)	Layton Report on strengthening technology awareness on architecture courses
1970	Club of Rome (limits to growth)	
1972	Concept of 'long life, loose fit, low energy' espoused by RIBA President Alex Gordon	Low-energy design in RIBA syllabus
1987	EU Architects' Directive	Environmental duty of care as principle
1992	Rio Summit (integration of energy, ecology and environment)	Environmental understanding introduced to syllabus by ARB criteria changes (1995)
1992	Maastricht Treaty (EU environmental policy)	
1997	Kyoto Protocol (global warming)	
2000	Urban Task Force Report (Rogers) Hague Conference (climate change)	Sustainability in syllabus as concept, increase in awareness of urban design
2002	Johannesburg Conference (sustainable development)	Further revisions to RIBA and ARB criteria for Validation especially at Part I
		Full range of sustainability issues in syllabus via revisions of 2003 affecting Parts 1 and 2
		'Environment' now a core theme of ARB Prescription

Fig 1.39
Self assessment form for the integration of sustainability and design criteria.

SUSTAINABLE DESIGN PROJECT SELF ASSESSMENT FORM

	Assessment Criteria	Max Points (per Criteria)	Student	Student Peer	Tutor
1	**Site Planning 1:1250 / 1:500**				
(a)	Architectural merit in site organisation and broad approach	15			
(b)	Specific merit in strategy to achieve a significant level of sustainability in design	15			
2	**Scheme at 1:200**				
(a)	Interpretation of opportunities in brief What merit does the design have as a piece of architecture?	15			
(b)	Environmental strategy for scheme as a whole	15			
3	**Detail design at 1:50 and larger scale**				
	Appropriateness of materials structure, envelope and level of understanding of sustainable construction and imagination used in its application	20			
4	**Quality and depth of supporting explanation**	20			
	Total	100% Max			
	Comments				

principles and body of knowledge (especially at undergraduate level), it would be easier to foster mutual understanding and interdisciplinary teaching across the industry as a whole.

3. Where sustainable design and construction is taught there appears to be little correspondence between knowledge acquisition via lectures, and knowledge

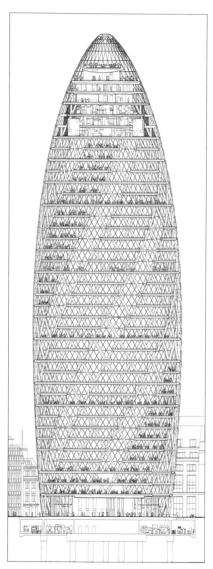

Fig 1.40
The Swiss Re building, London, consumes 50% of the energy of a typical office building.

application via practicals or design projects. Similarly, there is little correspondence between what is taught in the universities and the topics being researched under the umbrella of sustainability.

4. With a few notable exceptions, building development on university and college campuses rarely seeks to expose students (and staff) to the reality of sustainable design or good sustainable management. In spite of the *Toyne Report* (HMSO, 1992) the UK compares unfavourably with the rest of Europe in terms of green demonstration projects built on campus. As a result, there are few examples of the application of photovoltaic technology to new or refurbished buildings, or passive solar student housing, water or waste recycling or car-free campuses. Without a triangulation between teaching, research and development, the built environment student can hardly be blamed for not taking sustainability seriously.

5. Little interface seems to exist between further education and higher education institutions in the field of sustainable design, technology and construction. This is surprising given the extent of education available to building operatives (such as plumbers, electricians and bricklayers) in FE colleges. Although ladders exist between FE and HE in the area of admissions policy, no comparable exchange appears to exist in the pedagogy of sustainability.

So, in spite of initiatives from individual professional bodies, such as the RIBA, and encouragement from government, the broad agenda set out by the Toyne Report has yet to influence the wider culture of education for the construction and design professional. This is all the more regrettable given the interdisciplinary nature of sustainable development.

The Design Culture of Sustainability

The three main dimensions to sustainability – environmental, social and economic – have led to the regrowth and sustenance of architecture itself. Ecological design has proved a major regenerative force in architecture over the past decade. The fundamental precepts have been shaken by green currents influencing all aspects of the profession, from how we engineer buildings, to the design and shape of interior space, and the selection of materials used. Although it is possible to see sustainable architecture as a style – certainly green buildings are readily identified – green design is more than style. It is a fundamental reordering of basic design and technological principles and hence refigures architecture in all of its essential elements.

By exploiting the cultural possibilities of green architecture, architects have been able to help bring about acceptance of sustainability principles within society at large. One has only to look at how Richard Rogers, Nicholas Grimshaw and Norman Foster have used good design to 'shop-window' certain ecological principles. In the process they have created an environment of patronage which has helped younger practices and encouraged students to push at the frontiers of sustainable design. Few would doubt that the culture of architecture has been enlivened by green thinking but it may take another generation before the culture of cities is similarly altered.

The concept of sustainability embraces the notion of the environment as a holistic cross-disciplinary system.

Sustainability influences:

- how we design buildings
- how we construct buildings
- how we manage buildings

Sustainability challenges the fragmentary view of:

- low-energy design
- high art, high-consumption architecture
- profit at social or environmental cost

Sustainability supports:

- ethical view of architect's role
- multi-disciplinary approach
- community, social and cultural value
- new aesthetic language for architecture
- ecological thinking

Notes

[1]   Adapted from Brian Edwards, *Green Architecture*, AD Monograph, Wiley-Academy, London, 2001, p. 21.

[2]   Adapted from Brian Edwards, 'Design Challenge of Sustainability', *Green Architecture*, AD Monograph, Wiley-Academy, London, 2001, pp. 22–5.

[3]   http://www.eea.eu.int/main_html

[4]   Richard Saxon, 'Sitting on our assets', *Building Design*, 7 November 2003, p. 9.

[5]   Department for Environment, Food and Rural Affairs, *Achieving a Better Quality of Life: Review of Progress Towards Sustainable Development*, DEFRA, London, 2002.

[6]   Sustainable Development Commission, *UK Climate Change Programme; A Policy Audit*, 2003.

[7]   *ibid.*

[8]   John Egan, *Rethinking Construction*, The Construction Task Force, DETR, London, 1998.

[9]   G.B.S. Penoyre and S. Prasad, *Constructive Change*, 2000.

[10]   E. Vedung, 'Constructing Effective Government Information Campaigns for Energy Conservation and Sustainability: Lessons from Sweden', *International Planning Studies*, 1999, Vol. 4, pp. 2–7.

[11]   Mats Lundstrom and Maria Nordstom, *The City at our Fingertips*, Malmo, 2001, pp. 58–9.

[12]   Edgar Morris, *Seven Complex Lessons for the Future*, UNESCO, Paris, 1999, preface.

[13]   For *Eco Schools Handbook* see www.ecoschools.co.uk

[14]   *Action Plan for the Human Environment*, UN, Stockholm, 2003.

[15]   Paraphrased from UNCED Agenda 21, UNESCO, Paris, 2002.

[16]   Brian Edwards, *Green Buildings Pay*, 2nd edn, Spon Press, London, 2003.

[17]   Sustainable Development Education Panel, First Annual Report, 1999, p. 3.

[18]   *The Guardian, Environment Supplement*, 1 January 2000, p. 5.

[19]   Jonathan Theobold, 'Overgrazing has Stripped the Soil', *The Guardian, Society Supplement*, 15 November 2000, p. 11.

[20]   Reproduced (with amendment) from Brian Edwards, 'Sustainability and Education in the Built Environment' in John Blewett and Cedric Cullingford (eds), *The Sustainability Curriculum: The Challenge for Higher Education*, Earthscan, London, 2004.

[21]   Dean Hawkes, *The Environmental Tradition: Studies in the Architecture of Environment*, Spon Press, London, 1996, pp. 10–11.

[22]   Reyner Banham, *The Architecture of the Well Tempered Environment*, Architectural Press, Oxford, 1969.

[23]   Elizabeth Layton, *Report on the Practical Training of Architects*, RIBA, London, 1962, p. 2.

[24]   Derek Senior, *Your Architect*, Hodder and Stoughton, London, 1964, p. 23.

[25]   *ibid.*

[26]   *What Sustainable Development Education Means for the Professions*, HMSO, London, 2002.

[27]   Architects' Directive 85/384/EEC, clause 11.2; see also 11.3.

[28]   Brian Edwards, *Sustainable Architecture: European Directives and Building Design*, Architectural Press, Oxford, 1999, p. 9.

[29]   *Environmental Responsibilities: An Agenda for Further and Higher Education* (The Toyne Report), HMSO, London, 1992.

[30]   *Towards an Urban Renaissance: Report of the Urban Task Force*, E&FN Spon, London, 1999, Introduction.

[31]   *RIBA Journal*, 2002, p. 96.

Resources

2

2 Resources

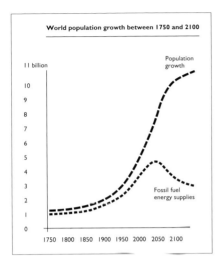

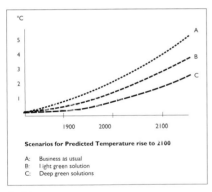

Fig 2.1
The long-term view: fossil fuels *(top)*, climate change *(bottom)*.

Energy Use and Global Warming

By the year 2050 it is expected that the world will double its use of energy. Much of this will come from an expanded market for fossil fuels (with consequent further pressure on price, and consequences in terms of global warming) but a growing percentage will be energy produced from renewable sources. Meeting the challenge of satisfying rising energy expectations in areas of the world such as China, Africa and India, which are currently undergoing industrialisation, requires action by architects to promote the exploitation of renewable energy in preference to oil and gas. The development of renewables offers an energy solution which does not damage human health (through air pollution), blight local environments (via petrochemical plants) or threaten natural systems (by global warming).

At present one-third of humanity (or 2 billion people) is dependent on biomass energy sources — typically firewood and animal dung – for cooking and heating. The consequences are felt not just in the area of poverty but in environmental stress. As trees are felled for firewood, the landscape becomes more arid with a decline in agricultural capacity. The downward spiral increases as further firewood is extracted, often involving lengthy journeys into the bush. As children are the usual gatherers of fuel, time spent on this activity eats into time for schooling.

The World Summit on Sustainable Development held in Johannesburg in 2002 set a target of halving fuel poverty by 2015. Part of the solution proposed is in the development of rural solar power systems. Since fuel poverty is most marked in relatively sunny, underdeveloped countries the potential of solar energy is obvious. What is being promoted by the United Nations Development Programme is a shift towards a low-carbon energy system based on solar power in developing countries, hydrogen fuel cells for already industrialised ones, and greater use of biofuels for world transport. Architects will be involved in these changes, not at the cutting edge of technological development, but in designing buildings able to accommodate fast-changing energy priorities. Buildings will be required to facilitate and test knowledge transfer from the science laboratory into the field. In this sense, buildings become exercises in applied research with all the subsequent monitoring that this entails.

Fig 2.2
Buildings help to test the performance of new environmental approaches. BRE building, Watford.
Source: Feilden Clegg Bradley

Research for sustainable energy design

Knowledge creation	Blue sky
Knowledge testing	Laboratory
Knowledge transfer	Design studio
Knowledge application and monitoring	Building
Knowledge sharing	Teaching

The particular problem of remote rural areas provides a distinct challenge for designers of schools, houses and local health centres. Grid-based energy systems rarely exist in rural areas – here electrical energy is generated from oil and heat from burning wood. Solar power provides an obvious solution in the form of photovoltaic (PV) generated electricity. Gridless electricity is necessary in remote areas, making local generation essential. Both wind- and solar-generated electricity suit people living in villages or remote homesteads and relieve pressure on local timber reserves. For governments and aid agencies, PV technology is the cheapest and quickest way to deliver electricity. With electricity come other benefits to rural communities – light for reading and study, connection to radio and television, and energy for cooking, boiling water and mobile phones. Off-grid solar power liberates the rural poor from dependency on imported and expensive non-renewable energy supplies. It costs about £800 to install a basic solar system to a house and £9,000 to a school in developing countries. Although, by the standards of other construction costs, solar installation costs are quite high (perhaps 20 per cent of the total building budget), the long-term benefits socially, economically and environmentally are significant. Although off-grid power is normally solar-driven in developing countries, it can also be wind- or water-driven.

It is ironic that about one-quarter of the world's solar panels are now manufactured by oil companies such as Shell and BP. If the world does double its energy consumption by 2050 it can do so only by diversifying the sources of energy production. In this period it is expected that developing countries will need five times more energy than at present, and most of this will have to come from renewable sources. Without the infrastructure of refineries, pipelines and power grids, large areas of rural Africa, Asia and Latin America will be dependent on non-grid supplies [1]. Such a demand may push down the price of PV panels to that of a few gallons of petrol. With the globalisation of architectural services,

Fig 2.3
Five approaches to electricity production
(*clockwise*): nuclear power; coal-fired power
station; energy from waste/combined heat and
power; photovoltaic cells; wind generator.

professionals in the developed world will need to learn how to use renewable
energy sources if they hope to work in the rapidly expanding developing world.

Barriers to energy conservation

- Awareness barriers
- Economic barriers
- Knowledge barriers
- Skill barriers
- Institutional barriers
- Technical barriers

Source: Adapted from Gerd Scholl, 'Sustainable Product Policy in Europe', *European Environment*,
Vol. 6, No. 6, Nov–Dec 1996, pp. 190–1.

EU Energy Directive

The EU Energy Performance of Buildings Directive, due to come into effect in 2006, promises to trigger fundamental change in the design and refurbishment of domestic property. Although the target of carbon-neutral housing is unlikely to be met within a generation, the display of energy ratings on buildings will encourage much more awareness of energy efficiency in both publicly owned and private property.

All new housing will have to disclose its predicted energy performance to potential buyers, leading to greater use of high levels of fabric insulation, controlled ventilation, condensing boilers, passive solar heating, photovoltaic systems and intelligent glazing technologies. The UK government has already signalled its intention to further revise the UK Building Regulations in 2010 (beyond the measures to be introduced in 2006) in order to comply with the Directive.

Changes to UK Energy Policy

In February 2003, the UK government signalled the introduction of a number of initiatives to improve energy efficiency and expand the use of renewable energy

Fig 2.4
Super-insulation and airtightness at the House for the Future designed by Jestico and Whiles.
Source: Jestico and Whiles

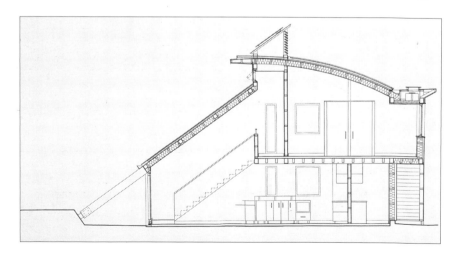

Amendments to Part L of the UK Building Regulations between 2002 and 2006. It is expected that a further 30% improvement will be required by amendments in 2010.

Standard	Wall U-value	Ground floor U-value	Window U-value	Roof U-value	Air-tightness at 50 Pa	Boiler efficiency
Building Regulations Approved Document Part L 2002	0.35	0.25	2.00	0.20	No standard	93%
Building Regulations Approved Document Part L 2006	0.25	0.22	1.8	0.16	0.36 ac/h	93%

Effect of changes to UK Building Regulations 2002–2010 on anticipated CO_2 emissions.

CO_2 emissions	Space heating CO_2 emissions (kg/yr)	Water heating CO_2 emissions (kg/yr)	Total CO_2 emissions (kg/yr)
2002 Building Regulations	813	746	1519
2006 Building Regulations	567	746	1313
2010 Building Regulations (anticipated)	397	706	1143

Source: *Prospect*, December 2004, RIAS/Camyx Group, p. 39

sources. The Energy White Paper set a target of cutting the UK's carbon dioxide emissions by 60 per cent by 2050 with 'real progress by 2020' [2]. The White Paper set out the framework for 'meeting tomorrow's challenges of a low carbon economy ... through the promotion of renewables' intended to make the UK largely self-sufficient in energy terms [3]. The political message in the White Paper is that of energy independence – making the UK less vulnerable to fossil fuel price increases, to fluctuating oil supply and political unrest in the Middle East. Since Britain is particularly well served by renewable energy resources (wind, wave, geothermal and solar), the government is signalling a massive investment in these supplies.

The White Paper has important implications for the practice of architecture. As part of the policy changes required, the government set up a 'Better Buildings Summit' in 2003 aimed at bringing key players in construction together to help develop strategies for achieving more sustainable practices. Topics considered by the task force included expanding the use of photovoltaics (PV cells) and local wind-generated electricity, combined heat and power (CHP), off-site construction technologies and taxation policy to increase the level of investment by the UK building industry in energy-saving practices.

Central to the new energy strategy is the emphasis on local generation of electricity (as against large, distant power stations). Microgeneration of electricity using PV panels on the roofs of houses for instance could, according to the White Paper, result in new houses having zero emissions of CO_2 in 20 years' time. However, with many of the UK's nuclear power stations (which currently provide 24 per cent of national electricity) being phased out between 2012 and 2015, there is likely to be increasing pressure on expanding local generation (i.e. at the building or nearby) well before 2023.

New UK energy legislation which will come into effect in 2006 implements the EU Directive on the 'Energy Performance of Buildings'. This Directive requires regular energy assessment in the use of existing buildings and the energy labelling of new ones. To meet the rigorous targets of the Directive, the UK government started to make wide-ranging revisions to Part L of the Building Regulations in 2004. Part L aims to improve the energy efficiency of buildings by addressing both the design and construction elements (prior to 2000 only the construction element mattered). However, what is proposed for the full revisions of 2006 is a common methodology for ensuring that the design actually delivers the energy savings predicted. This gives owners and tenants the evidence required to gain redress against the architect, system installer or builder for any failures in promised energy conservation. Further revisions to Part L are planned (in 2010 and 2015) to raise insulation standards still further, to encourage solar water heating and the use of photovoltaics, and to increase the standard of air-tightness. More immediately, Part L in 2006 is expected to require standards in building refurbishment to equal those in new buildings [4].

The government has stated that whilst energy efficiency is the 'cheapest and safest way' of meeting the Kyoto agreements on reducing CO_2 emissions, buildings have a critical role to play. Not only are the Building Regulations to be progressively upgraded, but public sector buildings are expected to act as examples of energy innovation for the private sector to follow. The design of schools, hospitals and universities will incorporate low-carbon technologies funded by new fiscal measures such as the Enhanced Capital Allowances Scheme.

Key goals of the Energy White Paper, 2003

- To significantly reduce carbon dioxide (CO_2) emissions
- To maintain the reliability of energy supplies
- To promote competitive energy markets in the UK and beyond
- To ensure that every home is adequately and affordably heated

Source: Adapted from *EcoTech*, Issue 7, Spring 2003, p. 22

Key targets of the Energy White Paper, 2003

- To have renewable energy contributing 20% of UK electricity by 2020
- To take steps to cut the UK's carbon dioxide emissions by 60% by 2050
- To ensure that more than half of the reduction in carbon dioxide emissions come from energy efficiency by 2020

Source: Adapted from *EcoTech*, Issue 7, Spring 2003, p. 22

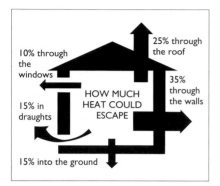

10% through the windows

25% through the roof

35% through the walls

HOW MUCH HEAT COULD ESCAPE

15% in draughts

15% into the ground

Fig 2.5
Typical domestic heat loss through elements of construction.

EU Directive on the Energy Performance of Buildings, 2003

- All EU governments to develop a common methodology for the integrated energy performance of buildings
- Set common minimum standards of energy efficiency for new and refurbished buildings by 2005
- Certify the energy performance of buildings every 5 years, with performance certificates for public buildings prominently displayed
- Require the regular inspection of boilers and air-conditioning systems over 15 years old

Source: Adapted from *EcoTech*, Issue 7, Spring 2003, p. 23

Although the White Paper responds to international obligations such as the Kyoto agreement, the main driving force is the EU Directive ratified in January 2003 on the 'Energy Performance of Buildings'. This Directive has far-reaching implications for the design, construction and management of buildings. In addition to the innovations listed earlier, it seeks by 2005 to implement a common methodology for the integrated energy labelling of buildings which will cover aspects of heating, lighting, cooling, ventilation and heat recovery simultaneously. In the past, poor energy performance could be offset by increasing the size of air-conditioning plant, and poor insulation standards by enhanced heat recovery. Under the proposed methodology all the elements which consume energy in pursuit of the environmental conditioning of buildings will be integrated into a single performance calculation.

Climate Change

Stabilisation of climate change may take a century after the last barrel of oil has been burnt. The time–temperature lag means that the world climate may be 4–5°C higher at the end of the fossil fuel age than at the beginning. Warming the Earth has serious consequences for agricultural production and fisheries, and as sea levels rise cities will not be immune from the effects. Greenhouse gases (GHGs) need to be stabilised in the short term and reduced in the long term. To achieve this we need to move towards renewable energy sources, to use more natural gas for power, less coal for heat and save oil for those things that cannot be met by other fossil fuels (such as plastics). We need, in the short term, a zero-carbon economy and zero-carbon buildings.

There are wide regional variations in the use of fossil fuels and hence greenhouse gas production. In the USA, GHGs are mainly the result of oil used in transportation and gas used in domestic heating. In much of Eastern Europe and China, coal is a major problem, in terms not just of GHGs but also of other pollutants such as SO_2 and SOx, which are responsible for respiratory diseases and acid rain. Coal is the basis of 70 per cent of China's energy, making China the second biggest producer of GHGs after the USA (although compared with the USA, China produces only about one-fifth per head of population).

In an attempt to limit GHG production, the Kyoto Protocol of 1997, ratified by over 100 countries (but excluding at the time the USA, Russia and Australia), established targets for greenhouse gas reduction based on a system of carbon trading between nations. The Emissions Trading System (ETS) allows one country to buy another's carbon credits, offsetting these against investment in the development of clean technologies. The Kyoto system, to be reinforced by a similar scheme for the EU in 2005, encourages investment in low-carbon energy projects in developing countries. Investors gain credits which allow the domestic market to buy international carbon emissions rights. The effect is to require architects to be aware not just of the energy consumption of a building but also of whether the energy is fossil fuel or renewable based. The global system of carbon trading may in time filter down to parallel a similar system for buildings.

CO_2 emissions have been increasing since the Industrial Revolution and continue to rise in spite of international obligations (such as those agreed at Rio and Kyoto). They continue to rise also in spite of improvements made to the energy efficiency of buildings. Three reasons are normally given for this:
- rise in human population (currently 6 billion and expected to reach 10 billion by 2050);
- the legacy of older, inefficient buildings (the existing building stock globally is replaced at a rate of under 2 per cent per year); and
- rising consumer standards, with the corresponding growth in air-conditioning, electrical gadgets of various kinds, and increasing comfort expectations.

If 50 per cent of global warming is caused by the burning of fossil fuels in support of the use of buildings, about 60 per cent of the remainder is generated in

Fig 2.6
The effects of climate change.

transporting people and goods to buildings. Cities, therefore, are responsible for 75–80 per cent of all anthropogenic CO_2 emissions, and it is these which are the main source of global warming. Debate currently centres on the degree of warming; estimates vary from 1.5°C to 4°C over 100 years. Bearing in mind the life span of buildings (typically 50–150 years), it is clear that many buildings designed today will need to survive quite different temperature conditions in the future. With a combination of global warming and a reduction in global dimming (the masking of the sun by air pollution), if the temperature of the planet were to rise by 4°C, it would lead to sea level rise of 5m by the end of the century.

The term 'global warming' suggests an even heating of the Earth. The reality is *climate change* and a great deal of regional instability. For example, the intensity of storms increases, with higher rainfall, stronger winds and less seasonal predictability for countries near the major oceans. Conversely, drought makes farming unsustainable in formerly productive areas (e.g. Texas, Sudan) and, as a result, nations become dependent on food aid, threatening health and prosperity. Global warming also heats up the seas, leading to the thawing of polar ice. As a consequence, sea levels rise due to melting ice and the thermal expansion of the oceans. This, in turn, alters the patterns of ocean currents, which cause further changes in the weather patterns.

Rising sea levels threaten our cities and, because most world cities (London, Sydney, Amsterdam, New York, Hong Kong, Cape Town) are at or near sea level, their very survival is at stake. These cities will, perhaps by as early as the next century, become the new Venices of human civilisation. It is not just the flooding of roads which will make these great urban centres untenable but the loss of the underground services upon which they depend – water supply, sewers, fibre-optic cables, underground transport. Even those who do not live or work in the city are affected. Most food production comes from the rich agricultural lands of former flood plains, and as sea levels rise much of this land will be lost by inundation. If 50 per cent of the global human population (the figure for the European Union is 80 per cent) now lives in urban areas, many of which are at or near coasts, climate instability threatens humanity's very existence.

Main effects of global warming

- Sea level rise
- Increase in storm activity
- Differential regional temperature rise
- Expansion of deserts
- Increase in episodes of high temperature, especially in unlikely places
- Increase in convective action (leading to soil drying)
- Stress on world forests

Source: Adapted from UN Inter-Government Panel on Climate Change (IPCC)

Fig 2.7
The Roman town of Palmera in Syria, which collapsed when the water supply failed.
Source: Syrian Tourist Authority

Buildings face a particular challenge. Many were designed when energy was abundant and the science of global warming was not developed. Their architects and engineers assumed that unlimited energy was available for heating, lighting, ventilation and lifts. In the commercial sector, these buildings were commonly fully air-conditioned and were deep in plan, thereby distancing much of the interior from natural sources of light, solar energy and ventilation. In the domestic sector, old patterns of dense city living (apartments, terraced housing) were replaced by detached and semi-detached dwellings. As a consequence, cities became widely spaced and unable to support public transport. Also, heat loss from one home was not the heat gain for another, as it would be in an apartment. With this dispersal went the separation of land uses. Journeys were necessarily made by car, adding to the overall carbon emissions. In many industrialised countries, such as the UK, USA and Australia, transport had, by 2000, begun to account for nearly 30 per cent of all global warming gas production.

Global reserves of fossil fuels

Oil	30 years + 40 years of tar sands
Natural gas	50 years
Coal	200 years
Lignite	300 years

Source: Adapted from *RSA Journal*, October 1994

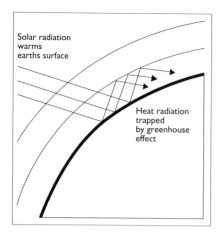

Fig 2.8
How global warming works.

The second most significant greenhouse gas by volume is methane. Globally, there has been a 1 per cent increase per year in methane emissions, part of which is attributed to the growth in domestic waste. Methane is particularly damaging since it depletes atmospheric chemicals which help to break down other greenhouse gases. In the UK, the construction process generates 48 per cent of all waste, with buildings in use being the principal source of the remainder (half a tonne of waste per person per year). There are several strategies that help to reduce waste generation and involve either reduction of waste at source or the exploitation of waste for energy or new material resources. The latter is what we refer to as recycling, reusing materials rather than dumping them in landfill sites, while the former involves the extraction of energy from waste (in, for example, local CHP plants).

How Does Global Warming Work?

The greenhouse effect is the result of a protective low-level envelope (known as the troposphere) which, positioned about 15 km above the Earth's surface, traps solar radiation. Only about half of all the energy of solar radiation is absorbed by the Earth, a process that alters the wavelength of the light. A proportion of the solar energy is converted into infrared radiation, which is then unable to escape into the outer atmosphere because of the presence of the greenhouse gases. The main greenhouse gases, which generally benefit life by allowing the Earth to trap the sun's radiation (hence the term the greenhouse effect), are CO_2 and methane, with lesser quantities of nitrous oxide and the manufactured chemicals chlorofluorocarbons (CFCs). The problem is that the effect of the natural production of these gases is being upset by the huge quantities added as a result of humankind's activities. Two hundred years ago there were 590 billion tonnes of CO_2 in the atmosphere; now there are 760 billion tonnes, resulting in an increase in the total solar energy absorbed by the Earth. It is this increase (and the fact that global tonnage of CO_2 is increasing rapidly) which has led to the prediction of warming by as much as 4°C over the next 100 years.

Without the protective shield of the troposphere, the planet would be over 30°C cooler. The troposphere is a delicate embrace that keeps us warm and sheltered from both the excesses of solar radiation and the chilling effect of night-time cooling. The trouble is that the system is being altered, with all the corresponding problems of climate instability. In this doomsday scenario, buildings (and how they are heated, cooled and lit) are the main culprits.

The Importance of Energy

Energy conservation is a central concern in the quest for sustainability. The burning of fossil fuels for buildings is responsible for about one-half of all energy use worldwide. Heating, lighting and ventilation require oil, gas or coal to be burnt either at the building or in a power station. It is the relationship between the combustion of fossil fuels and CO_2 emissions which is crucial, not energy as such. If society could generate all of its power needs from renewable sources there would be no problem. In the UK, the main sources of CO_2 emissions are:

- heating, lighting and ventilating buildings   46% ⎤
- building construction   5%   ⎦ = Total 51%
- transportation (of goods and people)   30%
- industry, agriculture   19%

Various intergovernmental agreements exist to limit atmospheric CO_2 release (see the section on Climate Change above). The Earth Summit at Rio (1992), the Kyoto Protocol (1997) and, more recently, the Hague Conference (2000) have all sought a consensus on international activity. An idea put in place at Kyoto concerned carbon trading, whereby a rich nation can buy a poor nation's CO_2 credits. This has allowed the USA to purchase the former Soviet Union's carbon allowances, permitting the USA to pollute at twice the European average and at 20 times the world norm. Typical CO_2 emissions per person per year are:

- USA   6.00 tonnes
- Europe   3.00 tonnes
- Japan   2.50 tonnes
- Russia   2.00 tonnes
- China   0.65 tonnes
- India   0.25 tonnes

There are three options available to reduce these levels: nuclear power, renewable energy and carbon conversion.

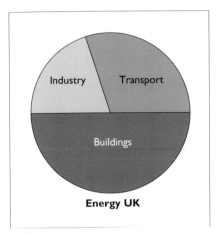

Energy UK

Fig 2.9
Energy use in the UK.

Nuclear energy, promoted initially as a clean energy source, has its own well-publicised environmental problems. Renewable energy, however, has much potential, to the extent that the UK government has set the following targets:

Year	Target
2005	5% of all energy from renewable sources
2010	10% of all energy from renewable sources
2050	50% of all energy from renewable sources

Source: National Energy Foundation, 2000

Carbon conversion is a valuable means of viewing the link between development and the carrying capacity of the land which supports it in terms of energy. The idea is based on the ability of trees and forests to convert CO_2 back into oxygen (which occurs via photosynthesis). Although the science is imprecise, the theory says that about 15 mature trees are required to convert the carbon emissions over a year of a typical car and 40 trees for a house. Much depends, however, on the size and type of tree and the energy efficiency of the CO_2-producing element. The conversion is based on an equation whereby 160 m^2 of trees are required to balance 1,000 kWh of energy consumed in heating, 900 m^2 for every 1,000 kWh of electricity used, and 1,200 m^2 for every 1,000 litres of petrol combusted. Typically, it means that every household requires roughly two acres of woodland to convert its CO_2 emissions back to oxygen. Using these figures, however, it quickly becomes clear that the carbon footprint of London alone exceeds the capacity of all the forests of the UK put together to achieve effective CO_2 conversion. Even if all of the UK was forested, it is unlikely that the national output of CO_2 would be balanced. This, of course, is why we have such a problem globally.

Climate Instability and Building Design

Buildings designed and engineered today will still be standing when climate change bites. By 2050, it is estimated that global temperatures may have risen by 2°C and by 2100 by perhaps as much as 4°C. Once triggered, the rise is exponential. Not only will there be an increase in temperatures overall in the UK but the incidence of storms and heavy subtropical rainfall will have increased. There will be pressure on drainage systems, on the building fabric itself, on land settlement patterns and on transportation. Apart from avoiding further building on flood plains, there are three principles to follow in designing buildings for climate change:

- the building shell and footprint is fundamental to long-term survival, adaptability and energy efficiency;
- build to a higher initial standard (better insulation, higher quality materials); and
- provide the means to upgrade building systems, especially in the areas of cooling and in the provision of renewable energy.

Although buildings in the UK are not regularly mechanically cooled (except shops and offices), there will be pressure, especially in the domestic sector, to cool buildings in the summer. Good design (for example, exploiting thermal capacity, good orientation planning) is essential to avoid the use of clip-on air-conditioning units that are commonplace in hotter climates. Such units are particularly expensive in electrical energy and, being short-lived and rarely recycled, pose further problems of resource consumption and waste disposal.

Renewable Energy

Renewable energy can be used to heat, cool or ventilate buildings instead of fossil fuels. The main sources of useful renewable energy for buildings are solar, wind

Fig 2.10
GLA building in London, designed by Foster and Partners, uses stepped section for shading (right) and spherical shape for natural cooling.
Source: Foster and Partners

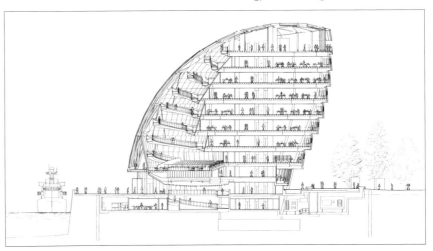

and geothermal resources. At a macro-scale, wave, hydro and tidal power are also available but are not always sufficiently exploited. The ready availability of fossil fuel sources has been a deterrent to the wider exploitation of renewable energy in the architecture and urban design realm. One trend noticeable at present is the shift from macro- to micro-scale application of renewable energy, thereby involving more building-related installation.

The combination of relatively secure long-term supplies (40–200 years, depending on fossil fuel type), low taxation and cheap prices has, until recent times, created complacency among consumers, developers and designers. The threat of global warming has, however, shifted the focus to unexploited, cheap and readily available renewable energy sources. Both the new CO_2 targets agreed at the Kyoto Conference in 1997 and incentives provided by the EU have played their part in the growing interest amongst architects in renewable energy. Consumers have also begun to link energy consumption with the wider question of healthy lifestyles, because renewable energy has particular advantages at a physical and psychological level.

Potentially, renewable energy could satisfy all of humankind's energy demands. The total energy of the sun far exceeds that required for human use. The problems, however, are to do with distribution, storage, conversion and application of this solar energy into a form useful for heating buildings, driving machinery and the countless other tasks which are now performed by burning fossil fuels. Renewable energy can be exploited for use in buildings in a variety of ways. It can be:

- extracted elsewhere and delivered through conventional delivery channels;
- extracted at or near the site of the building; and
- extracted via the fabric of the building.

To take advantage of these strategies, it is important to consider potential renewable sources at an early design stage. Sites for development can be selected on the basis of their access to renewable energy supplies – sun, wind, water power, geothermal, etc. A south-facing slope offers obvious benefits in terms of exploiting solar power just as a windy location provides the chance to develop local wind-generated electricity. After site selection, there are other design decisions that can help to maximise the exploitation of renewable energy. Orientation, building footprint and location on the site all allow for effective and cost-efficient harvesting of solar, wind and other sources of natural power. So, the first principle of renewable energy is to consider available sources and the method of exploitation at the briefing and sketch design stage (*RIBA Plan of Work* Stages A, B and C). Too often, renewable energy is considered only after the crucial decisions that affect its exploitation have been made. This is particularly true of passive solar design, where the geometric constraints are most marked.

Renewable Energy and Taxation

Carbon liabilities account for as much as 40 per cent of the market capitalisation of some companies. This suggests that their exposure to the tightening of government taxation to promote energy efficiency may limit their economic growth and stock market valuation. Companies which rely heavily on fossil fuels will find themselves increasingly heavily taxed as the government seeks to meet European Union obligations. The carbon tax (the result of Kyoto agreements embedded since 2002 into EU law) represents a major force for change in the design of buildings, especially for companies such as PowerGen, BP and Shell whose economy is largely carbon based. The UK Emissions Trading Scheme will result in investment in new cleaner technologies (such as renewable energy and fuel cell development) and the construction of more green buildings. Emissions trading allows one company to buy the carbon credits of another with the result that energy efficiency will figure in annual company reports. Since 15,000 companies account for 40 per cent of all EU carbon dioxide emissions, [5] there is likely to be pressure on these companies to reduce their dependence on fossil fuels. As these businesses comprise most of Europe's household names, new energy taxes will be a major driver of change in the design of buildings.

New laws, particularly from Europe, will activate change in energy production as well as its use in buildings. In fact, of the nine new EU environment policies introduced after the Maastricht Treaty (1992) three deal specifically with energy use and security. Here the emphasis is on renewable energy technologies – sun, wind and the hydrogen fuel cell. It is expected over the next generation that the fuel cell will have considerable impact on energy use not just in buildings but in replacing internal combustion engines and making obsolete highly polluting lead–acid batteries. Powered by a combustion of natural gas, photovoltaics and liquid petroleum gas, vehicles running on fuel cells are expected to be in use by

Fig 2.11
Use of renewable energy at the Taos Earthship, New Mexico, designed by Michael Reynolds.
Source: Sam Hughes

Fig 2.12
Solar space heating and earth sheltering at the Earth House in Milton Keynes.

2006 [6]. Individual fuel cells with a capacity of 1–25 kW can be stacked to produce the energy required to power a typical home. Since housing accounts for 27 per cent of all energy use in the UK, the benefits are obvious.

European Environment Policy after Maastricht

- Concept of 'sustainable development' adopted across Europe
- Environmental protection integrated with social and economic policy
- Consistent environmental laws between member states
- Control of cross-border pollution
- Consistent energy policy throughout Europe
- Action to maintain energy security
- Emphasis on renewable energy supplies
- European water framework
- Recognition of the cultural value of the European built environment

Main Types of Renewable Energy

Although there are many renewable energy sources, only the most easily exploited in buildings will be considered here.

Solar Power

Solar radiation is the basis of photosynthesis and the primary source of renewable energy. Solar power helps to create vegetation, which can be used as a fuel either directly or extracted from energy crops such as oil seed rape. More commonly, solar power is used passively in buildings to provide space heating, ventilation and lighting. Solar power is also used actively to heat water in roof-mounted collectors and to generate electricity with the use of photovoltaic (PV) cells. Since the sun drives the Earth's climate, solar power is also locked into wind and wave power. Sun power is also stored in geothermal sources and in fossil fuels.

Passive solar energy is commonly used in buildings but its full potential is rarely exploited. South-facing glazing provides useful space heating, creating about 20 per cent of the energy needs of a typical house. With enlarged windows to the south, the addition of conservatories or atria, and some ducting of the warmed air to the colder parts of the building, passive solar gain can provide nearly 40 per

Fig 2.13
Passive solar design at the House for the Future, Cardiff, designed by Jestico and Whiles.
Source: Jestico and Whiles

EU energy policies

- Cut CO_2 emissions by 8% by 2010
- Double the contribution (to 12%) that renewable energy makes to total energy demand by 2010
- Improve energy efficiency by 18% (compared to 1995) by 2010

Source: *Renewable Energy Systems* (EU), 1998, p. 28

cent (or 2,000 kWh/yr) of the primary energy heating needs of a typical house in the UK. For this to be most efficiently achieved, the solar energy needs to be stored in a building fabric of high thermal capacity, and the building should be well insulated and relatively air-tight. Simple measures such as southerly aspect, differential window area between north and south, and high levels of insulation can achieve a great deal of benefit at little extra cost. Necessarily, public rooms are placed on the south side and utility areas (kitchens, bathrooms, small bedrooms) to the north.

Passive solar design is exploited in the design of many building types. Schools frequently exploit its principles by placing highly glazed classrooms to the south, which are then vented at high level to a central corridor or circulation street. The plan maximises solar gain while the cross-section exploits stack-effect ventilation by using a stepped ceiling and high-level vents. By such simple measures, schools in the UK can save about 25 per cent of the energy normally used in space heating. In offices, passive solar design is employed by the use of atria and perimeter glazing to provide convective cooling currents which help to avoid the use of air-conditioning. Typically, modern commercial buildings are designed on the mixed-mode principle of passive solar, mechanical or fan-assisted ventilation, restricting air-conditioning to hot spots such as photocopying rooms. As with schools, these buildings employ hybrid systems of heating and cooling, producing in the process interesting new building typologies.

Solar energy is also used for lighting, and most designers combine passive solar design with the maximisation of daylight. Artificial lighting is a major source of energy use in buildings, sometimes approaching the energy consumption of space heating. Lighting can account for about one-half of all electricity consumed in a building. The cheapest way to reduce energy used in lighting is to take full

Fig 2.14
Environmental design to maximise daylight and
cross-ventilation at Law College, Cambridge,
designed by Foster and Partners.
Source: Foster and Partners

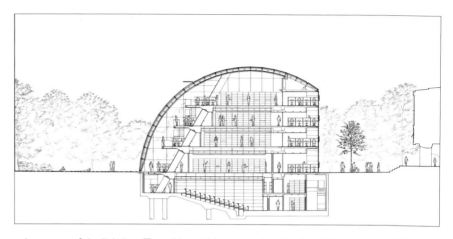

advantage of daylighting. To achieve this, room depths should not exceed 7m from an outside wall, and consequently building plans should be about 14m in depth (possibly 15m with an internal corridor exploiting borrowed light). Daylight penetration can be improved by the use of daylight shelves positioned on the outside of the building. Correctly designed, they can increase the level of daylight inside the building without glare or sharp contrast in the distribution of light from the window to the interior. Daylight shelves also frequently double up as solar shades, thereby reducing unwanted solar gain and the problem of sunlight penetration on work surfaces or computer screens. Such external shelves can also provide a window-cleaning gantry for building maintenance.

Active solar systems consist of flat plate water heaters and evacuated tube collectors [7]. Solar water heaters are normally placed on south-facing inclined roofs with the heated water taken directly into the hot water storage tank, which is usually positioned in the roof space. A few square metres of solar water heater can provide two-thirds of the hot water requirements of a typical household in the UK [8]. Outside the UK, community-based solar district heating systems are to be found. Here, solar collectors heat the water stored in large thermal (often underground) tanks during the summer, which, because of their size, retain much of the heat during the winter. This pre-heated hot water is then piped to adjoining buildings, where it can be heated further before use either in radiators or as domestic hot water.

Fig 2.15
Flat plate solar water heaters at the Taos, New
Mexico Earthship.
Source: Sam Hughes

Fig 2.16
Flat plate solar water heaters at the MacRae
House, Bristol.

Predicted expansion in renewable energy use in EU between 1995 and 2010

Type of energy	1995	2010
Wind	2.5 GW	40 GW
Photovoltaics (PV)	0.03 GW	3 GW
Biomass	45 Mtoe	135 Mtoe
Geothermal (heat pumps)	1.3 GW	5 GW
Solar thermal collectors	6.5 Mm^2	100 Mm^2

Key
GW: 10^9 watts
Mtoe: million tonnes of oil equivalent
Mm^2: million metres^2

Source: *Renewable Energy Systems* (EU), 1998, p. 29

Solar energy is increasingly being exploited with the use of PV panels. Their use in buildings is becoming more common as the cost of PV technology falls and confidence in its effectiveness rises. PV use globally is increasing by about 10 per cent every year, with costs falling, initially by 12 per cent a year and currently by around 4 per cent a year. There have been many showcase projects, such as the athletes' village at the Sydney Olympic Games, which had 665 houses heated, lit and ventilated almost entirely with electricity generated by rooftop PV panels [9]. Other showcase demonstration schemes include the Doxford Solar Energy Office near Sunderland, designed by Studio E Architects. Here, PV panels generating 70 kW are integrated on a large south-facing glazed wall which also employs passive solar technologies. Energy modelling of the building suggests that energy consumption will be 85 kWh/m^2/yr, producing 'a saving of one-third over typical offices in the region' [10].

Photovoltaics (PV): Issues and Choices
The key issues architects need to consider when contemplating the use of photovoltaic technologies in buildings are:
- How much will it contribute to the energy load?
- Is PV technology cost-effective over the lifetime of the building?
- Are the site and use appropriate?
- Is the technology reliable?
- Can PV technology be integrated into the design and other service strategies?

Fig 2.17
Photovoltaic and passive solar heating at the Doxford Solar office, Sunderland, designed by Studio E Architects.
Source: Studio E Architects

As a consequence of its benign nature and current government inducement, PV technology is attractive to clients and the public at large. With PV panels there are no emissions, no noise and no waste (except at the end of their lives). However, there are environmental costs in manufacture, but since most of the materials are recyclable – glass, aluminium, silicon – these are not considerable. Also, because of its modular nature, it is possible to start small and add PV modules later. In Europe in the period 2000–2004 annual growth in the use of PV technology was nearly 40 per cent, with most of the expansion in the area of architectural application, i.e. integration with buildings. Also, since PV systems are more efficient when they operate at low temperatures, much of the growth has been in sunny northern locations. To a degree, the temperature efficiency compensates for the loss of solar radiation away from the equator.

The main advantage of PV technology is the way that sunlight (or just light if it is bright enough) is converted into electricity. This allows lights, computers, TVs, microwave ovens, electric cookers and refrigerators to be powered without resorting to imported energy. In commercial applications where much of the energy load is electricity used for interior lighting and equipment there are obvious advantages. However, the main problem with exploiting all renewable energy sources within buildings is the intermittent nature of the supply (sun and wind) and the difficulty of storing the generated electricity. This is why it is important to ensure integration of the energy strategy with the design and day-to-day use of the buildings. In offices, for example, where lights are usually employed during the day, PV technology allows energy from the sun to be converted to electricity at the point of use. Hence, natural supply and human demand are in close proximity (unlike fossil fuel systems). Any PV-generated electricity which has not been consumed in the building is fed into the national grid, which acts as an energy store. In periods of low generation (at night or on cloudy days) the building user can buy back the electricity at a discounted rate. Hence, the efficient operation of a PV system requires access to the grid, otherwise expensive and space-consuming batteries are required for storage.

Before PV electricity can be used, either in the building or fed into the grid, it needs to be converted from DC to AC supply. This requires an inverter, which adds to the cost of installation and is more frequently the source of system failure than the PV panels themselves. Modern PV panels have a module efficiency of 15 per cent – that is, they convert 15 per cent of the primary energy of the sun

Fig 2.18
Section through Doxford Solar Office,
Sunderland.
Source: Studio E Architects

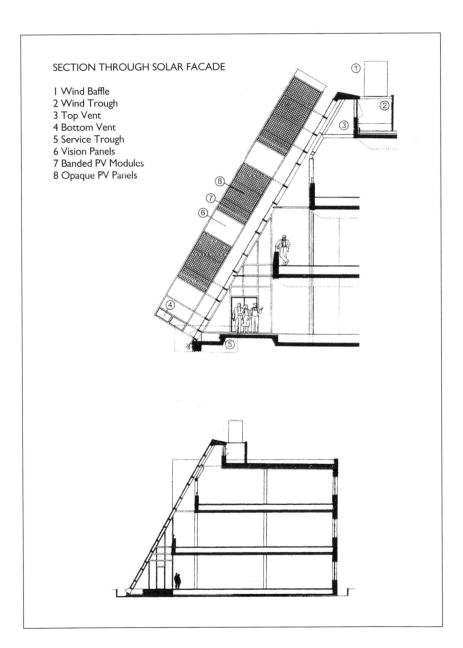

SECTION THROUGH SOLAR FACADE

1 Wind Baffle
2 Wind Trough
3 Top Vent
4 Bottom Vent
5 Service Trough
6 Vision Panels
7 Banded PV Modules
8 Opaque PV Panels

directly into electricity. As a rough guide, 8–10 m² of PV modules generate 1 kW of electricity all the time over a year, or put another way, the annual output in the UK is 750–800 kWh/kWp (i.e. kW hours per kW potential). However, output is reduced by shading, poor orientation and poor installation – hence the need to consider PV technology as a fundamental design issue as against a later 'bolt-on'. The peak output in the UK in high summer is 1.2 kW/m² of panel (or 9.6 kW in total with 8m² of panels), a level far in excess of energy demand at the time in a typical domestic building [11].

Cost of PV Technology

In the UK the cost of a typical domestic solar water system is £2,000, while a PV system generating a similar level of electrical energy costs £7,000–£9,000. For a small commercial building such as a petrol filling station, the capital cost of producing around 6,000 kWh/yr of electricity from PV panels is £35,000, [12] giving a payback period of 12 years at 2005 prices. However, the advantage of the

Fig 2.19 *(right)*
Sainsbury supermarket, Greenwich, an exercise in green design, designed by Chetwood Architects. Green issues were prominent in the brief, making integration possible from the outset.
Source: Chetwood Architects

Fig 2.20 *(far right)*
Sainsbury supermarket, Greenwich.
Source: Chetwood Architects

PV system is the type of power generated – electricity, essential for most modern appliances. Bearing in mind that 15 per cent of the energy of light is capable of being converted to electricity, whereas 45 per cent can be utilised for space heating and 30 per cent for water heating, the ideal answer is to employ a hybrid system as at Sainsbury's eco-store in Greenwich, designed by Chetwood Associates. PV and passive solar technologies used together provide an ideal system, especially when integrated with other green energy systems such as wood-chip boilers or geothermal energy.

There are, however, disadvantages at present, which grants from government, fuel costs and technological innovation may alter in the future. Solar electricity is two to three times the cost of fossil fuel power at the point of use. Relatively low oil prices mean that PV is (at present) disadvantaged. However, the creation of a large market in Japan for PV technology as a result of central and local government procurement policy has led to mass production by companies like Sharp. This in turn has driven down prices and improved both the efficiency and

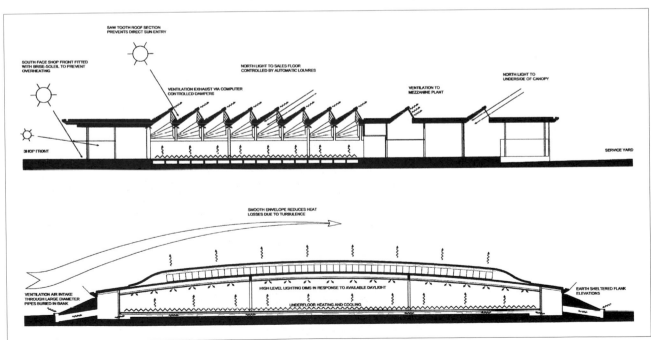

reliability of solar technologies. By 2050 it is expected that at current levels of technological innovation, PV will be employed in large solar electricity power stations, making nuclear and oil-based stations obsolete. Even in the domestic sector, PV installations will be competitive in 5–10 years' time (at current rising oil prices), and as an expanding market reduces unit cost, it may well be cheaper than oil and gas for non-domestic applications.

The payback time for the energy consumed in the manufacture of PV panels (the embodied energy) is recouped by the energy generated after five years of use. Over the typical lifetime of a PV system (put notionally at 20 years) four times more energy is produced than consumed in manufacture. And since this output is clean energy as against an input of 'dirty' energy (in manufacture) the wider environmental benefits are obvious. As a consequence of their advantages, companies which were oil-based, such as BP and Shell, now market themselves as energy companies complete with a division manufacturing PV panels.

Photovoltaics: the Need for Design Integration

With their ultra-modern aesthetic, photovoltaic panels are well suited to high-tech applications. Their ability to respond to sky conditions, their sheen and glamour (compared to other renewable energy applications) mean that many clients are happy to pay the extra cost of installation. Photovoltaic panels on a roof or tilted facade reflect favourably on a company, signalling a concern for the environment. This combination of aesthetics and prestige, added to the fact that most governments have generous grants available to help expand the market, suggests that photovoltaics will outstrip other renewable energy technologies.

The emphasis on energy, especially photovoltaic applications, has placed greater attention to the roof as an architectural element. Many see the roof as the fifth elevation [13] and one whose form and orientation are as important as the vertical elevations. Architects need to ensure that the technical aspects of PVs and the shape, orientation and angle of roofs are well integrated. The ad hoc effect of poor integration undermines the aesthetic potential of PV panels. With office buildings integration can readily be achieved, but with individual houses the effect can be less satisfactory. PV panel sizes are rarely in scale with domestic roofs, especially when a number of panels are required for efficient energy generation. As a consequence, some manufacturers such as Redland are developing roof tiles with integral photovoltaic cells.

Typical performance of roof-mounted PV system

Module efficiency	15%
System size	1.5 kW
South-facing roof at 30 – 40°	
System provides 50–60% of total energy use	
Cost of PV modules	£6/W of energy generated
Cost of PV roof tiles	£9/W of energy generated
Of total cost, 60% is cost of PV panels, 40% is cost of inverter and wiring	

Source: Northumbria Photovoltaics Application Centre

Disadvantages of PV systems

- Sunlight is intermittent
- Electricity is difficult to store
- System design is specific to location and building use
- Control and maintenance add to cost
- Costs are high at installation, low in use (opposite to traditional energy systems)

Source: Northumbria Photovoltaics Application Centre

In the high-tech arena, the concept of seamless engineering should be the ultimate goal. The dramatic curved forms of many modern buildings suit PV use since the sun is always moving and changing its altitude. Panels set at different angles can achieve optimum efficiency at different times of the day or the year. Also, since the glass of PV panels can be tinted in different shades, their colour and surface texture can be modified to suit the building. A kind of sexy integration is the key, with the needs of PV technology driving the basic shape and form of the building.

The UK is behind much of the world in PV application. There are expected to be only 6,000 applications in the UK by 2005 compared to 140,000 in Germany and 400,000 in Japan [14]. This is partly the result of lack of government incentives and

Fig 2.21
Combination of solar space heating, solar water heating and photovoltaic electricity generation at Integer House, Watford, designed by Cole Thompson.

the availability or price of alternative energy sources. It is also a cultural issue – Germany and Japan see themselves as high-technology countries, where to invest in PV engineering is a statement of national or corporate identity. In Holland, PV installation on houses is encouraged by a 2 per cent discount on normal mortgage interest rates [15].

Setting aside the fiscal measures which are encouraging wider application (from the USA to China), it is important that building design and photovoltaic use are integrated. The fundamentals of the building – its plan and section – should be shaped by the needs of this important new technology. This does not always mean flat solutions; curves and wave forms are often more energy efficient, especially when PV technology is combined with passive solar heating or cooling.

Wind Power

Wind can be exploited to generate electricity offshore, on land and at the building itself. Installation and maintenance costs have fallen to the point where it is now viable to use this technology at the site or on the roof of buildings. Various new technologies and windpump designs are available – some generate electricity directly, others are used for ventilation or for pumping water. Although wind energy has been demonstrated commercially over a wide range of geographical conditions, the UK is particularly well placed to exploit it. It is estimated that for 85 per cent of the year wind is available in the UK to power turbines, making the UK one of the best places in Europe for wind power.

Fig 2.22
Roof-mounted photovoltaic system at the University of Gloucester, designed by Feilden Clegg Bradley.
Source: Feilden Clegg Bradley

The principle of renewable energy from wind is similar to solar power. Electricity generated can be fed into the national grid and bought back on windless days. It can also be used to provide the power for lighting and electrical goods (though special circuits are needed). Normally, wind energy is turned into electricity and fed into large power grids but it can also be used in small grids serving an individual building (house, school, supermarket) or a village community. Here surplus electricity is fed into the national grid after local demand has been met. Wind energy is particularly important when fossil fuels are not available (e.g. on islands) or when electricity supply is intermittent. It is also useful as a complement to solar energy on the assumption that windy grey days occur when the sun is not shining. PV and local wind-generated electricity provide a wider range of self-sufficiency than solar power alone. However, unlike solar energy, which peaks when demand is at its lowest (in the summer), wind energy is most available when demand is greatest (in the winter). Wind turbines vary from small domestic appliances capable of generating 5 watts to large turbines with outputs of over 1.5 MW. Most commercial wind turbines are around 400 kW in capacity, and wind farms tend to operate most efficiently with several smaller turbines (300–500 kW) than one or two large ones. The same is true of buildings, where several micro-turbines are more effective than a single larger wind turbine.

Offshore Wind Farms

Concern over the environmental impact of land-based wind farms has encouraged the development of offshore facilities. The UK government wants 50 per cent of the 3,500 wind turbines planned to be erected by 2010 to be offshore with the remainder on land. Although the offshore sites are not without impact (on migrating birds and fishing) they offer clean energy without upsetting local communities. An example is the Noah Hoyle Offshore Wind Farm, developed by a consortium of National Wind Power and the Danish turbine manufacturer Vestas, which began producing sufficient electricity for 50,000 homes in November 2003. A further large offshore wind farm exists at Scroby Sands, 6 km into the North Sea near Great Yarmouth in Norfolk. These and 15 other offshore wind farms planned for 2005–2010 are expected to produce 5.4–7.2 GW of electricity, thereby helping to meet the UK government's target of 10 per cent of electricity from renewable sources by 2010. The construction of offshore wind farms is expected to create 20,000 jobs over the next few years, thereby compensating for the loss of jobs as a result of decommissioning of nuclear power stations [16]. As a general rule, one large offshore wind farm (of about 30 mega-generators) produces electricity for 50–60,000 homes and creates about 200 jobs locally (installation and maintenance) and 400 further afield (turbine manufacture). Hence, there is an economic argument in addition to the environmental one, with major turbine manufacturers arguing that 20 per cent of the UK's energy could readily be generated by the wind.

Micro-wind Generators

As an alternative to large-scale production there has been a growth in micro-wind generators suitable for building-related application. Typical are the products of a Scottish company called Windsave, which has developed a micro-wind generator system called 'Plug & Save' aimed at the domestic and small industrial market. At a

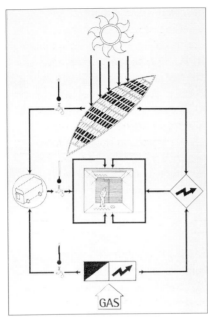

Fig 2.23
How fossil fuel and photovoltaic technologies work together at Duisburg Business Park, designed by Foster and Partners.
Source: Foster and Partners

Fig 2.24
Large-scale wind farm in Yorkshire producing electricity for 9,000 homes.

Fig 2.25
City scale vision of solar gain and climate protection as advocated by Buckminster Fuller at Expo67 in Montreal.

cost of £750 (in 2004), each unit produces 750 watts of energy over a typical year, saving, it is claimed, a tonne of carbon [17]. The turbine is fixed to the roof in the manner of a TV aerial and feeds power into the building at 240 volts. Unlike large wind-powered systems the surplus energy cannot be fed into the national grid but installers are eligible to receive government subsidies in the form of Renewable Obligation Certificates (which are tax deductible). Other systems are available which incorporate micro-generators into the ridge systems of buildings, sometimes altering the profile of roofs to maximise wind potential. As with PV technology, the designer needs to work closely with specialist manufacturers to ensure that aesthetic and engineering demands are equally met.

Other Renewable Energy Sources

Fuel Cells

An emerging technology which looks set to transform energy production is that of fuel cells. They work in a fundamentally different way to photovoltaics, fossil fuel combustion systems and normal lead-based batteries. Fuel cells rely on electrochemical technology and employ hydrogen gas mixed with oxygen to generate electricity. Hydrogen fuel, obtained from natural gas, methanol or petroleum, is combined with liquid oxygen to produce electricity, with heat and water vapour produced as by-products [18]. Potentially, fuel cells can provide electricity with minimal emissions and no moving parts – hence the technology is nearly as benign as photovoltaics.

A fuel cell consists of two electrodes separated by a polymer membrane electrolyte. A thin platinum-coated catalyst layer on each electrode allows the hydrogen fuel to disassociate into electrons and protons. The electrons generated are conducted into an external electrical current, with individual fuel cells generating about 0.6V, which is used directly or stored in a battery. According to the Building Centre Trust, hydrogen fuel cells will be in common use in 20 years' time for a wide range of uses from urban transport to lighting of buildings [19]. Rather than produce carbon dioxide as a by-product, the hydrogen cell produces hydrogen dioxide – water.

Geothermal Energy

Using a simple ground source heat pump (GSHP) it is possible to provide heating

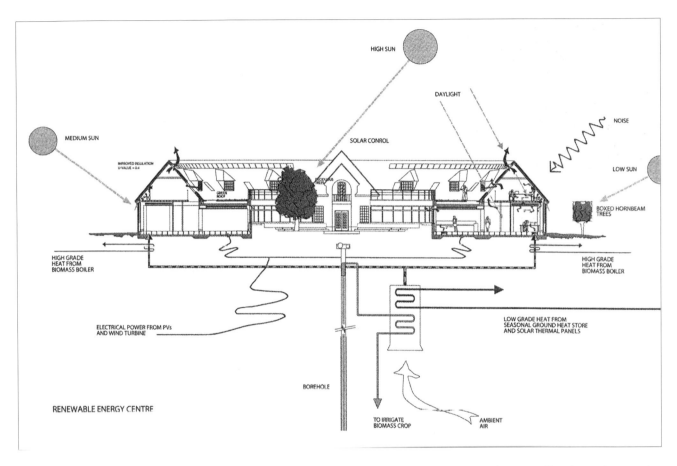

HIGH SUN

DAYLIGHT

NOISE

MEDIUM SUN

SOLAR CONROL

LOW SUN

IMPROVED INSULATION
U-VALUE = 0.4

DECIDUOUS
TREES

BOXED HORNBEAM
TREES

GREEN
ROOF

HIGH GRADE
HEAT FROM
BIOMASS BOILER

HIGH GRADE
HEAT FROM
BIOMASS BOILER

ELECTRICAL POWER FROM PVs
AND WIND TURBINE

LOW GRADE HEAT FROM
SEASONAL GROUND HEAT STORE
AND SOLAR THERMAL PANELS

BOREHOLE

RENEWABLE ENERGY CENTRE

TO IRRIGATE
BIOMASS CROP

AMBIENT
AIR

Fig 2.26
Geothermal energy used at the Renewable
Energy Systems Building, Kings Langley, designed
by Studio E Architects.
Source: Studio E Architects

and cooling for a building by exploiting geothermal energy. Geothermal energy is derived from heat which is generated in the Earth's core and radiates upwards towards the crust, where it is then harnessed for use in buildings. Since this energy is at a constant temperature of between 9 and 13°C in the UK, it can be employed to offset seasonal variations by acting as a heat reservoir in the winter and a heat sink in the summer. As such, it reduces primary energy consumption for winter heating and summer cooling [20]. Although the system offers benefits for all building types it is most useful for buildings like offices and shops where cooling is routinely required.

There are two main types of GSHP – a closed-loop system and an open one. The first circulates an anti-freeze liquid through a loop of plastic pipes laid in the ground either horizontally or vertically. The second uses groundwater from a supply well, which is passed through a heat pump to extract the available energy, which is then used for heating or cooling the building. GSHP schemes are more cost-effective than other renewable energy systems (such as photovoltaics and micro-wind generators) and are relatively emission-free. Since the technology avoids using high-tech gadgetry, maintenance costs are fairly low and reliability high. Compared to typical heating systems, GSHP can reduce carbon dioxide emissions by between 40 and 60 per cent. A typical GSHP installation for a new house using a horizontal loop system is about £10,000 [21]. However, a land area equal to about twice the footprint of the building is required for horizontal loop systems – limiting the use of the technology in built-up urban areas.

Biofuels

Biofuels are another renewable energy source gaining in popularity. They are either specially grown timbers or energy crops, or fuels based on waste of various kinds (municipal, agricultural or forestry). Energy crops are currently diversifying agriculture in the UK, providing fresh sources of energy and changing the ecology of the landscape. Biofuels provide energy through anaerobic digestion (producing methane) or combustion (producing heat). Because they tend to be produced locally from farming or waste collection, biofuels are best used in community-based power stations or directly in buildings. At its simplest, biofuel technology consists of wood-burning stoves, but it is also commonly employed in district combined heat and power (CHP) plants, which exploit the waste heat in electricity generation for district heating, and, less commonly, in gasifier units, which exploit the high temperatures of gas combustion. The integration of locally grown biofuels (such as coppiced willows), CHP plants and buildings provides an ecologically benign system for the future.

Woodchip Technology

Wood fuel has about 80 per cent of the calorific value of coal and represents Europe's main source of renewable energy. Approximately 40 per cent of domestic heating in Denmark and Austria is via efficient wood fuel stoves, and 20 per cent of primary energy production in Finland is derived from timber. Wood fuel comes in the form of logs, chips and pellets – the latter being made of compressed sawdust derived as a by-product of other timber processes. Since

Fig 2.27
Timber is a useful energy crop and building
material.

Geothermal heating: design points to consider

- Existing underground services must be located accurately
- Efficiency depends upon heat transfer rates. Solid ground is more effective than porous, and damp conditions better than dry.
- Horizontal pipe systems are cheaper than vertical
- GSHP should be sized to meet 60–70% of total energy requirements. A secondary heating/cooling system is required to meet extreme conditions.
- Watertightness is essential for the piping to avoid antifreeze loss
- Non-toxic antifreeze is essential with closed-loop systems
- Good quality groundwater is essential with open systems

Source: Adapted from *EcoTech*, Issue 8, November 2003, p. 21

timber derives from renewable sources (if properly managed) and returns oxygen to the atmosphere during the growing phase, it is an important element in any strategy for sustainable development.

Wood fuel can be used to produce heat or, via combined heat and power (CHP) technology, both heat and electricity. It has the advantage of being useful as a fuel at a variety of scales from the individual house to a school or as district heating. Timber production and processing is also relatively labour-intensive, having the secondary benefit of producing employment locally.

When burned as a fuel, timber releases into the atmosphere the carbon dioxide it absorbed during the growth stage. This means not only that timber as a fuel is carbon neutral but also that the forests from which it is derived are carbon dioxide stores, thereby helping to stabilise the global atmosphere. Compared to other fuels timber is low in net emissions, producing only 5 per cent of the carbon dioxide life cycle emissions (g/kWh) of gas, about 3 per cent of those of oil and 2 per cent of those of coal [22]. Added to this, wood fuel is low in sulphur and nitrogen (the main sources of acid rain). It produces ash at 1–2 per cent of dry weight of timber, which can be composted or used as a fertiliser.

Wood fuel is a local resource and its use supports local employment. Whereas oil, coal and gas are international products, creating employment sometimes thousands of miles away from source, timber fuels encourage a stable rural economy. People are employed in the forests, in wood processing, in community-based power plants, and in boiler manufacture and servicing. The employment chain becomes part of the sustainability network which architects and developers will be reinforcing by specifying wood fuel. Also, since much wood fuel derives from forest thinnings, the product of combustion is part of the waste chain of other industries. It is prudent to ensure that community-based wood fuel heating schemes (or CHP) are developed in partnership with forest owners. If there is a common interest (social and environmental as well as economic) between consumers and forestry companies the enterprise will have a better chance of succeeding.

In much of Europe and parts of Canada wood fuel is widely employed in biomass district heating schemes (BMDH). These are normally located in villages of up to 5,000 people or self-contained inner city communities of similar size. The usual pattern is to have a small number of BMDH plants on a circuit providing hot water to nearby houses. Each plant will generate 4–10 MW of power, the smaller amount being sufficient for about 500 inhabitants. Often larger buildings such as schools, factories or offices will have their own wood fuel heating plant, with many of them exporting their surplus heat to the community system.

District heating networks are usually twin pipes (flow and return) set about 600 mm below ground in a sand trench. The pipes are highly insulated, usually in foam, and able to withstand a temperature of 120°C. Since water conducts heat and reduces the insulation of the sand trench, there is normally an underground drainage pipe and filter mat. Water (and steam) is usually circulated at 12–16 bar pressure, leading to transmission losses of as little as 10 per cent per kilometre length. It is also commonplace for district heating networks to employ both biomass fuels and conventional fuels. This mixed energy economy allows oil or gas to be employed to even out peaks in demand when wood fuel on its own is unable to cope. As a general rule, the biomass share of total output should approach 70 per cent.

At the level of individual buildings, wood fuel is normally employed as part of underfloor heating schemes. Woodchips are fed into a pellet boiler to produce hot water, which is circulated in double or triple tubing placed directly beneath the floor finish but above an insulating layer of foil-faced insulation. Where wood fuel is locally available in high volumes (as logs, chips or pellets) it is cheaper to install and run than conventional oil or bottled gas boilers [23].

Leicester Community CHP Programme

Leicester was the first UK city to win support from the government's Community Energy Programme aimed at expanding the use of CHP. Funded through the Climate Change Levy administered by the Energy Saving Trust, the Leicester project-steered by De Montfort University's Institute of Energy and Sustainable Development, aims to heat university buildings, four local authority housing estates and 16 public buildings by a new CHP plant fuelled by locally grown energy crops. The grant of over £5 million (awarded in 2004) towards a project of £70 million will underwrite the viability of the project. Based in the St Marks area of Leicester, the new CHP installation will be fuelled by locally grown willow supplied by a consortium of Leicestershire farmers. Monitoring of the project will be overseen by De Montfort University and the Energy Saving Trust.

Strategies for Energy Efficiency

There are three broad factors which lead to greater energy efficiency in buildings: technology push, policy pull and enlightened self-interest. All three are evident to a greater or lesser extent in sustainable design, but the balance of importance of each varies according to the priorities of clients, the enthusiasms of architects and engineers, and the prevailing political ethos.

Normally, a green building will involve a combination of innovative technologies, connection in some way with UK or EU government policy (including any financial incentives which may be available), and a client who recognises the health or security benefits of low-energy design. It is this combination, for instance, which is behind the Hampshire green schools, green office projects such as the Barclaycard Building in Northampton designed by Fitzroy Robinson and Partners, and green housing schemes in South-West London such as Bedzed designed by Bill Dunster. Government policy on its own will not achieve the necessary changes – innovations in technology, construction and design are also required. Added to this, clients need to feel that there is a business case for sustainable design, which shows real benefits in the balance sheet. Hence it is important to integrate the three factors:

- technology push;
- policy pull;
- enlightened self-interest.

Importance of 'Technology Push' to the Architect

For the architect, energy technologies can usefully be divided into two types – new forms of energy and better use of existing energy. The former include renewable energy, new hydrogen-based fuels and biofuels. The latter includes greater efficiency in the use of existing energy (whether fossil-fuel based or renewable) by better design, from optimum orientation to super-insulation, and improved management of buildings from boilers to room controls. In the past, the architect and building services engineer were occupied mainly with improving the efficiency with which energy supplies were utilised, but today they are increasingly concerned with alternative forms of energy generation at the building itself (e.g. solar or wind power). In fact, some predict that in the future many buildings will be net exporters of energy rather than large inefficient importers, as was often the case in the past. The improved technology of generation of electricity from photovoltaic panels and micro-wind generators means that buildings will have an important role to play in meeting national energy needs over the next century.

Integrating the Three 'E's: Energy, Environment and Ecology

The UN Earth Summit in Rio de Janeiro in 1992 formalised the need to jointly address the imperatives of energy, environment and ecology. Until then, energy had been the primary resource concern, partly because of the threat of diminishing supplies, but increasingly as a consequence of global warming. The Rio agreement effectively widened the environmental debate to bring all resources into the frame, particularly the ecological well-being of the planet.

A look at the history of environmentalism underlines the gradual understanding of the importance of resource use at a global level, and the inclusion of more philosophical or spiritual concerns along with measurable criteria. Energy as a single topic has lost its supremacy and is now an element, albeit a major one, in the bigger picture of sustainable development. Other topics have begun to emerge as related aspects of environmental design, such as health, stress and productivity. Sustainability has become the intellectual framework for reconciling many competing interests. Although poorly defined, sustainability is a concept that embraces low-energy design and ecology, and places humans within nature's system rather than outside it, which was the tendency with the former emphasis on energy.

Fig 2.28
The three 'E's and three 'R's.

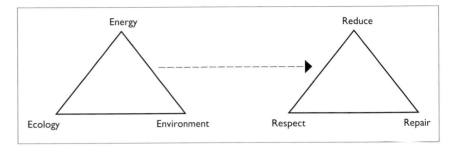

Development of environmental priorities

1970s	Energy scarcity
1980s	Global warming
	Concept of 'sustainable development'
	Ozone thinning
1990s	Water distribution and quality
	Rainforest protection
	Biodiversity
2000s	Health of cities
	Sustainable design and construction
	Sustainability and health

This broadening picture has led to a reassessment of the priorities between energy, other environmental resources and the ecological systems which hold them together. Humankind is also placed squarely within the system rather than adopting the typical Western view of a separation between humans and nature. The repositioning of environmental imperatives at the Rio Earth Summit forced a reassessment of key relationships, influencing not only the environmental sciences but also other areas such as business, farming and the world economic order itself. Although it takes time for the new order to become widely apparent or influential, the Rio Summit planted the seeds of change.

The Rio agreements formed a convenient three-point framework of global concerns, requiring human activities to be within it rather than outside it. Development, including building design, was to be informed by new concerns.

Fig 2.29
Three perspectives on eco-design:
energy, environment and ecology.

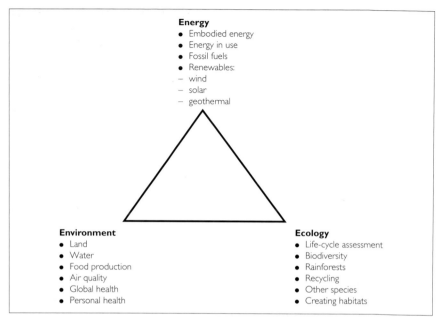

Energy
- Embodied energy
- Energy in use
- Fossil fuels
- Renewables:
  - wind
  - solar
  - geothermal

Environment
- Land
- Water
- Food production
- Air quality
- Global health
- Personal health

Ecology
- Life-cycle assessment
- Biodiversity
- Rainforests
- Recycling
- Other species
- Creating habitats

Architects now had to consider not only energy but also other environmental resources (particularly water use) and how the building impacted on the wider ecology (timber sourcing). For some the new agenda was too broad; for others it provided an inspiring fresh basis for architectural design.

Since the Earth Summit, ecological concerns have begun to impact on systems rather than resources. Although the agreements at Rio sought to protect endangered habitats, species and the genetic inheritance of all living things (genetic diversity within species), ecological design has taken on a broader remit. There is now a developing framework for assessing the ecological footprint of buildings and, though difficult, of whole cities. The concept of life-cycle assessment (LCA) is based on inputs, outputs and loops, and has at its heart the ecological methodology of cradle-to-grave measurement. Ecological design highlights the paucity of human design thinking. As a rule, nature creates the maximum of richness and complexity with the minimum of resources and the maximum of recycling, whereas humankind creates the minimum of richness and complexity with the maximum of resources and the minimum of recycling. As a consequence,

Main environmental agreements at the Rio Earth Summit in 1992

Energy	■ Global warming
	■ Future supplies
Ecology	■ Biodiversity
	■ Rainforest protection
Environment	■ Water resources
	■ Land and farming

Action to achieve the three 'E's: Energy, Environment and Ecology

Energy	■ Move from fossil fuels to renewable energy sources
	■ Employ low-energy design
	■ See building as generator of energy
	■ Consider all energy uses (heating, lighting, ventilation, transport)
	■ Use heat recovery
	■ Use orientation to reduce energy load
	■ Consider embodied energy and energy in use
Environment	■ Consider environmental impact on broad front
	■ Consider resource conservation (land, water, materials)
	■ Restore land and buildings as part of development process
	■ Avoid pollution through design
	■ Design for durability, flexibility and recycling
	■ Design for health, comfort and safety
Ecology	■ Consider effect of choice of materials on biodiversity
	■ Link design systems to ecological systems
	■ See development as closed loop with recycling of waste
	■ Maximise diversity from minimum resources
	■ Use development to extend or create natural habitats
	■ Use planting for shelter and energy efficiency

mature systems in nature (rainforests, coral reefs) are beautiful and life enhancing (for all species). Humankind's mature systems (cities) are rarely beautiful or life enhancing. Normally, they are polluted, alienating and divisive. Ecology provides a useful framework to bring mankind and nature closer together.

There are internal conflicts between low-energy design, ecology and environmental design. The materials employed for energy efficiency, such as glass fibre, polystyrene and foaming agents used in insulation, have a big environmental impact. The use of hardwood, often employed as a window product in low-energy design, has ecological consequences. There are also potential conflicts between quarrying (to provide local materials) and ecology. But not all impacts are negative. The extraction of gravel and clay can provide useful wetland habitats to compensate for those lost during 19th century land drainage. Even quarries can create nesting sites for birds of prey and undisturbed cliff faces for endangered flora.

The important point is to balance the agendas of energy, ecology and environment, rather than to pursue one aspect at the expense of the others. This is the path to a richer, more environmentally responsive, humane architecture than the former obsessive pursuit of energy efficiency.

Importance of Indicators

Many assessment techniques, such as the Building Research Establishment Environmental Assessment Method (BREEAM) in the UK and the Leadership in Energy and Environmental Design programme (LEED) in the USA, increasingly recognise the complexity of choices or decisions required. As an environmental assessment tool for offices and other building types, BREEAM has moved from concentrating solely on energy issues to widen its scope to reflect the multifaceted nature of ecological choices. In the process, other topics have emerged as influential, such as water conservation and occupancy health. As the issues to be addressed have become more wide-ranging, the tendency has been to use indicators rather than measure every possible impact. Indicators are a useful assessment tool as they provide a guide to the bigger picture. Indicators come in two types:
- as an indication of the attainment of a goal; and
- as an indication of fluctuations in a system.

Fig 2.30
The roof as habitat and extra layer of insulation.
Source: Erisco Bauder

Both types are used in the construction industry – the first at the design stage and the second as a monitoring tool once the building is occupied (such as the CIBSE PROBE Studies based on post-occupancy evaluation).

A good indicator of energy efficiency at the design stage is the measure of units of energy consumed per square metre (normally expressed as kWh/m^2). The same figure can then be used to measure performance and modify the building services management system on completion. But the source of the energy is not taken into account, so a further indicator might be necessary, such as the percentage of energy generated by renewable means. This could well change over the occupation of the building, allowing CO_2 emissions to be reduced compared to initial expectations. The same indicator (energy), therefore, could be a useful guide to the designer, to those who manage the building by providing a measure for performance enhancement, and to government as a target for national CO_2 reduction. Health, too, can be an indicator – the health both of construction workers (there are many health risks from different construction materials and techniques) and of building occupants, whose health can suffer as a result of poor environmental design. Local biodiversity is another useful indicator. The full ecological picture from excavation, production, construction, use and disposal of a building material is difficult to measure. For example, in brick manufacturing, there is the ecological impact of clay extraction, but with good management and design, valuable wildlife habitats can be created, perhaps exploiting the cleansing of 'grey water' from local industry or housing areas. What is important here is to consider the full life cycle and to use sample species for measuring environmental impact rather than complete habitats, which are necessarily complex.

Fig 2.31
Roman Mosaic floor in Morocco which charts the diversity of species, with man at the centre.

Self-assessment sustainability toolkit for architecture students

Theme	Topic	Score	Multiplier	Sub-Total
Energy	Orientation		×3	
	Shelter		×3	
	Super-insulation		×3	
	Glazing area		×3	
	Passive solar gain		×3	
	Passive solar cooling		×3	
	Renewable energy		×3	

	Heat recovery	x3
	Other (specify)	x3
Materials	Waste minimisation	x2
	Local sourcing	x2
	Reuse (of buildings)	x2
	Recycling (of parts)	x2
	Embodied energy	x2
	Maintenance	x2
	Other	x1
Resources (land)	Brownfield site	x2
	Density	x2
	Biomass	x1
	Other	x1
Resources (water)	Low-water appliances	x1
	Grey water recycling	x1
	Rainwater collection	x1
	Other	x1
Access	Disabled	x2
	Public transport	x2
	Cycling	x2
	Walking	x1
Health	Natural materials	x2
	Natural ventilation	x2
	Natural light	x2
	Stress	x1
	Contact with nature	x1
Total		

To avoid being swamped by statistics, the designer needs a simple toolkit for assessment based on readily understood principles and values. These already exist but few are sufficiently simple to provide a useful guide, especially at the sketch design stage (when key decisions on the environment are made). The problem with BREEAM and other toolkits is that they often come into operation only once the fundamentals of footprint and location have already been decided. There is a need for simplicity in initial assessment and the use of multipliers to give priority to certain values (see the sustainability toolkit above developed by the author for use by architecture students). Since not all projects need to give equal weight to energy considerations, the addition of multipliers allows adjustments to reflect political and client values or the priorities which may flow from the nature of the site, building function or occupant need.

Eco-innovation and its impact on the design of buildings – the 4 'E's

Eco-innovation (design approach)	Resulting building
Less energy	Efficient
Fewer materials	Elegant
Greater recyclability	Equitable
Design with nature	Ecological

Water: Tomorrow's Oil?

The attention given to energy conservation over the past few years has deflected attention away from concerns about water. The construction industry has started to come to terms with global warming but has yet to face up to its responsibility with regard to water conservation. Water is potentially as important as energy and, globally, water scarcity is a more pressing problem than energy supplies. Unlike energy, water impacts directly on health and food production, and, although there is a link between fuel, poverty and health, the connection is by no means as direct as that with water. In Africa, most of Asia and even parts of Europe, water is the most pressing resource crisis: is it tomorrow's oil?

Fig 2.32
Typical water-stressed settlement in North Africa.

Water: Poverty and Health

In the world today one in six people do not have access to clean water, nearly one-half of all people lack proper sanitation in the home, and every 15 seconds a child dies from a water-related disease [24]. Architects working outside the UK need to take water as seriously as they do energy, and those working in Africa, parts of Asia and Latin America will find that water engineering and domestic plumbing are often intractable problems. Many students of architecture who gain employment with non-governmental organisations (NGOs) such as Oxfam find themselves helping to dig wells or install rudimentary water systems in countries such as Uganda, where 40 per cent of the population still lack proper supplies. Water, not oil, is the priority – first, creating clean unpolluted supplies and, second, providing sanitation either in the form of community latrines or domestic toilets.

In countries like Kenya, Tanzania, Sudan and Rwanda architects need to address the infrastructure of water before they can approach the task of designing buildings. The NGO Water Aid provides advice on digging wells, laying pipes and supplying remote rural communities, but it requires architects, engineers and mechanics on the ground to install the equipment and supervise the work. A modern well can be dug in Uganda for about £800, and with clean water come health, education and more effective farming [25]. Hence, water is the key to a chain reaction of benefits for some of the most impoverished regions of the world.

The main water-related diseases are cholera, dysentery, typhoid, bilharzia, hookworms and trachoma. These cause death, stunted growth or blindness, and are the result of either contaminated water or lack of water leading to poor sanitation through insufficient supplies for hand washing. Hence, the answer is not just to provide clean supplies of water but to provide the basic sanitation of toilets, wash basins and sewage systems to ensure a healthy lifestyle. Although engineers are involved mainly in the supply of new water infrastructure, architects have an important role to play in providing sanitation in public buildings such as schools, which can be models for other buildings.

Water is the key to overcoming the poverty trap which holds millions of people to subsistence farming in large areas of rural Africa. Not only are the residents impoverished by lack of water and the expanding grip of Aids, but their demands on other resources, such as timber to boil what water is available, stress the environment further. Hence, poor water leads to poor health, and overlarge families to compensate for premature death, which in turn leads to forest and scrub clearance. The cycle is one of growing poverty, desertification and political instability.

The situation is often as bad in large Asian cities. In Dhaka in Bangladesh about 3 million people live without the simplest drainage or sanitation. Many of the new homes for the inward-migrating rural poor (often driven from ancient farming areas by rising sea levels) are built on parts of the city which were formerly rubbish dumps. The present population of 12 million is expected to rise to 23 million within a decade with only 50 per cent having basic services of water and sanitation [26]. Such statistics demonstrate the scale of environmental stress caused partly by global warming and partly by the lack of proper planning of infrastructure in rural Africa and urban Asia.

At present, nearly 20 per cent of the world's population in 30 countries face severe water problems, and by 2025 the figure is expected to rise [27] to 30 per cent in 50 countries [28]. Unsafe water is the world's biggest killer and, besides disease, poor sanitation leads to lack of human dignity and quality of life. As many children spend a great deal of time gathering water for their families, inadequate water provision leads to poor education and a spiral of poverty. Also, in poor parts of the world the cost of water is greater than in affluent countries, with bottled water costing about 10 times that of municipal supplies. Families can spend 20 per cent of their income on water, and as the water-table drops (due to excessive extraction of groundwater supplies), this percentage is expected to rise. Taking a global view of world problems, water is likely to be tomorrow's oil.

Global water stress

■ Human population	6 billion
■ Population lacking basic sanitation	3 billion
■ Population lacking clean water where water-related disease is prevalent	1 billion

Source: UN Refugee Agency, 2000

In the UK, we have taken water too much for granted. Our wet maritime climate provides a relatively assured supply of domestic, agricultural and industrial water.

Water use – some facts

Water used in agriculture
- Globally, 67% of total extracted
- In Africa, 87% of total extracted
- In the UK, 13% of total extracted

Soft drinks
- 2.5 litres of water are required to make 1 litre of soft drink
- 0.5 litres of oil required to make 1 litre of soft drink

Drinking water
- In a typical building only 4 litres of the 150 litres of water per person consumed per day is used for drinking

Recent floods confirm, however, the unpredictability of our water resources: we have had eight drought years in the past fourteen, and although 2000 and 2004 were wet years, the trend is towards less rainfall in the south and east and more in the north and west. Climate change, the result of the fossil fuel/global warming equation, is clearly altering rainfall patterns. As the planet gets warmer, the distribution of rain varies both within continents and within countries. Global warming means more global rain, but it falls in the wrong place. The extra precipitation does not reach the centre of continents, which are becoming hotter and drier. The UK is on a water divide, with some parts wetter and some drier, but all areas are having to face up to change in the water regime.

Water consumption in the UK

- 150 litres per person per day
- 51% of extracted water goes to public water supply
- 36% to power generation
- 13% to agriculture
- Architects influence directly or indirectly 50% of water use in UK

Why water matters in the 21st century

- Essential for public health
- Essential for agriculture
- Increase in human population puts stress on water supply
- Climate change is altering patterns of rainfall
- Rising living standards mean more water demand per person
- The 4.1 million new households in the UK required by 2016 have huge water demand implications
- Water use also means energy use (in supply and in waste)

Water use in a typical household in the UK		Water use in a typical office building in the UK	
Activity	% of total	Activity	% of total
Washing and hygiene	40	WC flushing	43
Toilet flushing	30	Urinal flushing	20
Laundry	11	Washing	27
Washing dishes	6	Canteen	9
Gardening	4	Cleaning	1
Drinking	4		
Miscellaneous	5		

Source: *BRE*, 1998

Changing rainfall patterns are only part of the problem. We now consume more water per household than ever before and we have more premises demanding water (housing, offices, schools, supermarkets). There is growth in the consumption of water per person and, as a consequence, per building. Suddenly, we have become aware of a potential water shortage even in rain-drenched Britain. Suddenly, too, we have discovered that around 50 per cent of all water use in the UK occurs in buildings. Just as with energy, buildings are responsible for half of all consumption and architects and designers have to take this water issue on board as an environmental imperative.

Water conservation is no more difficult to achieve than energy conservation. Although cost is a major impediment, not just of the equipment necessary for collection and recycling but also for the extra space and structure required, the reality is that with rising water bills attention to water conservation makes financial sense. However, while for many institutional clients water bills are too low for expensive conservation strategies to be worthwhile, significant economies of water use can be achieved with modest measures (such as reduced flow taps).

Design for water conservation

Technological	Reduced-flow taps
	Self-closing taps
	Low water-flush toilets
	Compost or vacuum toilets
	Waterless urinals
	Sensors for urinal flushing
	Showers rather than baths
	Low water-use domestic appliances
Grey water systems	Recovered wastewater (recycled water)
	Rainwater collection at site
Engineering design	Pervious paving to feed groundwater supplies
	Landscape design to soak up rainwater
	Soft water catchment to 'sponge' rainfall peaks
Management	Monitor use (metering)
	Leakage detection
	Education

But on many urban sites the space simply does not exist for reed beds, and any collected water from roofs may be too contaminated by air pollution for use in the building. There are, however, many possibilities that could be explored, such as the relationship between renewable energy and rainwater conservation. For example, wind energy could be used for pumping water and solar energy for cleansing it. If this were to happen, buildings would be genuinely holistic in their approach to sustainability, integrating strategies for energy and water saving. The principles of water conservation are similar to those of energy conservation (or any other resource, for that matter). There are four stages:

- harvest renewable or local sources;
- reduce the level of usage;
- reuse primary supplies; and
- recycle the wastes.

Domestic Water Collection

Water consumption in the UK rose by 75 per cent between 1960 and 2002 with annual rainfall decreasing by about 8 per cent over the same period. In southern England the supply situation is particularly acute, especially over the summer. A simple answer is to use domestic roofs to collect water, which is then stored in a basement. About 150 litres of water per day are consumed by a typical person, resulting in levels of around 600 litres per day for a typical household. With the UK's rainfall pattern, a storage tank of about 200,000 litres is required to meet expected demand over a year. Using a simple sand filter and pump the stored water can then be used for flushing toilets (the main water use in a typical house), washing machines, garden irrigation, showers and baths. Mains supply will still be required for drinking water and cooking but, by diversifying water sources, there is reduced demand on the water grid, and domestic consumers will face lower water bills. The main problem with rainwater collection is not the level of rainfall (as it is in Spain) but the area required for water storage. Since the water tank is heavy, storage has to be at ground level or below. However, the thermal capacity of the stored water can have a beneficial impact on energy performance, especially in an age of rising global temperatures.

Design Solutions for Harvesting Water

The first obvious step is to collect the rainfall in tanks and use this for a variety of water purposes. There are four problems with this, however.

- Tanks are large, heavy and take up valuable space which could be used for other purposes. Storage is viable only in new construction where basements can be constructed for storage. In existing buildings, the weight of stored rainwater is prohibitive.

- Rainwater may not be of potable quality (water is strictly regulated under EU and UK law). Quality depends on catchment surfaces (lead and copper are clearly unsuitable), the storage method and the biological treatment. Often, the water needs to be boiled before drinking or subject to ultraviolet light (radiation cleansing). This adds to cost and, importantly, CO_2 production, demonstrating the link between water and energy use.

- The cost of water self-sufficiency is expensive in construction terms. The capital outlay may not be recovered quickly, especially when the invisible costs are computed. However, with water bills rising (in well-designed modern houses, the water utility bill is often higher than the energy bill) over the lifetime of the building, the initial cost will be recovered. At the Hockerton Energy Village near Newark in Nottinghamshire, designed by Robert and Brenda Vale, considerable efficiency was gained by putting water high on the environmental agenda at the briefing stage.

- The building will need to be designed to exploit water catchment. This will entail large gutters, the ability to access the system at key points (to clear leaves, etc.), and the use of roof pitches which do not add excessive velocity to the flowing water or unduly slow down its path to the tank. As a consequence, water conservation, just like energy conservation, has aesthetic ramifications.

Reducing Water Demand

Water consumption can be reduced by adopting simple design and management measures. By dividing water into potable and non-potable use, it is possible to gain the benefit of harvesting, reusing and recycling water without any associated cost or health problems. This strategy includes water use reduction, employing simple measures such as low-flush or dual-flush toilets. A useful measure for all public buildings is to use sensors in public toilets to avoid urinals flushing when not in use (e.g. Birchanger Green Service Station on the M11). In the domestic setting, dual flush systems respond to the different flushing needs of toilet uses and can reduce domestic water consumption by 40 per cent. Use reduction is also encouraged by water metering, which provides an immediate measure of water usage as a benchmark from which improvements in water efficiency can be made. Research shows that meters reduce water use by around 20 per cent on average, and more for poorer households. It is also worth remembering that reduced water use means less waste, and less waste requires less energy to process sewerage.

Changes to UK Water Regulations

Appliance	1986 Water Bye-laws	1999 Water Regulations
WC	7.5 litres/flush	6 litres/flush
Washing machines	150–180 litres/cycle	120 litres/cycle
Dishwashers	7 litres/place setting	4.5 litres/place setting
Showers	None	Meter if more than 20 litres/min

Source: Environment Agency, UK

Benefits of water conservation in buildings

- Lower water charges
- Groundwater supplies conserved for future generations
- Reduced stress on water supply infrastructure
- Reduced pressure to build reservoirs
- Reduced use of hot water (saving energy)
- Reduced use of water in supply and sewerage systems (saving energy)

At Hockerton, high-grade (i.e. drinking) water needs are met by the collection of rainwater from conservatory roofs, which is then stored and mineralised (passed through light and carbon filters) before use. The shared storage tanks assume 5 litres consumption per person per day and provide sufficient drinking water capacity for two-thirds of the year. Typical water use in the UK is 150 litres per person per day; at Hockerton, low-grade water needs (i.e. toilet flushing) are met by a reservoir served by drainage from other roofs, roads and surrounding fields. Here, the water is fed through a sand filter before use. The reservoir stores 150m³ of water which provides the village with a secure 100-day supply for flushing toilets, clothes washing, and so on. Water conservation is made viable by the use of flow restrictors, low-water washing machines and, for garden irrigation, the use of soiled water.

Fig 2.33
Hockerton Energy Village, Nottingham, designed by Robert and Brenda Vale, integrates a number of sustainable design principles.
Source: Hockerton Energy Village

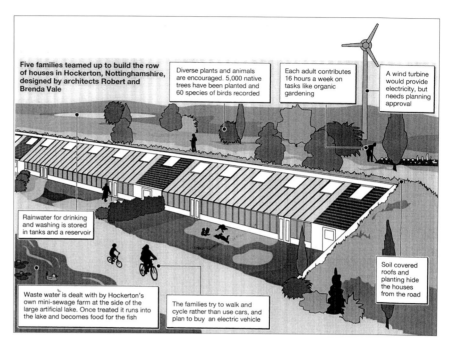

Five families teamed up to build the row of houses in Hockerton, Nottinghamshire, designed by architects Robert and Brenda Vale

Diverse plants and animals are encouraged. 5,000 native trees have been planted and 60 species of birds recorded

Each adult contributes 16 hours a week on tasks like organic gardening

A wind turbine would provide electricity, but needs planning approval

Rainwater for drinking and washing is stored in tanks and a reservoir

Soil covered roofs and planting hide the houses from the road

Waste water is dealt with by Hockerton's own mini-sewage farm at the side of the large artificial lake. Once treated it runs into the lake and becomes food for the fish

The families try to walk and cycle rather than use cars, and plan to buy an electric vehicle

Recycling of Water

Water is commonly recycled as low-grade water but not as high-grade (drinking) water because of the possible health hazards. Recycling allows cleansed water to be put back into effective use – for irrigation, recreation, amenity, and ecological diversification. Typically, recycling consists of passing low-soiled water (i.e. with no solid wastes) into a reservoir via reed beds or other biological cleaning processes. The water has to pass slowly through the system for the bacteriological breakdown to occur. The usual set-up in domestic development positions the reed bed after the septic tank. In commercial development, the reed bed is positioned after the water separation in the building and before the most polluted water is taken to public sewers. For recycling to work, there needs to be a highly active ecosystem – one which is not threatened by groundwater contamination. Alsop and Störmer's Water Works Pavilion at the Doncaster Earth Centre demonstrates how this kind of system operates, from the visitor toilets to the local river system, including internal water tanks, external reed beds and willow thickets.

Fig 2.34
Housing in London's Docklands that makes a
virtue out of development on the flood plain.

Fig 2.35
Domestic water harvesting from a sedum
planted roof at an eco-house in Bristol designed
by Bruges Tozer.

Grey Water Recycling

Reed beds work by cleaning the soiled water biologically. The roots of reeds (and other plants) supply oxygen to the naturally occurring bacteria in the water, which then digest any pathogens present. Faecal coliforms are broken down with the residual matter, supplying nutrient-rich water to a lake (as at Ecolonia in Holland, masterplanned by Lucien Kroll [29]), which can then provide a habitat for wildlife or a resource for a fish farm.

At the Barclaycard Building in Northampton, designed by Fitzoy Robinson and Partners, the cleansed water is used as part of the chilled ceiling system [30]. In this example, water is taken from a lake on the north side of the building (where it remains cool), passes through pipes in the ceilings, and is returned, warmed, to the lake only to be naturally chilled again (see Fig 4.15). Like all robust water systems, the loop is complete and balances the needs of the building with those of the wider ecosystem.

The Need for Integration of All Resources

There is embodied energy in water; in other words, considerable amounts of energy are invested into getting clean, potable water into our taps. Much of the world's water supply comes from fossil fuel driven desalination plants. Where this happens, embodied energy can represent 50 per cent of the water content by volume (i.e. it takes half a gallon of oil to produce a gallon of desalinated water). Water is a valuable resource in drought-stricken areas like the Middle East and is behind many regional conflicts. Even if we in the UK do not face such challenges, it is prudent, given the life of buildings (50–150 years), to plan to accommodate future changes in rainfall or consumer use patterns. Both input (rainfall trapping) and output (water use) strategies are needed, but more crucial still is the importance of combining energy and water design as a coherent package. This is largely what happens at Hockerton, where a heat pump, which exploits air warmed by the conservatory, heats the communal water supply, providing preheated water to the five dwellings. The system takes advantage of the capacity of large volumes of stored water to stay warm for a long time, resulting in an overall energy saving of 75 per cent. Similar systems operate in Denmark, where large tanks of water (often collected rainwater for domestic non-potable use) are stored partly underground but roofed in glass to maximise the chances of the sun

Fig 2.36
The Water Arch at the Sydney Olympics sought to raise awareness of water conservation in Australia.

warming them through what is known as 'passive solar gain'. This preheated water is either distributed by pumps to adjoining houses or taken to small CHP plants. In either case, the efficiency gained from integrating energy and water strategies is considerable. It is a policy behind the Cole Thompson design for the Integer House, Watford, which applies a balanced approach to all resources, from energy to water, and also that of the Hockerton Energy Village in Newark.

There is one other benefit of addressing water as a design challenge. Recycling water is a more visible medium of resource conservation than energy. It can be tracked, felt, seen and reused more directly than energy. As such, water conservation demonstrates sustainable practice in a very tangible way, making sustainability visible (unlike aspects of energy conservation). Buildings that do not confront its agenda are not facing one of the overriding design issues of the 21st century.

Notes

[1] For more information on United Nations initiatives see www.undp.org.
[2] *Energy and Environmental Management*, January/February 2004, p. 7.
[3] *ibid.*
[4] *ibid.*, p. 8.
[5] *ibid.*, p. 5.
[6] www.cerespower.co.uk.
[7] Peter Smith, *Options for a Flexible Planet*, Sustainable Building Network, Sheffield University, 1996, p. 24.
[8] For further information see *New Scientist*, 17 September 1994 and 9 July 1995.
[9] Brian Edwards, *Sustainable Architecture*, Architectural Press, Oxford, 1999, p. 117.
[10] The quote is from David Lloyd Jones, *RIBA Journal*, June 2002, p. 62.
[11] Northumbria Photovoltaics Application Centre, 2003.
[12] *The Architects' Journal*, 10 May 2001.
[13] Randall Thomas, *RIBA Journal*, June 2002, p. 62.
[14] *ibid.*
[15] *ibid.*
[16] *Energy and Environmental Management*, January/February 2004, p. 7.
[17] *ibid.*, p. 6.
[18] Penny Lewis, 'Renewables', *Prospect*, March 2004, p. 33.
[19] www.buildingcentre.co.uk/energy/research
[20] *EcoTech*, Issue 8, November 2003, p. 20.
[21] *ibid.*
[22] www.thecarbontrust.co.uk
[23] Cliff Beck, Highland Birchwoods, personal communication, 24 November 2002.
[24] Angelique Chrisafis, 'A handful of hope', *The Guardian, Environment Supplement*, 23 August 2003, p. 1.
[25] *ibid.*
[26] *ibid.*, pp. 2–3.
[27] www.unep.org/vitalwater. See also World Health Organization and UNICEF websites.
[28] John Vidal, 'Sanitation', *The Guardian, Environment Supplement*, 23 August 2003, p. 3. See also www.wateraid.org.uk.
[29] Brian Edwards, 'Ecolonia', *Architecture Today*, No 67, April 1996, pp. 10–15.
[30] Brian Edwards, 'Green goes mainstream: Barclaycard headquarters', *Architecture Today*, No 80, July 1997, pp. 20–30.

Sustainable Design and Construction

3

3 Sustainable Design and Construction

We spend at least 80 per cent of our lives in buildings and most of the remainder in cities. Seventy-five per cent of the European population is now urban, and the year 2000 marked not only the six billionth human but also the first time the global human population was a predominantly urban rather than rural species. With the growth in city living comes a distancing from the land. We have lost sight of seasonal cycles, of the struggle for food or warmth, and instead we have become interested in culture, sport and media. Architecture, too, has broken free of its old bonds to locally sourced materials, vernacular traditions, and the union between buildings and the land. Cities owe no allegiance to the carrying capacity of the landscape in which they are sited. They draw upon food, water, resources and human energy from all corners of the globe. Successful cities measure their wealth and enterprise against international yardsticks, not local ones. As a consequence, the ecological footprint of London now exceeds the productive rural capacity of all of England, and Canary Wharf's carbon conversion footprint may well be bigger than the area of London. Cities and buildings are increasingly disconnected from the landscape in all but visual terms.

Several techniques have been advocated to achieve a better balance between town and country. There is the system of carbon accounting, whereby CO_2 emissions are balanced by the conversion back into oxygen by forests, as discussed in Chapter 2. For every house, half a hectare of deciduous forest is needed; for a supermarket, perhaps 40 hectares. If this ratio is not sustained, the carbon becomes locked into the upper atmosphere where it contributes to global warming. The problem with carbon accounting, an idea which emanated from the 1997 Kyoto Conference, is that rich countries such as the USA can buy the carbon credits of the poor ones (e.g. Russia). It allows the wealthy to carry on polluting and holds the poor in a cycle of debt.

Life-Cycle Assessment

More practical perhaps is the technique of life-cycle assessment (LCA), a process that brings ecological principles into the development process. LCA is used to evaluate the environmental performance of buildings from the cradle to the grave. It measures the ecological costs of resources such as energy, or of a manufactured product such as a brick, which are then evaluated against environmental criteria. For a building, LCA brings into focus the complex impacts in construction, use and

Fig 3.1
Life-cycle impacts of a brick.

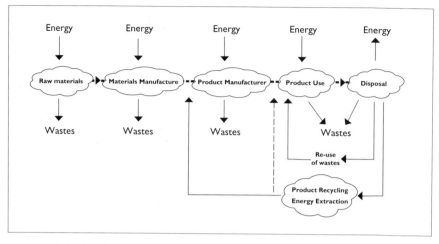

decommissioning. The technique has two main benefits: it can be used to guide architects and facilities managers over the lifetime of the building; and it can help to identify potential cost savings by reducing the building's exposure to future environmental legislation or maintenance problems. A development of LCA is life-cycle costing (LCC) which looks at the cost of a building over its full design life (30–50 years). In reality, LCC is the net value of the design, construction, operation and maintenance costs calculated over the full lifetime of the building. Rather than focusing on initial cost, LCC puts into the equation the operational costs (heating, lighting, ventilation) and the building maintenance costs (servicing of air-conditioning units, etc.). As such, it is responsive to rising oil prices and the cost of upkeep of mechanical plant, and potentially provides a basis to measure the enhanced productivity by the occupants of the building. LCC is a sophisticated tool which measures cost and asset value over the full life cycle, rather than the initial cost of construction.

Architects, like many construction professionals, are under pressure from clients and others in the supply chain to reduce the adverse ecological impact of their buildings. Growing environmental awareness has led to a more demanding public (clients and building users) who expect better environmental performance without additional cost. LCA highlights the total lifetime cost. Capital cost (i.e. the actual construction cost) can be seen in the context of a building's overall lifetime cost, allowing cost, environmental value, maintenance, recyclability and reuse to

Fig 3.2
Traditional brick and tile works in Morocco.

Fig 3.2
Traditional brick and tile works in Morocco.

be considered jointly. Too often, buildings are measured against the initial, capital cost, not their operational costs over the 50 or more years of their lives, and, more rarely still, the cost which is carried by others (pollution, waste, ecological damage). LCA has three advantages as an assessment tool:

- it brings time into the equation, allowing impacts and recycling loops to be readily comprehended from cradle to grave;
- it allows energy, ecological and environmental impacts to be analysed and set in the context of social and economic benefit;
- it is a holistic tool, which bridges design services, manufacturing, construction and building maintenance.

However, there are problems with LCA. The process looks at elements of construction (steel, concrete, ceramic tiles, paints, etc.) developing precise statements of the ecological impact over time for each element. Unfortunately, construction is more complex than that, involving materials used in unison, and the life-cycle benefit of one may be at the detriment of another. For example, painted steel reduces the ease with which it can be reused, and bricks bedded in a cement mortar cannot be recycled. The Dutch have overcome this problem by using *Eco-Quantum*, [1] a system which assesses the life cycle of whole units of construction such as glazing systems (glass, frames, mastic), structural walls (bricks,

Fig 3.3
Eco-house in New South Wales designed by
Lindsay Johnston, which combines locally
sourced heavy materials (stone) and globally
sourced lightweight ones (aluminium).

mortar, foundations) and interior partitions (plasterboard, framing, paint). There
are four parts to an *Eco-Quantum* audit:

- extraction of raw materials, waste;
- impact on health, toxicity, global warming;
- life-cycle assessment of equipment and appliances; and
- transport and material impacts in use.

Whether LCA or the *Eco-Quantum* technique is used, the goal remains the same,
to be better informed about the ecological impacts involved during the life of a
building. They are not decision-making tools but decision-aiding ones.

A Working Definition of LCA

LCA identifies *the material, energy and waste flows associated with a building over its
entire life in such a fashion that the environmental impacts can be determined in
advance* [2]. The flows described are from the extraction of raw materials for use,
reuse, recycling or disposal. Normally, there are three choices at the end of a
building's life:

- to reuse the parts in new construction;
- to recycle the material (e.g. as aggregate for new concrete); or
- to demolish and dispose of it in landfill.

Reuse is preferable to recycling (because of the energy costs of reforming a
material), and recycling is preferable to disposal. Disposal is a last resort, since
landfill sites are increasingly scarce, landfill taxes are rising, and the methane
production and other off-gassing from landfill sites contributes to global warming.
It is occasionally possible to extract energy from waste or to compost organic
waste. What LCA highlights is the opportunities that exist at the end of a
building's life, and it allows these benefits to influence choices made by the
designer at the beginning of the process.

LCA differs from other environmental auditing systems by measuring impacts
away from the site [3]. Not only are all the ecological factors over time considered
but also those over a wide geographical area. Take the example of a brick. There
are many environmental impacts of a brick, both during its life and spread over a
large area (extraction, baking, transport, use, reuse, etc.). LCA puts these into an
easily comprehended framework which architects can readily grasp at the design
stage. It also avoids the problem of shifting adverse impacts to other areas and

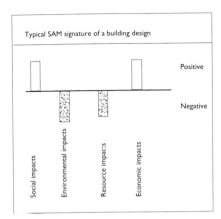

Typical SAM signature of a building design

Positive

Negative

Social impacts | Environmental impacts | Resource impacts | Economic impacts

Fig 3.1
SAM assessment.

thus making the development appear benign, such as can happen with high-tech green buildings which source their materials from around the world, often from places with lax environmental legislation.

Other Environmental Management Tools

Sustainability Assessment Model (SAM)

There are several assessment tools available to help predict the sustainability of a project. Some are energy-focused, others take a broader view. Among the techniques which adopt a wider perspective is the Sustainable Assessment Model (SAM) developed initially by Inchferry Consulting and the University of Aberdeen [4]. SAM assesses the project over the full life cycle under four headings, grouped into 22 performance indicators. The headings map onto the triple bottom line of sustainable development – environmental protection, social progress and economic prosperity – but with the addition of 'resource availability'.

They embrace the following issues:
- **Resource use impacts**, which include an assessment of the intrinsic and inherent values of the resources employed, especially their security, cost and environmental impacts. This allows decisions to be made between different construction materials (steel, concrete, glass), between different energy sources (oil, gas or renewables), and between different forms of capital (nature, social and intellectual).
- **Environmental impacts**, which include four assessment criteria: pollution; ecological footprint and impact on biodiversity; nuisance (noise, smell and visual); wastes. These are weighted and measured to form indicators.
- **Social impacts**, which include the social and community benefits, the direct and indirect jobs generated, and the health and safety impacts.
- **Economic impacts**, which include the benefits arising from the products or services provided, the contribution towards productivity, asset accumulation and economic growth.

The four main headings are broken down into 22 key indicators, which are then measured and given a score. Each project (or alternative design) then has a signature which can be compared with best practice in the type and subsequently modified. Such tools are relatively easy to use and versatile. They allow designers, clients and regulators to understand the complex impacts raised by a typical project. Also, since the indicator can be represented graphically, SAM provides a visual picture of the likely impacts, raising public awareness of sustainable development issues. It is a tool which can also be used to measure the decommissioning of a building or to assess the sustainability impacts of adaptation as against demolition.

Other sustainability assessment tools can be developed for particular types of building project, for example, for tourism, schools, higher education, health buildings, etc. Each will have common generic characteristics but with a weighting of indicators or the addition of extra ones to reflect specific impacts. For example, with tourism visual impact may be given particular attention, with hospitals the impact on social welfare and health, with education the impact of teaching and learning.

Eco-Management and Audit Schemes (EMAS)

There are other generic environmental assessment tools, such as Eco-Management and Audit Scheme (EMAS) and specific ones for different building types (BREEAM for offices, SEAM for schools). Architects and engineers are more familiar with the management systems developed to measure the environmental impact of buildings at the design stage than with the more broadly based systems. However, both have a part to play under specific conditions. For example, the environmental management system developed under ISO 14001 is useful in terms of operating an office to good ecological principles or in terms of choosing a contractor or supplier with sound environmental practices. However, it is not helpful in assessing the ecological impact of a specific project. So it is important to apply both the building-specific auditing tools (such as BREEAM in the UK and LEED in the USA) and the generic ones. Of the former, probably the most useful is the Environmental Management System (EMS) approach. This normally involves five actions which are externally audited but not normally made available to third parties: [5]

- develop an environmental policy;
- set objectives and measurable targets;
- implement the objectives and targets;
- monitor performance and take remedial action as necessary; and
- review the policy on a systematic basis.

The EMAS auditing system is, however, the preferred model in the European

Union. Both LCA and EMAS share a common basis but under EMAS the environmental performance is required to be publicly reported, as well as externally audited.

Three requirements of registration under EMAS

- Establish an environmental management system
- Produce an environmental statement
- Have both system and statement independently audited

Eco-labelling is another useful tool for the designer, especially in product selection. It, too, is an EU initiative and seeks to make all environmental claims by manufacturers conform to the same evaluative criteria. Eco-labels are intended to guide purchasers or specifiers and share some characteristics of LCA, although eco-labels are always product-specific [6]. Eco-labels cover certain product types used in the building industry such as paints, ceramic products and light bulbs, and are assessed on the basis of an independent audit carried out to common EU standards.

Content of environmental statement under EMAS

- Description of company's activities
- Assessment of significant environmental issues.
- Statistical summary of emissions, pollutants, impacts, etc., on environment
- Other factors pertinent to environmental performance
- Timescale of monitoring
- Name of accredited environmental officer

No matter what environmental auditing scheme is adopted, the objectives remain much the same. For an architectural practice, EMAS provides the measures needed to decide how to reduce environmental impact directly and indirectly through the choice of contractors or suppliers. For a manufacturer of building products, LCA and eco-labelling help to identify areas where energy can be saved, waste reduced, pollution prevented and, as a consequence, money or liability saved. Design practices and manufacturers can both benefit from the improved public image that follows from an environmental auditing scheme.

Specific Building Type Environmental Assessment Tools

There are many tools available to assess particular building types, and most share a common basis. Those developed in the UK have come mainly from the Building Research Establishment (BRE) and cover common building types – housing, schools, offices. Although they were initially concerned primarily with energy conservation, they have been expanded to embrace a wide range of environmental, ecological and health issues.

BREDEM

This is the environmental assessment system developed by the BRE for domestic buildings. BREDEM is a software package designed to calculate the heating load of different housing configurations based on gains, losses and boiler systems. It takes into account locational and latitudinal factors, insulation levels (in walls and roofs), air-tightness, window area and orientation. It is mainly an energy design tool but can be adapted to shed light on comfort levels and humidity, as well as energy used in transport. It is not as comprehensive as other design assessment tools (such as BREEAM) and is cumbersome to apply. For a simpler manual tool, the BRE produces Method 5000 but, again, it avoids ecological and wider environmental issues.

BREEAM

This is the auditing system most commonly used by UK designers for office and other buildings. It is comprehensive yet simple to use and results in a scoring system that allows different design strategies to be compared before construction begins. The measures span global atmospheric pollution down to local impacts, including those which affect human health. The different factors are weighted but embrace amongst others:

- CO_2 emissions with quantified benchmarks;
- healthy building features;
- air quality and ventilation;
- minimisation of ozone depletion and acid rain;
- recycling and reuse of materials;
- ecology of the site;
- water conservation;
- noise;
- risk of Legionnaires' disease;
- hazardous materials;
- lighting.

Fig 3.5
Although metal and glass have high quantities of embodied energy, both can be readily recycled. Wessex Water Building, near Bath, designed by Bennetts Associates.

As with all environmental assessment tools, BREEAM is useful both to the designer and to the client. The benefits to the construction industry as a whole are numerous:

- developers can promote the high environmental performance of their buildings and thus increase sales;
- designers can quantifiably demonstrate the environmental achievements of their work;
- landlords can audit the property from an environmental point of view with the aim of making cost savings; and
- employers can reassure employees that their working environment is healthy and of high quality.

Potentially, these benefits could lead to a better legacy of built assets, healthier office environments (and, hence, a more productive workforce), and reduced adverse environmental impacts at a global level. Developers in particular have used high BREEAM scores to promote their buildings, appealing to the widening environmental concerns of consumers [7].

SEAM

This is the environmental auditing system developed in the UK by the Department for Education and Skills (DfES) for schools. It, too, covers a wide range of environmental and ecological interests. SEAM allocates points on environmental issues from energy use to water economy, timber sourcing and recycling. The maximum number of points available is 45, and designs are classified as either Class A (with scores of over 35), Class B (with scores of over 25), or Class C (with scores of over 15). The auditing scheme is linked to an action plan and regular monitoring of the school in use. At the time of writing the topics under SEAM and their weightings are as given in the table overleaf [8].

Measuring the Environmental Impact of Materials Used in Construction

Materials used in building construction have a big environmental impact – in extraction, processing, transport, use and disposal. This impact exists at a global, regional and personal level, affecting climate and biodiversity on the one hand, and the health of people on the other. Natural resources used in construction (roads and buildings) account for about one-half of all resource consumption in the world. Architects and engineers cannot claim to be sustainable practitioners without addressing the complex and sometimes contradictory demands of building materials.

No single methodology exists to guide those who specify construction materials. Frequently, the concept of 'embodied energy' is employed, but over the life of a building the embodied energy of the materials employed represents only around 10 per cent of the total energy consumed by the building in use. However, the concept of embodied energy does highlight the high energy transport costs of bulky materials (stone, aggregates, brick, concrete products) and the high energy processing costs of some commonly used lightweight materials (aluminium). There are three important principles that come from an understanding of embodied energy.

1. **Source heavyweight materials locally:** Stone, aggregates, bricks, etc. should be specified from quarries or manufacturers located near the construction site. This saves on energy use in transportation and reduces the overall environmental impact (disturbance, noise, pollution). Ideally, materials will be made on site (such as sun-baked bricks commonly produced in Africa and the Middle East as part of the construction process) or sourced within a reasonable radius (10 km). Apart from the reduced environmental damage, this principle will revive local building traditions and employ local people, allowing the development to be seen as belonging to the local community.

2. **Source lightweight materials globally:** Most embodied energy relates to transport costs but this is not the case for lighter materials. In the case of aluminium, for instance, the bulk of its embodied energy is the result of the manufacturing process, with a ratio of about five to one in the amount of energy consumed per unit weight of aluminium. Embodied energy is high in other lightweight materials such as PVC. However, it must be remembered that, once the energy has allowed the manufacture to take place, society has a stock of material resources that can then be used, reused or recycled (see below). This represents a capital reserve trapped in buildings which can be released at the end of the building's life. During their life, lightweight materials also perform a useful energy service which reduces the embodied energy load. Aluminium used, for instance, in conservatory construction can help trap solar energy, giving a valuable payback, and over time more than cancels out the

Measures used in the Schools Environmental Assessment Method (SEAM)

New buildings	Maximum no of points
Sites selection	1
Sources of hardwoods and softwoods	4
Low NOx combustion equipment	1
Use of recycled materials	1
Ozone-depleting chemicals	2
Volatile organic compounds	2
Harmful substances	1
Lead-free paint	1
School grounds	3
Recycling facilities and waste disposal	2
Ventilation	3
Lighting	
— high quality integrated design of daylighting and electric lighting	2
— lighting controls or switching arrangements	2
Water economy	1
Water quality	2
Legionellosis (including Legionnaires' Disease)	1
Health and safety legislation	2
Maintenance	
— complete set of record drawings and maintenance manuals	2
— caretaker training	2
Energy (CO_2) rating	7
Home to school transport policy	2
School environmental policy	1
Total number of points	45

Fig 3.6
The stone and timber in this school in Tibet can
be recycled. Notice the bolted fixings.
Source: Arup Associates

cost of its embodied energy. Similarly, aluminium used as an external louvre can effectively shade a building, reducing, in the case of an office or school, the cooling load. So, in considering embodied energy it is important to understand the full lifetime energy equation, and to remember that this varies according to building type, orientation and location.

3. **Recycling potential: Life-cycle assessment** (LCA) has highlighted the complex picture of cradle-to-grave environmental impacts. Taking energy as a single issue, the impact of a material depends on initial energy costs (input costs) and the final energy costs (output costs). There is embodied energy at the beginning but also embodied energy at the demolition stage of a building's life. Two actions are needed: first, to ensure that the potential for reuse and recycling influences the material choices made at the beginning by designers; and, second, to ensure that any residual embodied energy is extracted before the material is placed in a landfill site. Residual energy may be extracted via burning, perhaps in a waste incinerator plant, producing electricity, or via composting (where the energy breaks materials down into useful chemicals or by-products).

Resources which go into the manufacture of a building material can be retrieved and converted back into a useful product at the end of the building's life. This is true of plasterboard, concrete and, of course, steel. The easiest ways to achieve energy saving in construction materials are to design for reuse (of the whole building or its parts) and to detail for recycling. Reuse is a term normally employed for a material which is given a new life without substantial remanufacture (e.g. a reused steel beam). Recycling is when a material is reprocessed into a new product of the same material type. Aluminium and copper are both commonly recycled, with over two-thirds of all new copper consisting of recycled old copper. The degree of recycling is dependent on world commodity prices – aluminium is currently cheap and abundant, providing a disincentive to recycle. Copper, on the other hand, is relatively expensive and there are measurable limits to the world supply of copper ore. So, whereas only 40 per cent of aluminium is currently recycled, 75 per cent of copper is. Irrespective of market forces, architects should select materials on the basis of their recycled content since recycling is less energy demanding than the full process of extraction, processing and manufacture.

Energy is a useful measure of sustainability in the selection of construction materials, but it is not the only one. There are other impacts to consider such as air and water pollution (both commonly the result of building material manufacture), damage to the visual, ecological and cultural landscape (of quarrying or felling of forests), and the scarcity of future supplies. The Brundtland definition of sustainable development introduced the concept of 'futurity', or considering the resource needs of future generations. One immediately thinks of fossil fuel energy supplies but it applies equally to metals (copper, lead, zinc), to hardwood timber sources and to water. The latter is not normally considered a pressing environmental issue but, as groundwater supplies are exhausted, we face the prospect of using ever-increasing amounts of recycled water with the consequent growing risk to health. One of the main sources of global water pollution is from buildings, especially the manufacture of materials and the construction process. Eventually, the global construction industry may wish to develop an embodied water methodology (similar to energy) or at least recognise the pollution impacts of the manufacturing processes involved in making building materials.

There are long-term future supplies of sand, stone and softwoods [9]. Global scarcity does not exist in these areas, and hence they should be selected in preference to metals, plastics and hardwoods. This will lead to a particular aesthetic and architectural style (a kind of updated vernacular architecture) and, when combined with globally sourced high-tech lightweight materials, the

Fig 3.7
The use of a variety of materials suggests an understanding of differential environmental impacts. Greenwich Millennium School designed by Edward Cullinan and Partners.

combination has the potential to generate energy-efficient, resource-friendly and responsive buildings. The marriage of local sourcing of commonly available bulky materials and international sourcing of specialised lightweight ones (such as photovoltaic panels or intelligent glazing systems) will be the basis of architecture in the 21st century. High and low tech will co-exist in the same building rather than being hostile neighbours along a street.

Waste

Waste from construction accounts for about one-half of all waste going to landfill sites in the UK. Although trends suggest a reduction in this percentage as a result of increasing levels of recycling, construction and demolition waste is one of the areas of priority identified in the government's sustainable construction initiative.

Architects can contribute to waste reduction in four broad ways:
- They can design out waste by, for example, specifying materials which do not need to be cut on site. The use of standard components and modular construction reduces the need for modification and, hence, waste. However, the need to address packaging becomes more important as prefabrication increases. A useful measure of waste is to record the number of skips per £100,000 of construction and to monitor where these are dumped (landfill, recycling yards, etc.). Architects should seek to specify the waste chain as well as the production chain.
- They can specify reused, recycled or reclaimed materials. Designing using reused components, structural members and materials can reduce costs but add to the complexity of site operations. Questions need also to be asked of the performance and reliability of recycled construction products. However, increasingly common materials such as bricks are recycled for use in new construction, and old concrete is broken down to form new construction aggregate. Architects could help to expand the market for recycling by specifying reused or reclaimed materials.
- They can design their buildings to be easily dismantled at the end of their life. This requires attention to the type of fixings employed and the finish given to materials. By bolting rather than welding steel junctions, by screwing rather than nailing timber and by using lime rather than cement mortar, a whole range of recycling possibilities is opened up with little extra design thought.

Fig 3.8
House in Findhorn, Scotland, based on reused whisky vat.

- They can design buildings which are inherently flexible and capable of reuse at the end of their functional life. Since the structural life of a building is usually longer than its economic life (100 years as against 50), architects should design for functional change. Reusing the whole building obviously saves on waste and helps maintain visual, social or cultural continuity. However, reuse of the whole structure requires attention to the quality of construction and the robustness of materials over long periods of time. The pressure to build cheaply under government initiatives such as Egan can militate against long-term benefits. Waste is too rarely part of the financial equation which dictates the design of buildings.

Waste disposal is both an environmental and a health issue. Waste exhausts the availability of new resources, it adds via methane to global warming, and it is a source of water, soil and air pollution. Local pollution around waste disposal sites can have adverse impact on the health of nearby residents, on agricultural productivity and on local biodiversity. When one remembers that 50 per cent of all waste is the result of the construction industry, the professionals have an ethical responsibility to address the issue.

Over the next generation, waste will become as important as energy to construction professionals. Under the Waste and Emissions Trading Act 2003, the UK government made a commitment to reduce levels of landfill in 2020 to 35 per cent of that in 1995. This demanding target, required to meet the standards set by the EC Landfill Directive, puts pressure on all member states to address the problem of waste generation and disposal.

Complexities of Designing for Waste Reduction

All forms of construction provide opportunities for waste recycling, reuse or reduction. Structural steel offers the obvious advantage of reuse, either as new structural members or by recycling old steel at the foundry. However, the protective coatings employed and the method of fixing can be a significant inhibitor to reuse. Aluminium offers similar advantages, although all the metals have high embodied manufacturing energy costs and some use dirtier processes than others. The architect could help the environment by specifying new steel with a high recycled element or requiring steel or aluminium from manufacturing plants that employ 'clean-burn' fuels.

Fig 3.9
The Earthship Community at Taos, New Mexico designed by Michael Reynolds uses construction based largely upon waste. *Left to right:* Walls are built of recycled bottles, or tyres and rammed earth; the resulting house and village, which challenge normal measures of architectural excellence.
Source: Sam Hughes

Structural concrete offers an alternative range of potential benefits. Concrete is very long lasting (if correctly specified), and hence concrete buildings lend themselves to recycling either in whole or as a structural frame. Concrete does not normally require a finish so there are fewer health risks and, being environmentally stable, it offers climatic advantages over some other forms of construction. Concrete, too, can be recycled to form high-quality aggregate, although the costs are relatively high and there are often noise and dust problems. From the point of view of 'industrial ecology' – the ability to use waste from other industrial processes and to recycle itself – concrete offers benefits which the green architect can exploit. In particular, the 300 million tonnes of materials quarried each year in the UK to provide the aggregates and cement for concrete could be reduced if architects specified a percentage of waste (such as glass fibre or fuel ash) in the aggregate. Also, by specifying locally produced concrete products, the embodied energy costs of transport would be greatly reduced. At the Earth Centre in Yorkshire, 2,000 tonnes of recycled concrete was used in the convention centre design by Feilden Clegg Bradley with Bill Dunster. Also, it should be remembered that, in the UK, all of the reinforcement in concrete is from recycled steel scrap.

Timber construction is often regarded as the best environmental option. However, it has limited application for a wide range of building types where size, height, fire risk and climatic factors reduce timber's overall penetration into the UK construction market. Where timber is widely used – in housing and similar smaller projects – it provides considerable potential for reuse. Also, being an organic material with high energy content, after use it can be burned as a fuel or allowed to compost. However, the preservatives and protection required to safely use softwoods (such as pine and spruce) pose health risks to construction

Fig 3.10
Cob-wall house near Worcester, designed by
Associated Architects. Elevation *(top)* and
section *(bottom)*.
*Source: Associated Architects with kind permission of The Architects'
Journal.*

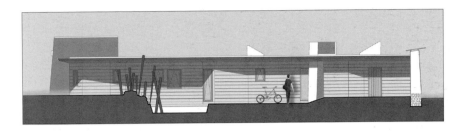

workers and the wider environment. Although hardwoods (such as oak and
beech) require little or no protection, fixings should be employed to allow for
ready dismantling at the end of the building's life. Timber waste forms a large
percentage of typical construction skips because of the amount of on-site cutting
normally employed.

Features of sustainability

- Mankind and nature are locked into a dynamic asymmetrical system
- Human society has never been sustainable
- The nature of unsustainability is always changing
- The complexity of sustainability is a barrier to progress
- Human society is living on the 'capital' of the planet, not its 'interest'
- Political decisions are short-term, natural systems long-term
- Short-term damage requires long recovery time

Brick construction offers endurance and satisfactory appearance over long time-
scales. Brick buildings are relatively healthy (no additional finishes) and can be
readily recycled at the end of their lives and easily repaired during them. The

Fig 3.11
Life-cycle impacts of steel construction.
Source: Corus

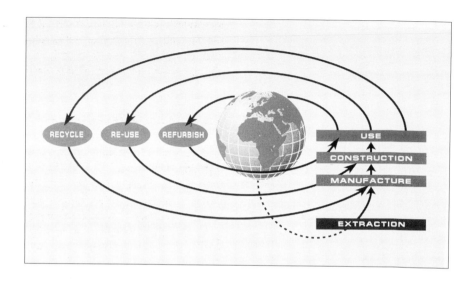

Fig 3.12
Example of steel bolted construction at the IPI
Building, University of Bradford, designed by
Rance, Booth and Smith.
Source: Rance, Booth and Smith with kind permission of Architecture Today

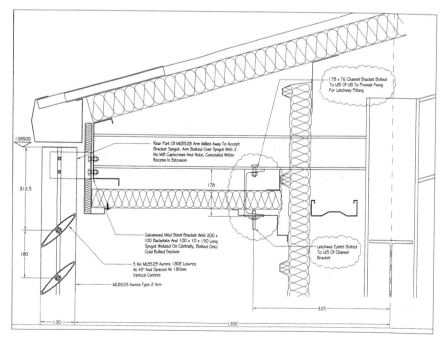

individual brick can also be reused if the building is dismantled but only if lime mortar (rather than cement) is employed. If the mortar joint is stronger than the brick then the only recycling option is as low-grade aggregate. Landfill often contains a large element of brick waste.

Which is the Greener: Steel or Concrete?

Architects face a dilemma when choosing a construction material, a fact highlighted by an examination of the use of steel in construction. Steel is often seen as a poor relation to concrete because of its high embodied energy and poor performance with regard to thermal capacity. However, since steel can be recycled indefinitely, thereby allowing the embodied energy to be traded across generations, and the thermal capacity of concrete is overrated (except for office buildings), steel may, in fact, be a wise green choice. To be sustainable, the design of steelwork should be such that it can be readily dismantled (bolted not welded connections) and of uniform length for reuse.

The embodied energy of steel is about 20 times higher than that of concrete (unreinforced) and about one-quarter that of aluminium. But embodied energy needs to relate to the weight/strength potential of the material and to its ability for subsequent material reuse. Both steel and aluminium have high energy costs in manufacture but relatively low recycled energy costs. You can do a lot more structurally with a tonne of steel than with a similar weight of concrete, and, as many architects will testify, you can achieve a great deal more tectonic construction as well.

Comparison of embodied energy by construction material

Material	Embodied energy (kWh/tonne)
Steel	7,000
Aluminium	28,000
Copper	18,000
Timber (in use)	1,000
Glass	2,000

Fig 3.13
Demolition of concrete buildings provides the opportunity to reuse waste as aggregate in new buildings.
Source: George Mills

It is said that most of the steel needed for the future already exists in the form of existing buildings and other structures. New steel manufacture is needed merely to top up the supply we already have. So embodied energy is not as critical as many claim, as long as the design provides the facility for reuse (of the member) or recycling (of the material). In fact, nearly 50 per cent of all new steel today consists of recycled material, as does around 70 per cent of aluminium.

If you run the aluminium or steel manufacturing process through a full LCA, you get some interesting outcomes. First, embodied energy is relatively insignificant as a proportion of total energy used in a building. The amount of energy needed to produce a building (manufacture, transport and erect) is only a fraction of that consumed by the building in heating, lighting and ventilation during its life. Typically, embodied and in-use energy have a ratio of about 1:10 in buildings (unlike washing machines, where the ratio is 1:2).

Also, some manufacturing plants use hydro or geothermal power, thereby adding further to the complexity. LCA also highlights the transport energy costs, which are largely related to weight. Steel, being lighter than concrete, requires much less transport energy, and the same is true for aluminium. So an inverse equation appears: the higher the embodied energy, the lighter the material and the lower the transport costs. Other materials like concrete may have low embodied energy (in manufacture) but high energy transport costs. So weighty materials (such as concrete, bricks, etc.) should be locally sourced.

LCA also highlights other impacts. Steel consumes far less water than concrete and its manufacture is less of a pollutant in water systems. At most steel manufacturing plants, water is held in a closed system and is used and reused in a cycle, while the manufacture of concrete requires extraction and aggregate washing, which affects both water quality and quantity. As we have seen, water is becoming an important environmental issue, and it is time that we developed an embodied water equation as we have done for energy.

A typical steel building weighs about half that of a concrete one. Weight is a useful rough measure to assess general environmental impact. Pollution, dust, nuisance and noise are generally weight related – the heavier the building, the greater the environmental damage. The trick with environmental assessment is to reduce pollution, not transfer it, and to see environmental impacts as total systems with feedback loops. The three stages in the life of a material or building – manufacture, use and disposal – all have their impact interactions.

Recently, manufacturers have developed a system of cheap, flexible, low-maintenance steel-framed housing for use in developed and developing countries. Steel offers advantages over brick, timber or concrete homes on cost, speed of construction and recycling potential. Steel is increasingly employed as an ecologically sound high-tech material capable of generating sophisticated climate-responsive buildings. Some of the best recent buildings from an ecological point of view are mongrels not thoroughbreds – they use steel and concrete or steel and bricks. The choice of materials is made on the basis of what is 'appropriate' rather than 'consistent'. At Doxford, near Sunderland, Auketts with Studio E Architects have designed three-storey modern business units with load-bearing brick perimeter walls (for thermal performance and appearance), a steel frame (for flexibility and speed of construction), pre-cast concrete floor/ceiling panels (for thermal cooling capacity) and photovoltaic facades (for local electricity generation). The result is material diversity with enough energy complexity to ensure sustainability.

Fig 3.14
The Integer House, Watford, has high levels of insulation and pre-cast concrete construction which promotes reuse of structural members.
Source: Cole Thompson/Architecture Today

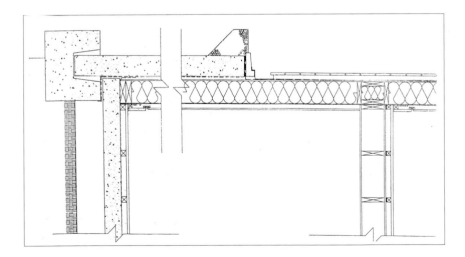

The Four 'R's – Reduce, Reuse, Recycle and Recover

If the current world population of 6 billion people increases to 10 billion by 2050 as predicted, the human race will have four times the environmental impact that it has today. This frightening prospect is based on the assumption that the World Trade Organisation's expectation of 2 per cent global economic growth per year will be realised in spite of resource shortages or sink limits (the ability of natural systems to absorb pollution). The world's ecosystems are already under great stress, and society needs to adopt a strategy which brings improvement in living conditions without global disaster. Quality of life can be maintained, but only through the adoption of the four 'R's – reduce, reuse, recycle and recover.

Environmentalists have long advocated the three 'R's, but the fourth, recover, was added more recently because so much of the human habitat needs to be repaired and recovered from contamination. This is especially true of cities, which have become the global focus of pollution and waste. Since the construction industry is mainly concerned with urban areas, it carries a particular responsibility to address the agenda of brownfield sites.

Reduce

Society has to reduce the demands made on all non-renewable resources – fossil fuels, water, mineral ores, agricultural land and geological deposits. A reduction in consumption means that supplies will be available for future generations. It also provides extra time to develop alternative supplies. For example, by conserving energy, we reduce the demand made on the finite reservoir of fossil fuels (oil, gas, coal) and we give ourselves more time to develop renewable sources of energy.

Society needs a culture of reduction, not ever-growing consumption. The consumer-led economy may benefit share prices and create global employment but it strips the environment of its resource capital. As we have already seen, there is at present a conflict in the world economic system between economic capital and natural capital. Architects and engineers need to strive towards creating a better balance in buildings between resource use and performance. Mies van der Rohe's famous aphorism 'less is more' should refer to reduced material and energy use and more comfort and value. A strategy of reduction, supported by stricter building regulations for existing and new buildings, is a necessary condition of global ecological well-being.

Fig 3.15
Reusing whole buildings offers many
environmental benefits.

Reuse

Once a building or city is created it becomes a capital asset. Within its bricks and concrete lie resources and human investment which should be reused over generations and across changing building use priorities. This means that the buildings should be robust in form and construction, should be socially valued (and hence desirable objects to reuse), and should be well located. Reuse of the whole or recycling of parts is preferable to total demolition. Where the whole building cannot be reused, the elements of construction from which it is made should be designed so that they are capable of reuse.

Reuse, as opposed to recycling, requires the architect or designer to address the design task differently. Conventionally, the architect forms a building plan to suit the precise needs of a brief. The building matches the brief in the specifics of layout and construction. However, in a period of rapid social and technological change, such closely tailored buildings quickly become redundant – either the social or economic expectations on which they were based evaporate or new technology makes them obsolete. Obsolete buildings are normally demolished, adding to future resource stress, disturbance, pollution and waste. The better path is to reuse the building, but it must have been built in a certain way for this to happen. A building is more likely to be reused if:

- it makes good use of natural light and ventilation;
- it is well serviced by infrastructure of various kinds (public transport, utilities, etc.);
- it does not contain toxic materials;
- it is well constructed, preferably using 'natural' materials;
- it has attractive spaces and character; and
- it has access to renewable energy resources (solar, wind).

Clearly, some buildings perform better than others, but the task for the designer is to create a structure with the inherent characteristics that make it suitable for reuse. Architects need to realise that their drawing-board decisions often close options for subsequent alternative uses. What is needed is a rebalancing of the form/function contract to allow for possible future functions to shape the initial form. Considering their impact on resources, buildings should be primarily robust intergenerational assets rather than objects with an inflexible singularity of function. This means greater concern for process (following Egan principles [10]), an understanding of sustainability at all levels, and 'loose-fit' functional solutions.

Fig 3.16
Restoring older buildings in locations undergoing renewal, as here at Yokohama, helps conserve resources while also providing cultural continuity.

Reuse also entails the rescuing of elements of construction (steel beams, timber, bricks, etc.) for use in other buildings. Not many new buildings are designed or constructed to encourage reuse. Steel members are welded (rather than bolted) and given toxic finishes (oil paints, powder-coated epoxy resins). Bricks, too, are used with cement mortars that are often stronger than the bricks themselves, thus preventing their reuse. The use of a weaker mortar (one containing lime) and the avoidance of plaster finishes greatly enhance the chances of reuse. Since the embodied energy of a brick would drive a car five miles, the consequences are enormous for the millions of bricks created (and wasted) every year. A reused brick saves on:

● the excavation of clay;
● the baking of bricks (consuming fossil fuels and causing air pollution); and
● landfill waste at end of life.

So the reuse philosophy requires a change in how we design our buildings and a corresponding change in how we construct them. Architects could create a major demand for reused components simply by specifying them. This would not only generate a market for reused components but also lead to buildings of greater aesthetic richness and social value.

Recycle

Recycling is the next step. It involves rescuing the useful parts of a material by extraction and re-manufacture. In the case of aluminium, it entails melting aluminium scrap and reforming the material into further useful products (aluminium structural members, clips, etc.). Unlike reuse, recycling requires further energy in the reforging process but is preferable to the total loss of the material.

Certain construction materials, especially those with high embodied energy, are commonly recycled: steel, aluminium, lead, copper. Corus, Europe's major steel manufacturer, claims that one-half of all new steel is recycled old steel and all new steel reinforcement in the UK consists of recycled steel. The degree of recycling is partly dependent on market forces, but designers could help by specifying materials with a large recycled component. Since metals tend to be recycled, their use is preferable over concrete for large construction frames. However, as mentioned earlier, concrete offers other benefits (such as thermal capacity) and can be locally sourced (using aggregate and cement from nearby). Also, concrete can be recycled by breaking down old concrete into aggregate for use in new building or road construction.

Fig 3.17
Squatter housing in Tokyo made from salvaged
building materials covered in plastic sheets.

Recycling often involves the extraction of energy from a material and the separation of other parts for subsequent reuse. Old timber can be incinerated, perhaps in waste-based power stations, and plasterboard can be reformed. It is important to consider the recycling potential, the environmental impacts at each stage, and the full life-cycle costing characteristics of the options of reuse and recycling.

Recover

Half of the global human population lives in cities, most in conurbations of over a million. Urban areas are a major source of air pollution and, as a consequence, pose an increasing risk to human health. In the EU, for example, poor air quality in cities is now the second major cause of death because it leads to heart attacks, cancer and bronchitis. Much of this air pollution originates in buildings or as a consequence of the need to travel to buildings. Any strategy for recovering cities needs to encompass the contribution building design can make to healthier living. There are obvious areas that urban design can address, such as: the avoidance of deep planned offices, with their high-energy loads and pollution costs; the lack of pedestrian and cycle-friendly spaces; and the poor public transport provision. Urban air quality is also improved by planting trees, which act as air cleansers, climate modifiers and shading devices.

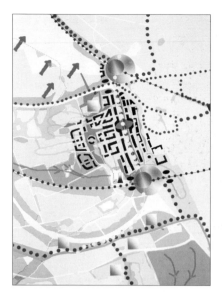

Fig 3.18
Masterplan by students at the Edinburgh College of Art's School of Architecture, which provides a green framework for the recovery of brownfield land on western edge of Edinburgh.

Building, landscape and urban design can, in unison, help to recover cities from pollution, chaos and alienation. The city is now home for most people: we spend 80 per cent of our time inside buildings and the remainder mainly in polluted urban areas. The human habitat is now predominately urban, and architects have a key role to play in creating civilised, clean and productive cities. Many modern polluted urban centres (Hong Kong, Tokyo, London) are the result of a lack of regulation and poor design. If the 20th century saw the fashioning of cities as we know them, the 21st will witness unprecedented action to reclaim them from pollution and chaos.

The second major arena for recovery is contaminated land, the so-called brownfield sites. Air pollution is fairly readily dissipated (to become someone else's problem in the form of acid rain or climate change) but land pollution remains static and persists, blighting large areas. It is estimated that 20 per cent of land in most Western cities lies vacant and underused, often because of contamination. Old industrial cities (Detroit, Glasgow, Turin) have extensive tracts of contaminated land. It often forms a ring around the commercial centre (e.g. Manchester) or wedges, which run from the centre to the outskirts along former industrial corridors (e.g. Sheffield). Since the latter are often based on river courses, there are valleys of pollution affecting water, land and air quality.

Action by all agencies (governmental, professional and private) is needed to tackle urban land contamination. In Western cities such areas stand idle and neglected; in Eastern and Southern cities they are often colonised by squatters, who establish townships on the land nobody else will use. Like air pollution, contaminated land is a threat to human health as well as being ecologically degrading. The degree of pollution depends on the chemicals or agents present. There is often arsenic where chemical plants were located, radiation on sites of former factories or hospitals, heavy metals (cadmium, lead, mercury) at steel or large-scale manufacturing plants, and asbestos at former power stations. As industry has moved out of cities it has often left behind sites suffering from a range of unknown and often toxic forms of pollution.

To enable this land to be put into productive use again, it needs to be retrieved from its polluted state. Expertise is required to survey and analyse this land, to deal with the contamination, and to design buildings that reduce exposure to any surviving sources of pollution. Architects are frequently involved in advising on site selection and subsequently in design, and so need to become familiar with the problems associated with contaminated land.

Many brownfield sites contain elements of contamination (land, water or air). If the land is to be recovered, different design strategies are needed depending on the source or type of contamination. The main methods employed fall into four categories:
- removal of toxic material, often soil soaked in chemicals;
- capping and sealing the source of pollution including the contaminated soil;
- cleansing the land using biological methods; and
- cleansing the land using chemical methods.

There are advantages and disadvantages with each, and often all four strategies are used on the same site. Removal of toxic material simply takes the pollution to somebody else's backyard (either a private or a local authority waste site). Either way, it sweeps the problem under the carpet rather than solving it. The effectiveness of capping is dependent on proper seals and, given the life of buildings (50–100 years), architects need to feel confident that underground bunkers or tanks are resistant to corrosion or fracture. Biological methods are the most benign and are based on toxin-neutralising plants (alder, willow, poplar, reed) which either naturally break down pollution or absorb it. The planting can then be cut down and the pollution transported to locations where it can be effectively treated by combustion or composting. The method is ecologically safe but requires time. Chemical treatment involves the use of synthetic agents that break down the pollution source or make it more accessible. It can then be treated by other means (such as incineration) or removed. Cost and time are key factors in remedial land treatment but it is vital that environmental factors such as spillage or run-off are not ignored.

The four 'R's brought together as a package help to focus on the interconnectedness of the options available. Good ecological design consists not in considering issues in isolation but in combining them into a systemic whole. Typically, an architect will have to employ elements of each 'R' in a brownfield project and will need to balance the 'R's according to cost, programme and time constraints. However, by bringing each part together, the building will enjoy the consequent environmental benefits. A mixed use of environmental measures is infinitely preferable to the chasing of single green goals.

Fig 3.19
Masterplan of the Earth Centre, Yorkshire, built
on a former coal pit and quarry site.
Source: Grant Associates

UK government sustainable construction policies

Key priorities

- Benchmarking sustainable construction
- Reducing CO_2 emissions
- Improving productivity of non-domestic buildings
- Reducing resources used in construction by maximising recycling

Secondary priorities

- Conserving water
- Increasing use of renewable materials (timber, etc.) used in construction
- Treating and remedying contaminated land
- Reducing pollutants from construction processes

Source: DETR, *Sustainable Construction – Opportunities for Change*, 1998

Buildings, Health and Construction Materials

Health is defined by the World Health Organization (WHO) as *a state of complete physical, mental and social well-being* [11]. Buildings contribute to this state and it follows, therefore, that they have a profound impact on quality of life. Any design which subjects users to health risks is both unethical and exposes the architect or engineer to potential litigation. Such a broad definition of health poses certain dilemmas but, at the same time, opens up fresh avenues of architectural development. Health in the context of cities has already been discussed; here the emphasis is on the building, its details and its impact on personal wellbeing.

Health is emerging as a new catalyst in building design. The environmentalists' former emphasis on global warming, pollution and resource depletion placed personal health well behind that of planetary well-being. Buildings were to be energy efficient in spite of the use of potentially toxic insulation, of reduced levels of ventilation and reduced window area. Green building did not embrace either the physiological or psychological dimensions of health. Now, however, a new philosophy is emerging from the ecological design movement, one which balances energy efficiency with human health. The new emphasis is not on energy efficiency at any price but on more holistic solutions that bring natural (and hence healthy) systems into the equation [12]. Health is dependent on adequate comfort levels, but comfort alone does not promote healthy living or working environments. The three key components of healthy building environments are:

- comfort;
- being free of pollution; and
- being responsive and stimulating to human needs.

Each of these components has its own principles, science base and practice in construction, but they cannot be considered in isolation.

Comfort

This concept is central to the creation of healthy human environments. Comfort embraces thermal comfort, humidity, ventilation and lighting. We need to feel comfortable, to be able to see without glare or dimness, and have the right balance of humidity and ventilation. Healthy environments are normally those based on natural sources of light, ventilation and materials.

Fig 3.20
Art Lover's House, Glasgow designed by
Charles Rennie Mackintosh – a study in healthy,
stimulating design.

Comfort can be achieved by other means (in much of the world, air-conditioning is needed to maintain comfort levels) but, wherever possible, natural systems and technologies are preferable to mechanical ones. For example, comfort can be enhanced by improved levels of insulation, by adopting 'breathing wall' principles whereby the building acts like a lung in response to fluctuating external conditions, and by eliminating unwanted air movement (draughts).

The lack of comfortable conditions can promote mould and bacteria growth. High levels of moisture, insufficient ventilation and the presence of bacteria lead to mould colonisation. In its wake come dust mites, which eat the mould and excrete tiny droppings. These are then inhaled by occupants, leading to respiratory problems and other forms of ill health caused by bacteriological contamination. The root of this problem, which manifests itself in sickness or allergy, is poor design.

Being Pollution-free

If buildings are polluted they are not healthy, even though they may be energy efficient. Pollution comes in many guises: toxicity (poor air quality), noise pollution, and, to a degree, space pollution (the psychologically stressful effect of overcrowding). All three are legitimate design concerns, especially taking the WHO definition of health into account. Air pollution occurs indoors by:

- the entry of external air pollution;
- contamination of air which is the result of planned combustion (boilers, cooking, etc.);
- contamination resulting from unplanned combustion (smoking);
- off-gassing of chemicals used in construction or furnishings; and
- radon entering the building through the ground.

Although each is important and can affect human health, it is the cocktail of chemicals which probably poses the greatest risk. Also, airborne water vapour enhances the absorption of the chemicals into our bodies through breathing. VOCs (volatile organic compounds) are commonly ten times the level inside buildings than outside, leading to allergies and sick building syndrome. VOCs occur as a by-product of manufacture and are slowly released into the atmosphere during the lifetime of the building. Their release is accelerated by wear and tear, cutting or drilling, and stresses caused by temperature variations.

Fig 3.21 *(right)*
Office building with high levels of natural light
and contact with nature. Wessex Water
headquarters, near Bath.

Fig 3.22 *(far right)*
Supermarket building that provides natural light.
Sainsbury Supermarket, Greenwich, designed by
Chetwood Architects.
Source: Chetwood Architects

What is good for the building is good for the occupant. To put it another way, if
there are mould attacks, outbreaks of timber rot, or fabric cracking due to an
excessively hot or dry indoor climate, it is bad news for the building and bad news
for those who use it, too. Another important principle is to take a cautionary
approach. If there is doubt, err on the side of caution: do not expose people to
unknown risk. Since many construction materials have not been in existence for
more than a few years and many new ones are introduced onto the market each
year, it is wise to exercise caution or scepticism in their use. The final principle to
follow is that of naturalness. Materials taken directly from nature (timber) or those
from organic or inert sources (bricks and clay tiles) are inherently safer than
synthetic materials (plastics).

Buildings, as we have seen, last a long time and the pollution placed in their fabric
at the start (i.e. in construction) can blight the building throughout its life. Glass
fibre quilt insulation, for example, desirable as an energy-efficiency measure, poses
a greater health risk than insulation based on organic materials (cellulose fibre,
sheep's wool). However, poor detailing in the use of organic materials can lead to
decay, which threatens both the building and its occupants. So, with natural
materials, particular attention must be paid to moisture levels, ventilation and
rodent control.

Radon is a problem in parts of the UK. A radioactive gas, it occurs naturally in much of Cornwall and Devon, Derbyshire, large areas of Wales and the Highlands of Scotland. It is odourless and is a major source of lung cancer, especially for those who also smoke. It enters the building through the ground. Poorly ventilated underfloor cavities can result in a build-up of radon, which then permeates the building through cracks in floorboards or through service runs.

CFCs (chlorofluorocarbons) are commonly found in buildings even though the Montreal Protocol of 1989 banned their manufacture [13]. CFCs and the material used as a substitute, HCFC (hydrochlorofluorocarbons), are highly damaging to global and personal health. They have 20,000 times the global warming impact of the same volume of CO_2 and are responsible in addition for the thinning of the ozone layer. The ozone layer protects us from ultraviolet light, and as the ozone layer is depleted and as more of this waveband of light reaches the surface of the Earth, there is an increase in skin cancer and eye cataracts. Skin cancer is now the UK's second most common cancer and, though it is not a big killer, it leads to considerable disfigurement. An extra 60,000 cases of skin cancer in the UK per year are attributed to ozone thinning. One-half of all CFC use is related to buildings — either as a chemical used in cooling or as a foaming agent employed in the manufacture of insulation products.

Although CFCs are no longer specified, they remain in many existing buildings, especially those with air-conditioning. CFCs can be retrieved safely at demolition to prevent release into the atmosphere, and many local councils offer a free CFC recovery service. Unfortunately, there is a black market in CFCs and it is still used in less regulated parts of the world. As for asbestos, we only became aware of the health problems late in the day: it confirms the importance of exercising caution when new products are brought onto the market.

Responsive and Stimulating Environments

Since health has a psychological dimension it becomes incumbent upon designers to create environments which reduce stress and which respond positively to user need. Occupational stress can be the result of overwork, of environments which are difficult to moderate, or of the loss of contact with natural cycles (daylight, sunlight, night-time). Sensory stimulation can provide a natural counterbalance to our frequent reliance on artificial stimulants (alcohol, caffeine), which contribute to stress. Natural stimulation comes from the play of sunlight on walls, from well-ventilated rooms bathed in daylight, from the presence of plants inside and contact with trees and shrubs outside. Quantitative indicators of healthy environments need to be matched with qualitative ones [14]. It is the subtle play of space and light which comes closest to natural conditions and which is at the root of forging stress-free buildings.

The interaction between mind and body is as important as that noted earlier between body and building. Inevitably, these connections are not fully understood but it is essential that the architect creates spaces that reduce stress, which can be done by employing technologies that are under the control of building users. Research suggests that in office buildings those closest to windows suffer less stress and are, as a consequence, more healthy and productive than those further away from windows. Similar research from hospitals establishes a parallel correlation between the personal control of light and ventilation by patients and the rate of stress, antisocial behaviour and recovery [15]. In the home, where the bulk of life is conducted, it is important to avoid systems, materials, products and processes that frustrate or damage health.

Responsiveness is partly achieved by user-friendliness. Over-complex controls lead to stress and alienate people from their environment. As a result, instead of turning down heater controls, people open windows and, instead of setting timers, they leave systems running when they are not needed. A responsive environment is not only a natural one (i.e. natural light and ventilation in the day rather than artificial light and mechanical ventilation) but also a simple one. A balance is needed between simplicity and stimulation: an overly simple interior may be soporific. Light (particularly sunlight), space (particularly vertical space) and interior planting (especially exotic species) can provide a stimulating well-tempered environment. Add to this the sound of leaves rustling or the smell of aromatic plants and the responsive feel of the space is complete. A visual and audible interaction between the interior and exterior world is also important, although not if the exterior environment is hostile, in which case it should be excluded.

Fig 3.23
Interior of Barclaycard office, Northampton, designed by Fitzroy Robinson. A stimulating and energy efficient working environment.

Fig 3.24
Traditional windcatcher used for ventilating
courtyard housing in the Middle East. The
airflow can be reversed for night-time cooling.

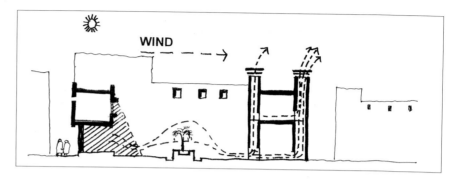

Windcatchers

By maximising the use of wind and sun, windcatchers make a major contribution
to sustainable design. Through the skillful utilisation of renewable resources,
windcatchers provide natural ventilation in modern buildings where air-
conditioning or mechanical systems normally predominate. Windcatchers have an
ancient pedigree, being employed from about the second century BC in parts of
the Middle East, and are still common in the region. They work by catching the
wind at high level and drawing ventilation through the building at low level
because of the different air pressure. Windcatchers are primarily wind driven but
also utilise temperature gradients, and can be solar-assisted as well as wind driven.

Windcatchers break the mould of window or vent-based, low-level, cross-
ventilation. They use instead controlled ventilation at high level, taking advantage
of the wind pressure which is invariably present. As a consequence of their shape
and position, windcatchers can normally utilise wind from any direction and, via
the use of dampers, of any speed.

Windcatchers can be a more effective means of ventilating large, deep-plan
buildings than side window vents. The rate of ventilation can also be more readily
controlled and integrated with other ventilation strategies such as the stack effect.
Hence, wind and sun can be jointly employed to reduce the demand made on
mechanical ventilation systems. In this regard, windcatchers have become popular
with green architects, and their presence on the roof of a building (as at Portcullis
House, London by Michael Hopkins & Partners) is a sure sign of a natural
ventilation strategy.

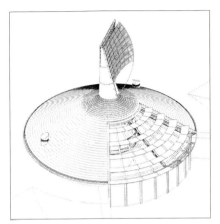

Fig 3.25
Wind cowl used to ventilate ICI Visitor Centre in Runcorn *(above)*, designed by AMEC Design and Engineering, and Brighton Library *(right)*, designed by Bennetts Associates.
Source: AMEC Design / Bennetts Associates / AJ

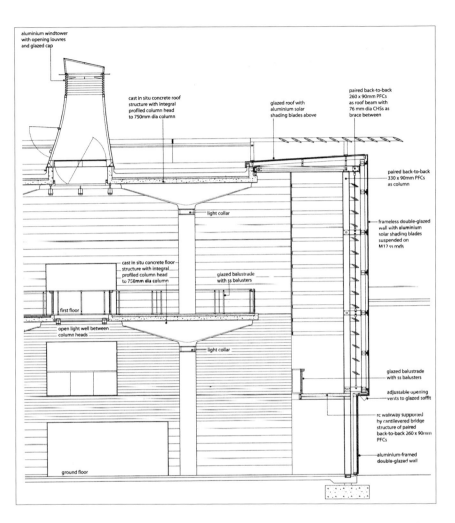

aluminium windtower with opening louvres and glazed cap

cast in situ concrete roof structure with integral profiled column head to 750mm dia column

glazed roof with aluminium solar shading blades above

paired back-to-back 260 x 90mm PFCs as roof beam with 76 mm dia CHSs as brace between

paired back-to-back 330 x 90mm PFCs as column

light collar

frameless double-glazed wall with aluminium solar shading blades suspended on M12 ss rods

cast in situ concrete floor structure with integral profiled column head to 750mm dia column

glazed balustrade with ss balusters

first floor

open light well between column heads

light collar

glazed balustrade with ss balusters

adjustable opening vents to glazed soffit

rc walkway supported by cantilevered bridge structure of paired back-to-back 260 x 90mm PFCs

aluminium-framed double-glazed wall

ground floor

As a general rule, the catchment area of a windcatcher is the same as that which would have been provided by wall openings (i.e. windows and vents). Since the roof-mounted windcatchers are unobstructed (unlike windows), manufacturers claim that there is a constant flow of fresh air irrespective of wind direction. However, the combination of windcatchers and traditional windows means that in the summertime windcatchers act as exhaust vents for the warmed air using the stack effect. It is this combination which is increasingly attractive as temperatures rise under the influence of global warming.

Windcatchers are normally internally divided into two chambers – one for incoming air, the other for exhaust air. The external wind movement creates a negative pressure or suction zone to one side while pressurising the other. As a consequence, air is driven into the building and controlled via dampers at ceiling level. The volume control dampers determine the amount of air flow and can be adjusted mechanically or via a computer program depending on internal and external temperature levels. Windcatchers can be integrated with suncatchers, a system which brings natural light into the building via a silvered sun pipe placed in the centre of the windcatcher unit. It has the advantage of conveying natural light and natural ventilation simultaneously, providing a useful technology for deep-plan buildings.

Specialist design advice should be sought when considering the use of windcatchers. The number, size and position of units is important, and how they interact with solar-assisted stack effect strategies via atria should be the subject of computer modelling. One particular problem is that of excessive night-time cooling with cold air entering the building via the units. Dampers and windjammers are required to ensure that the desirable effect of night-time cooling does not become an excessive energy demand on the building in terms of day-time heating.

Windcatchers are an environmentally friendly, energy-saving technology of particular relevance to deep-plan buildings where external obstructions or other problems such as noise or ground-level air pollution restrict the use of window vents. They can be useful also in more traditional situations as long as wind and solar systems are integrated. Since no power is required to move the air, the total energy load of ventilation or air-conditioning is greatly reduced. However, it is unusual to employ windcatchers on their own. More normally they form part of a mixed economy of ventilation techniques (windows, atria, mechanical backup). It has been claimed that the use of windcatchers can reduce the energy load of ventilation by 40 per cent with initial capital costs 15 per cent lower than conventional solutions. There is also less space required for plant rooms and, due to the simplicity of windcatcher technology, maintenance costs are significantly lower [16].

Fig 3.26
View of wind cowls and photo-voltaic panels at the Jubilee Campus, Nottingham, designed by Michael Hopkins and Partners.
Source: Michael Hopkins and Partners

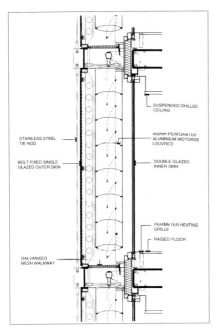

Fig 3.27
Window detail at the Helicon Building, London, designed by Sheppard Robson.
Source: Sheppard Robson

Window Design

The design of windows is a great deal more complex than simply satisfying U-value requirements. The U-value standard of 1.8 for windows required under Part L of the UK Building Regulations (2006) ignores the interrelationship between heat loss through windows, solar gain, daylight penetration and air infiltration. Windows are complex design problems requiring attention to size, shape and position as well as the angle of splays, position of blinds (internal and external) and the size of openings. Added to this, the type of glass and its coatings (Low-E and Pilkington K Glass, for example) have a big impact on energy performance.

The tightening of standards for windows to match those elsewhere in Europe under amendments to the Building Regulations in 2002, and the application of the new standards to refurbishment as well as new construction, have resulted in considerable carbon savings. The energy efficiency of windows is, however, better assessed using the European Window Energy Rating Scheme. This evaluates the energy performance of windows on the basis of their thermal insulation, useful solar gain and air infiltration [17]. The resulting assessment provides a rating number which is specific to a location rather than universal. Hence, orientation, exposure and other factors are taken into account. The scheme offers more sophisticated evaluation than under Part L of the Building Regulations.

Healthy Materials

As a general rule, natural building materials are also healthy ones. The problem is that the lack of technical performance from organic materials often results in architects selecting manufactured products. However, traditional materials, some neglected because of fashion or poor performance, are being revived as a result of their undoubted healthiness. As they are revived, new techniques are being developed to use them in new ways. The main organic materials are listed below [18].

Earth Products
These range from earth blocks, sun-baked bricks and clay mortars to earth-based plasters. They have been used for centuries in Europe and are low embodied energy materials with zero toxicity and, with careful detailing, enjoy long life.

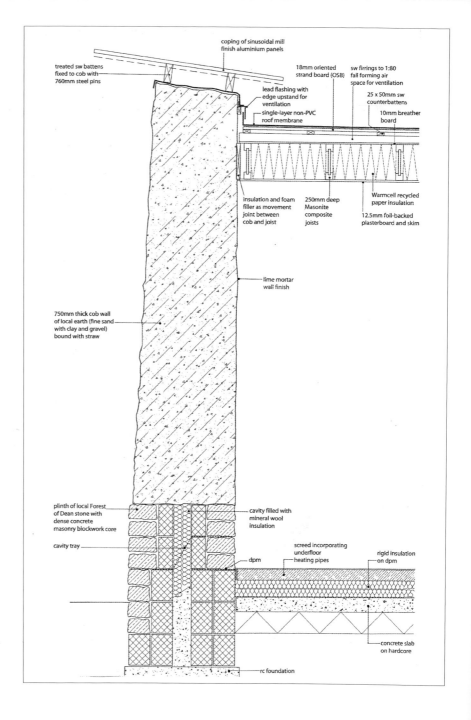

Fig 3.28
Detail of contemporary cob wall (sand, clay and straw) at a house near Worcester, designed by Associated Architects.

Source: The Architects' Journal / Associated Architects

coping of sinusoidal mill finish aluminium panels

treated sw battens fixed to cob with 760mm steel pins

18mm oriented strand board (OSB)

sw firrings to 1:80 fall forming air space for ventilation

lead flashing with edge upstand for ventilation

25 x 50mm sw counterbattens

single-layer non-PVC roof membrane

10mm breather board

insulation and foam filler as movement joint between cob and joist

250mm deep Masonite composite joists

Warmcell recycled paper insulation

12.5mm foil-backed plasterboard and skim

lime mortar wall finish

750mm thick cob wall of local earth (fine sand with clay and gravel) bound with straw

plinth of local Forest of Dean stone with dense concrete masonry blockwork core

cavity filled with mineral wool insulation

cavity tray

screed incorporating underfloor heating pipes

rigid insulation on dpm

dpm

concrete slab on hardcore

rc foundation

Fig 3.29
House in Zanzibar built using greenwood and
basket-making techniques.
Source: Edward Cullinan

Fig 3.30
Model of John Makepiece House at Hooke,
Dorset, designed by Edward Cullinan and
Partners.
Source: Edward Cullinan and Partners

Stone

Stone walling and structural members have long been employed in construction. They are the basis of many ancient buildings and have stood the ravages of time and human use well. Few have given rise to health problems. Because it occurs naturally, stone is healthy, enduring and attractive. Health problems can occur in quarrying and site cutting (especially the inhalation of dust) but generally stone poses little pollution risk. Quarrying is, however, visually and ecologically damaging, and there are large transportation energy costs involved. There are long-term sources of limestone and sandstone in the UK and, provided quarries are local, stone is an obvious choice of material to use in construction. Stone is also readily recycled, and its high thermal capacity, combined with its endurance, makes it an attractive choice for many reasons.

Timber

Wood-based products and timber structural members form the basis of much vernacular and modern construction (not just in the domestic realm). Timber is a sustainable, self-renewing product and, as living wood, helps in the conversion of CO_2 back into oxygen (thereby reducing global warming). Timber, however, needs to be sourced from a reputable supplier to prevent habitat loss, especially distant rainforests. Locally grown hardwoods are increasingly used in UK construction, especially green oak, which has benefits of ease of workmanship and pliability if used before fully seasoned. Softwoods are more generally employed but may need chemical treatment, which raises health and pollution problems.

Lime Mortars

These have long been used in buildings and, until the introduction of cement in the late 19th century, were the major bonding element for stone and masonry. Lime is also used as a plaster and external wall finish. Lime (as putty, hydraulic lime or lime mortar) has many applications and, if used as brickwork or blockwork mortar, allows the bricks and blocks to be recovered and reused.

Organic Insulation

Natural products can be turned into building insulation for use especially in roofs and walls. Various materials form the basis of organic insulation – e.g. cellulose fibre, vegetable fibre, sheep's wool. Unlike manufactured insulation (such as expanded polystyrene), natural insulation materials are low in embodied energy, are not toxic, and do not release ozone-depleting chemicals.

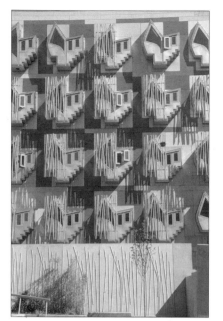

Fig 3.31
Façade of the Scottish Parliament Building in
Edinburgh designed by Enric Miralles / RMJM,
using locally sourced building materials which
make reference to the Scottish landscape.

Water-based Paints

Paints and varnishes that are not oil-based are now widely available. Being water-based, they pose little threat to the health of construction workers or building occupants. Oil-based paints are particularly toxic: professional painters have a 40 per cent higher incidence of lung cancer than other workers [19]. An alternative is to use natural resin oil as a paint primer or water-based equivalents.

The market for natural materials in the UK is relatively depressed compared to much of Europe. In Germany, the use of water-based paints is 20 times that in England and, in Denmark, natural insulation products account for 10 per cent of the market while in the UK they make up only 1 per cent [20]. It is not sufficient, however, to simply specify green products: new construction techniques are also required. The design of the building needs to recognise the potential health problems posed by everyday construction detailing. As concern over health begins to drive the sustainability agenda beyond that of low-energy issues, it carries a fresh generation of construction materials, details and site techniques in its wake.

Green materials: choices and conflicts

- Health versus ecological criteria
- Direct impacts versus indirect impacts
- Immediate versus long-term impacts
- Measurable single assessment methods versus unmeasurable complex ones
- Embodied energy versus energy saving in use
- Attractive appearance versus allergic reaction

Notes

[1] Brian Edwards, *Sustainable Architecture*, Architectural Press, Oxford, 1999, p. 213.

[2] This definition is adapted from the Environmental Technology Best Practice Programme guide *ET257: Life-cycle Assessment – An Introduction for industry*, 2000, p. 2.

[3] *ibid.*, pp. 2–3.

[4] *Energy and Environmental Management*, January/February 2004, pp. 10–11.

[5] Environmental Best Practice Programme, DETR, London, 2000, p. 7.

[6] *op. cit.*, Edwards, pp. 207–9.

[7] Brian Edwards, *Green Buildings Pay*, 2nd edn, E&FN Spon, London, 2003.

[8] *Schools Environmental Assessment Method (SEAM)*, Building Bulletin 87, DfEE, London, 1996, p. 56.

[9] Eoin O'Cofaigh and Owen Lewis, 'The Principles and Practice of Sustainable Architectural Design' in *European Directory of Sustainable and Energy-efficient Building*, James & James, 1999, p. 61.

[10] John Egan, *Rethinking Construction*, The Construction Task Force, DETR, London, 1998.

[11] http://www.who.int/en/

[12] Neil May, 'Energy efficiency and Ecology in the Renovation of Vernacular Buildings', *Building for a Future*, Spring 2000, p.63.

[13] *The Montreal Protocol Foreign Office Command Paper*, Treaty Series No. 19, HMSO, 1990.

[14] *op. cit.*, Stevenson and Williams, pp. 70–1.

[15] C. Gates, 'Design speeds recovery', *Building Design*, 25 April 2003, p. 6, see also 'Assessing benefits in the health sector' in Sebastian Macmillan (ed.) *Designing Better Buildings*, Spon Press, London, 2004, pp. 100–6.

[16] 'Passivent' brochure C1/SFB (57), March 2001, p. 3.

[17] *EcoTech*, Issue 8, November 2003, p. 5.

[18] The author here is indebted to the Natural Buildings Technologies Company for the list and summary.

[19] *op. cit.*, Stevenson and Williams, p. 68.

[20] Quoted by Neil May at the *Green Buildings Pay* seminar, Aylesbury, Buckinghamshire, 18 October 2000.

Design Solutions

4

4 Design Solutions

Space, Time and Sustainability

Sustainability is increasingly seen as the only legitimate design issue in architecture in the 21st century. The argument is both spiritual and practical. Physically, Planet Earth is under great ecological stress from global warming. No architecture has moral validity unless it addresses this problem by being environmentally sustainable. Of course, as we have seen, sustainability also has social and aesthetic dimensions. The role of technology is to bridge the two worlds of social advancement and ecological harmony. Out of this compact comes a new architectural order – a fresh typology for many building types and the new technologies within them. Out of it also comes a new agenda for design, one where human habitats and nature at last find reconciliation.

Technology holds the key to architecture's green future. Designers are busy testing and developing new construction technology based on solar cells, intelligent facades, breathing walls, thermal mass and natural ventilation. The new order of sustainability, translated to the macro and micro levels, influences every decision. There are three key forces in this liberating new world for design and construction:
- the use of ecology as a system;
- the broadening of sustainability agendas beyond the issue of energy conservation; and
- the interaction between people, space and technology within a sustainability paradigm.

All three influence architectural culture in important ways. They introduce designers to the idea of reuse and recycling, to considering the source as well as the use of materials, to water conservation, and to the health of both construction workers and buildings' occupants. This new thinking requires new technologies, be they borrowed from other industries, alternative technologies, revivals of old technologies (such as lime mortars – brought back to life by the demands of sustainability) or others that have yet to be developed. All of this gives rise to fresh perspectives. One such is the recognition that healthier buildings are also more productive ones. The human environments that architects create influence health   both physical and psychological. Buildings can lead to stress or relieve it; buildings can cause cancer or help prolong life. Productivity, technology and sustainability are being recognised as an important package of interactions,

Fig 4.1
Ken Yeang has set an example of using new sustainable technologies to reinvigorate skyscraper design.
Source: Ken Yeang

especially in working environments. Green buildings pay, not just in terms of energy conservation but in health promotion and social cohesion, too.

The technologies that designers employ are a cultural statement. Building construction is not value free – it is influenced by many factors, such as cost, buildability, sustainability and aesthetics. The sustainable design movement (such as embodied energy and recyclability) is the way it has moved from big decisions (such as urban density, plan depth of buildings and energy saving) to smaller ones. The choice of every component and every element of construction and assembly is now subject to green examination. 'Eco-architecture' runs the risk of becoming 'eco-tech', with a reliance on technology alone. However, true sustainability changes everything – the space plan, section and details of construction. If this new ecological agenda does not change social space and city form, it will have failed to become mainstream. Technology is the key to sustainable construction just as urban design is the key to sustainable cities. Only when green issues change the politics of city form, when social space and social equity are taken seriously, will we finally have fully reclaimed the city from 20th-century excesses.

Technology is the single most important generator of design. It is not what buildings are but what they do and how they do it that are the major concerns of sustainable development. Building science and functionality have been the two dominant strands of form generation for at least a century. Since function in a world of rapid social and economic change becomes quickly obsolete, space has become more elastic and less specific. Buildings are increasingly big volumes without specific use (e.g. the Millennium Dome). At a fundamental level, technology allows us to convert resources into useful artefacts (from cities at one end of the scale, to mobile phones at the other). Technology is the blend of science and design – there is a human dimension imparted by the creative thinkers who imagine the designed future. Designers impart cultural value – their role is to fashion technology. The challenge is to make this process more ecologically conscious, to see buildings as a marriage not only of use and technology but also of biology and fashion. In this sense, architects give legitimacy and expression to a style that uses ecology to provide the fundamental order.

Sustainability as a Key Quality Indicator

Sustainability is not a stand-alone feature of design but one of several characteristics to which an architect should aspire. Since design quality is dependent upon available resources, sustainable design is about generating better value over a longer time scale with the resources available [1]. Design quality indicators (DQIs) bring together the linked attributes of function, building quality and impact in such a way as to allow for the rational measurement of sustainability from three key perspectives – social, economic and environmental. After all, a design is not economically sustainable if it does not effectively serve a function; is not environmentally sustainable if it lacks robustness in construction; and is not socially sustainable if it is not enjoyed by users. The Vitruvian triangle of firmness, utility and delight shares similarities with the modern-day triangulation of sustainable development.

Fig 4.2
The Vitruvian triangle shares similarities with the triangulation of sustainable development.

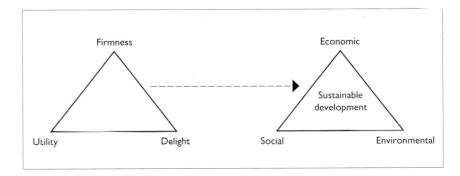

It is important that performance measurement tools take account of present-day resource impacts and possible future scarcity. Fitness for purpose may well vary in the future as different resources come under strain and as the climatic environment changes. A material or energy system that is selected today may not be the best choice in the future. Therefore, predictive tools such as BREEAM, LEED and Eco-points need to recognise life-cycle issues in an unstable world. Whatever tools are employed, there is an urgent need to make buildings more resource efficient and flexible whilst also contributing to human satisfaction and to business performance [2].

Fig 4.3
Design is a cultural statement which addresses many agendas. Selfridges department store, Birmingham, designed by Future Systems.

The UK government has sought to link design quality with sustainable development in its recent *Planning Policy Statement 1: Delivering Sustainable Development* (PPS1), which states that 'high standards of building design help achieve sustainable development' [3]. The emphasis on design is a welcome change – a succession of British governments failed to acknowledge the social, economic and environmental advantages of good design. PPS1 requires architects and planners to cooperate more to help promote economic development, social inclusion and environmental protection. As mentioned in Chapter 1, evidence from teaching suggests little in the way of cross-professional cooperation.

Action for Sustainable Design

The dual imperatives of climate change and fossil fuel depletion place a responsibility upon architects and engineers to design more elegant, fitter, ecologically resourceful and adaptable buildings. Existing buildings are inevitably more difficult to change than are those on the drawing board. As a general rule, the older the building the more difficult it is to adapt. Given that the life of a building is typically at present 100 years (as against the design for life of 50 years) they will be around in a period of climate and resource stress. The rules to follow for constructing a generation of fitter, more adaptable buildings are listed below:

- **Apply green principles from the outset:** Green principles must be put into the brief at the very beginning to ensure that costs will not be increased. If sustainable technologies are bolted on later, building costs will rise.
- **Avoid functional specificity:** Although function is the basis of form (and building character) it is also relatively short-lived compared with the structural life of buildings. Over-specific buildings are inherently inflexible.
- **Maximise access to daylight and natural ventilation:** Green buildings are those that are not too deep in plan, too high or too irregular in shape. Buildings should be no deeper than 12–15 m and generally no higher than 4–6 storeys. A combination of narrow floor plate construction and atria can enhance access to daylight and reduce energy use through stack-effect ventilation.
- **Design for simplicity of operation:** Over-complicated buildings are not fit in the long term (although they may be for short periods). The means of servicing and the degree of user control of the interior environment are important considerations. Simplicity of service and constructional systems allows for

Fig 4.4
The Solar House, Wakeham, designed by
Robert Adam Architects, combines classical and
modern approaches to energy design.
Source: Robert Adam Architects

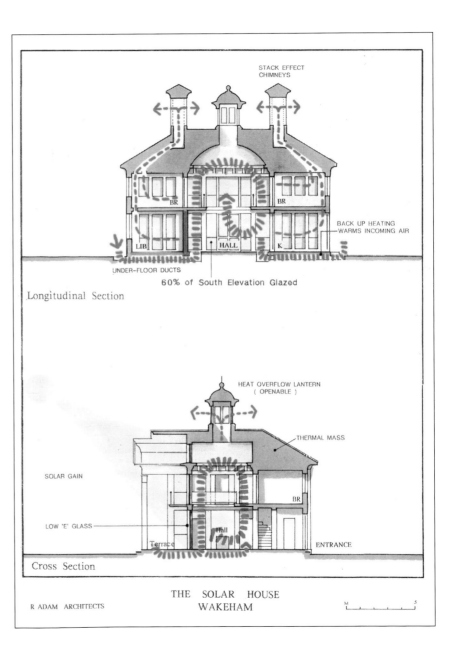

periodic upgrading and permits building users to understand the building, generating respect over its life span.

- **Design for long life:** Since buildings last at least as long as people, they obviously affect future generations. Low-quality construction can become a burden on subsequent generations. Long-lived, low-maintenance buildings may entail higher costs at the outset, but over their life they are a wiser investment. Long-lived buildings save on energy and waste.

- **Maximise use of renewable energy:** Although solar energy generation may not be exploited in the first decade in the life of a building, it is likely to be added over subsequent decades. It is imperative that maximum access is provided for renewable energy (sun, wind and possibly geothermal). Wind and sun are both readily available in the UK, and when one is not accessible the other generally is. Buildings have the potential to be not only self-sufficient in energy but also exporters of energy (through the generation of electricity supplied to the National Grid). To maximise renewable energy exploitation, buildings should be correctly orientated (south on a major facade), angled appropriately in section (30–40° roof slope, 60–70° facade slope), and spaced to give access to the sun (especially winter sun at about 18°). In terms of wind energy, it is necessary to avoid obstruction to air-flow, such as by tall buildings or trees, and roofs should be designed to support wind generators.

- **Replaceability:** Since buildings always eventually fail, in part or whole, it must be possible to upgrade or replace a component or system. The materials of construction must allow for simple replacement. Flexible, demountable construction is more easily renewed than monolithic construction. Obstacles to replaceability are rigid adhesives, welded (as against bolted) connections, the use of over-strong cement mortars (as against lime-based ones) and specially tooled proprietary details. At the design stage, allow for separate structural, component and servicing life cycles.

Lessons from Vernacular Architecture

The traditional architecture of the world represents a resource that has considerable potential for helping us to understand the principles of sustainable design and construction. Vernacular buildings are made of locally available materials, employ local, mainly renewable, sources of energy, and adopt construction practices that favour recycling and respect for nature. These characteristics are to be found in rural housing as well as in urban buildings, and in Africa and Asia as well as in pre-industrial Europe. The lessons from vernacular architecture concern both the individual building and the urban layout, and also the relationship between villages, farms and natural resources.

Putting aside the historical interest of old towns and rural buildings (whether ancient or vernacular), the principles or lessons that can be identified from them are described below.

Energy

Most of the energy required to heat, light or ventilate vernacular buildings is locally sourced. It comes in a variety of forms, including carbon-based fuels, such as wood, coal, methane and straw-based fuel (e.g. dried animal dung), and renewable energy in the form of sun and wind. These various sources are combined in ingenious ways, with local variations to suit different climatic requirements. Hence in the cold north the chimney will be used for heating, whilst nearer to the equator its primary role will be that of ventilation. Likewise, in the north the courtyard plan may be employed for shelter from cold winds, whilst in the hot south the same plan, though with subtle variation, is likely to be the result of the need to provide shelter from the sun's heat.

The position of the building within a plot, its orientation and plan, and the location of windows, doors and fireplaces are all likely to be determined by energy considerations. The regional variations reflect different energy sources and different energy strategies. By learning about these variations it is possible to gain perspectives on future energy design.

Construction Materials

Vernacular buildings normally employ locally sourced construction materials. These may be gained directly from the ground or forests or may be modified through baking. The first group includes stone and timber, the second includes bricks and tiles. Traditional construction normally consists of a combination of virgin materials and those that have been modified. For example, a vernacular house may have brick walls and a timber roof covered in thatch. Alternatively, it may be a timber-framed house with a brick fireplace and chimney, or a bamboo house with a hand-moulded clay stove. Vernacular construction contains a high

Fig 4.5
Traditional solution to solar screening in Cape Town.

Fig 4.6
Modern approach to solar screening in Cape Town.

percentage of indigenous materials, which over time assume cultural meaning in parallel with their practical purpose.

Since transport costs in the past were high, vernacular buildings are normally constructed of locally sourced materials – those that could be carried by hand, by cart or over water. Water was often the key to the location of settlements (for transport and power), for food supplies and sanitation. As a general rule, the weight of construction materials not only determined how far they were carried but also influenced the shape and size of construction elements. Hence, heavy materials were produced in units that could be readily transported. Clay was formed into bricks, while timber was split into planks that could be floated on rafts or carried through the forest. The length, size and shape of construction materials were directly related to the means and capacity of the transport system.

Where materials were very heavy, it was common practice to build near the source rather than to transport the material to a distant site. Hence, where stone was the predominant building material houses, farms and towns were built near quarries (or quarries were opened up to serve them). Similarly, in marshy areas buildings were constructed on stilts to take advantage of the reeds and bamboo on the doorstep.

Settlements that used construction materials with a short life span tended to move in response to the availability of the resources, both for construction and for energy or food. With intermittent settlement went a light touch in terms of environmental impact, which in turn gave time for the ecosystem to recover.

Local Crafts

Distinctive patterns of building grew up in response to locally available construction materials and different regional climatic conditions. The result was a flourishing industry of building crafts, which was equipped to extract the maximum potential from available resources – energy, water and materials. Since the crafts had their own practices and bodies of knowledge, the skills were inter-generational and, in time, the products of labour became cultural as well as material assets. Innovation was slow since materials and climate did not change. As a consequence, building failure was rare and architecture was respected as embodying wider social and cultural values. Examples today can be seen in the courtyard houses of the Middle East, the sun-baked earth buildings of Central

Africa, the timber farm buildings of southern Russia, and the bamboo dwellings of the Philippines.

The crafts have both a construction role and a symbolic one. Traditions grew up which give identity to the vernacular buildings of the world. Details of construction, decorative elements and distinctive forms help define regional variations in vernacular architecture. These are invariably the result of functional or practical considerations as well as artistic ones. However, the distribution of built forms and their supporting crafts reflect human and material resources in a way that illustrates sustainable practice. Since there is wide regional variation in vernacular building, the geography of vernacular architecture challenges the universality of modern global architecture with its imported materials, energy and labour.

The reuse of construction materials is a feature of vernacular architecture. New buildings often incorporate parts of older buildings, whether in the form of structural members (such as timber beams), cladding material (such as stone slates) or built-in fittings (such as store cupboards). Recycling was encouraged through local scarcity and made possible by the use of reversible fixing techniques. For example, timber was pegged rather than nailed together, bricks and stone were cemented using lime mortar, and doors and windows were held in place using wedges. A culture of recycling existed until modern times and often consisted of the reuse of materials from outside domestic architecture; timber from ships was used in houses, and when corn mills were upgraded the millstones were employed as doorsteps. Materials from rich houses also found their way into poor ones as the former were rebuilt, and from modest houses to farm buildings.

This approach to construction survives today in many parts of the world. Perhaps as many as one building in eight in the world is made from recycled or waste materials. Plastic, cheap sheet metal, timber packing cases and cardboard boxes are frequently modified to form the basic structure and enclosure of houses built in the expanding squatter villages of Africa, Asia and Latin America. Resourceful people with little income build shelters from waste as a stepping stone from a life of rural hardship to one of urban possibility. Their towns, usually built without planning permission or sanitation, in time become settlements that are adopted by the local authority, which then provides water, roads, electricity and schools for populations that can be counted in millions. These are towns that are truly vernacular in spirit and which owe their origin to the creative exploitation of urban waste as a physical resource.

Design Approaches for Key Building Types

The following sections describe differing approaches to the design of sustainable buildings in three key sectors: office accommodation, schools and housing.

The Green Office

It is arguable that sustainability has altered the design of offices more than any other building type. There are two reasons for this: first, the relative inefficiency of earlier typologies, with their dependence upon air-conditioning, electric lighting and mechanical ventilation; and second, the new awareness of the beneficial effects of more natural methods of lighting and ventilation upon psychological stress levels and, as a consequence, upon worker productivity.

Typical energy consumption of office buildings in the UK

Travel to work	50%
In-use energy	39%
Embodied energy	11%

Typical annual investment associated with office buildings in UK

Salaries	80%
Buildings	7%
In-use energy	4%
Equipment, etc.	9%

Fig 4.7
Green office in Glasgow, with shallow floor
plates and narrow atrium: interior *(right)*,
exterior *(far right)*, section *(below)*.
Source: McEwan Smith

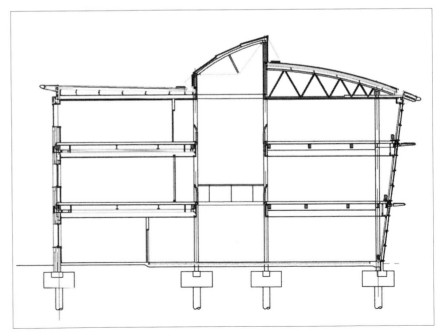

General characteristics of green office design

- Shallow floor plates (12–15 m) for maximum daylight and ease of cross-ventilation.
- Use of atria or glazed malls to promote solar-assisted ventilation.
- Height to promote stack-effect ventilation.
- Orientation on east–west axis to give long north and south elevations.
- Solar control by means of external screens and internal blinds.
- Use of thermal capacity to moderate temperatures.
- Air-conditioning restricted to 'hot spots'.

The general characteristics of green office design are supplemented by a range of specific constructional strategies which can be modified to suit different types of office, level of occupation and extent of IT use. They can be categorised according to four sustainable design themes – energy, water, materials and health. Not all of the general or specific features can be incorporated in a single project, but as a rule of thumb it should be possible to achieve 75% compliance with the options in these tables.

Fig 4.8
Typical section for green office. British Energy building designed by Fitzroy Robinson and Partners.
Source: Fitzroy Robinson and Partners

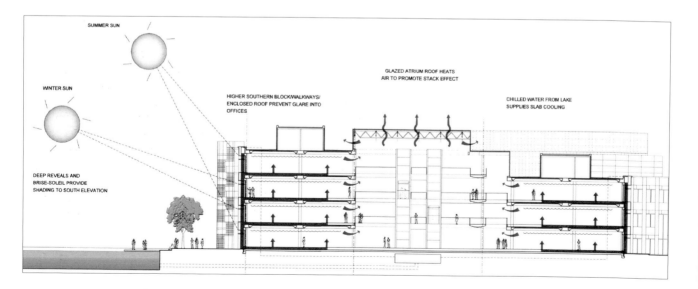

Specific characteristics of green office design

Energy	Natural or displacement ventilation
	Optimum use of daylight
	High thermal mass, preferably exposed
	Solar shading and light shelves
	Waste heat recovery
	High levels of insulation
Water	Dual-flush toilets
	Spray taps
	Urinal sensors
	Rainwater collection
Materials	Use of recycled/reused/renewable materials
	Local sourcing of materials
	Construction for disassembly
	High-tech materials for energy engineering
Health	Limited automation of environmental control
	Low-toxicity materials
	Natural environment/materials
	Social space as well as work space
	Nature visible inside and out

Since the bulk of energy used in a typical office is derived from electricity (lighting, fans, computers), it is here that particular efforts to reduce energy consumption should be directed. The easiest economies are to optimise the use of daylight and to use low-energy light fittings. Daylight penetration can be enhanced by the use of daylight shelves outside, by improving the design of window soffits and reveals, and by profiling the ceiling. Daylight cannot be projected beyond a distance of 7m (depending upon level of external illumination), thereby restricting the depth of an office to around 14m (assuming windows on both sides). However, the use of high ceilings can enhance light penetration. Normally, offices deeper than 14m are subdivided by glazed courts or atria. These provide a source not only of daylight but also of sunlight, the heat from which can be employed to provide natural ventilation via the stack effect.

Fig 4.9
BRE office, Watford, designed by Feilden Clegg Bradley. *Left to right:* façade detail, façade section, view, floor section.
Source: Feilden Clegg Bradley / Brian Edwards

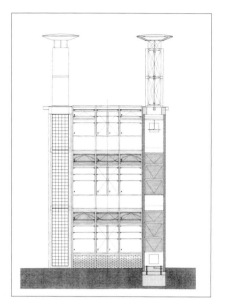
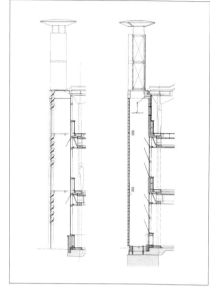

Research suggests that office workers placed near to windows suffer less stress than those further away. Being close to windows increases access to natural light (including sunlight), natural ventilation and views – all properties which promote physical health and a sense of psychological well-being. Research also confirms the importance of lighting, humidity and ventilation switches being under the control of the office worker. Often, such controls are automated and adjusted by a building management system triggered by sensors. Although this may help reduce energy use, it can frustrate workers, who like to feel they can alter their workspace to suit their own needs. This 'feel good' factor of green design has only recently begun to influence workspace design.

The correct orientation of an office building is also important. Difficulties can occur when the sun is at a low angle, particularly excessive solar gain, glare and light reflection on computer screens. Ideally, offices should be aligned to an east–west axis so that there is one long south elevation and a long north elevation. The south facade can then be protected by solar screens, vented at the top through a deep double or triple wall, with light levels adjusted by mechanically controlled louvres or blinds. Conversely, the north facade can be clear glazed

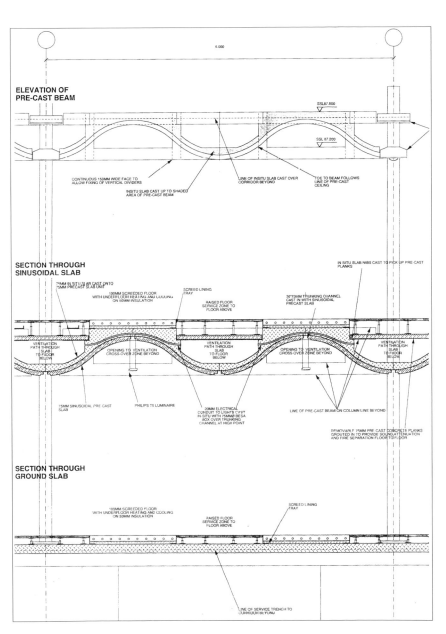

Fig 4.10
Attention to the quality of the working
environment as well as energy efficiency leads
to productivity benefits.
Source: Foster and Partners

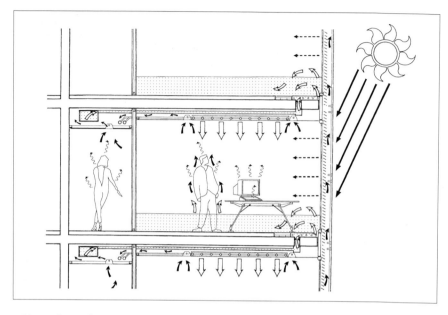

without fear of provoking any of the complications associated with sunlight. The
east and west facades, being narrow, can contain accommodation such as
photocopy rooms or toilets. Their special needs can be matched by a facade that
is more solid in character.

Office buildings that are glazed on all facades, often in order to maximise daylight
penetration and external views, can experience difficulties. Several strategies can
be employed to achieve relatively high levels of energy efficiency, such as double
skins that incorporate different types of glass according to orientation, translucent
insulation and self-venting facades. Increasingly, the office envelope consists of
intelligent facade technology controlled by a computerised management system.
As already described, such systems give the benefit of better energy efficiency but
have the disadvantage of being indifferent to the variety of human needs.

Office buildings also commonly employ a system of external grilles which,
irrespective of orientation, provide three functions in one device – solar
protection, daylight shelves and walkways for building maintenance. The system
has the advantage of simplicity, and being fixed in nature it does not suffer from

Fig 4.11
Attention to quality of daylight penetration at
the Wessex Water headquarters, designed by
Bennetts Associates: exterior sunscreen *(right)*,
façade section *(far right)*.
Source: Bennetts Associates and Brian Edwards

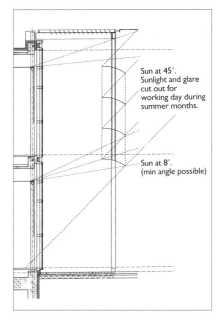

Sun at 45°.
Sunlight and glare
cut out for
working day during
summer months.

Sun at 8°.
(min angle possible)

the high cost of maintaining moving parts. Another benefit of this combined
system is the uniformity it can give to facade design, thereby aiding prefabrication
and cost reduction. A permanent walkway constructed to project beyond the
glazing line in the proportion of 1m width for every 3m ceiling height helps to
keep windows clean and shaded from the midday sun. Many urban offices suffer
from a loss of energy efficiency (approaching 15 per cent) as a combined result of
dirty glass and the cooling load needed to deal with solar heat gain.

Planting is often used to moderate the environment. External tree planting can
provide useful solar shade in the summer, but when the leaves drop in the
autumn the same trees offer little obstruction to the penetration of winter
daylight and desirable solar gains. Trees planted in atria and shrubs positioned in
office areas have the benefit of purifying the air and of reducing stress levels
associated with sterile working environments. Internal planting also encourages
social exchange, which can enhance the sense of community within commercial
buildings.

Advantages of concrete office buildings

- Stable indoor environment due to high thermal capacity.
- Attractive and healthy indoor environment.
- Ability to exploit natural light through pale-coloured concrete soffits shaped as light scoops.
- Ability to incorporate water-filled cooling pipes or air ducts within concrete structures to reduce cooling load.
- Ability to design out suspended ceilings and air-conditioning (reducing costs by 5–7 per cent).
- Potential to improve staff productivity by better levels of natural light and enhanced air-quality (improvement of 6 per cent claimed)

Source: *Eco concrete*, British Cement Association, 2001, p. 6

Natural cooling systems in office buildings

Technique	Energy benefit (W/m² of floor area)
Exposed soffits of floor slabs, coffered to maximise heat exchange area	25
Air ducting through concrete slabs (e.g. Termodeck system)	40
Water cooling through concrete slabs (embedded pipes)	64

Source: *Eco concrete*, British Cement Association, 2001, p. 6

Comparison of benefits of natural cooling systems over air-conditioning

- 50% reduction in carbon dioxide emissions
- 20% reduction in building services component of construction costs
- 5–7% reduction in building maintenance costs
- Potential staff productivity benefits

Source: *Eco concrete*, British Cement Association, 2001, p. 6

Fig 4.12.
This low-energy office for the Ministry of
Defence near Bristol designed by Percy Thomas
Architects sets a good example of enlightened
procurement.
Source: Percy Thomas Architects

Clearly, there are many strategies available to achieve the green office. The depth of floor plates is important; so is access to daylight, sunlight (in atria spaces) and natural ventilation. Orientation is also important, especially in suburban development, and planting can aid energy efficiency. The use of alternate office floors and glazed atria begins to recall the pattern of streets and malls found in cities. The dynamics of big offices are, after all, like those of small cities in the way that the number of people employed leads to a sense of community, which design can consolidate. Atria, important as they are for low-energy design, are equally valued as social spaces by the people who work in buildings that have them. At the Barclaycard Building in Northampton, which accommodates nearly 3,000 employees, for example, the internal galleria successfully provides a variety of environmental and social functions [4].

Economic Benefits of Green Office Design [5]
The main benefits of investing in environmentally smart office buildings are:
- reduced investment risk through changes to environmental legislation and rising fuel prices
- improved rental income through better image for the building;
- increased lettable area through a reduction in the volume of building services

Fig 4.13
Design for a green office of the future by ECD
Architects.
Source: ECD Architects

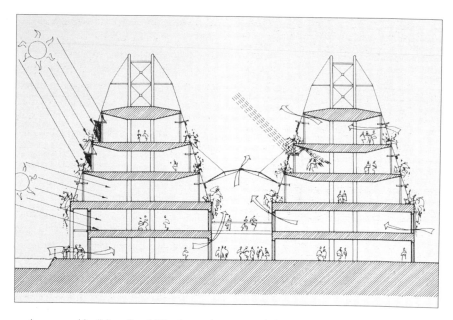

- improved building flexibility through structural simplicity
- lower construction and maintenance costs by avoiding air-conditioning
- enhanced company profile
- better productivity of the workforce through improved working environment

Against these benefits, however, are a number of concerns, such as:

- noise problems as a result of open plan and atrium configurations
- overheating problems as a result of reliance on natural cooling and ventilation, a problem exacerbated by climate change
- lack of occupant control over working conditions due to computerised building management systems
- lack of thermal mass due to the drive towards prefabrication and the speed offered by steel construction.

As a general rule the greater the naturalness of the working environment, especially with regard to natural light and ventilation, the greater the economic benefits through enhanced productivity [6]. Studies indicate that a well-designed green office needs an intelligent system of controls to achieve overall energy efficiency, but that a means of overriding it should be provided for the person

Fig 4.14
Portcullis House, London, designed by Michael Hopkins and Partners. One of the first UK government offices to apply green principles.
Photo: © Richard Davies

who works in that particular space [7]. Another issue is the relationship between energy conservation and noise disturbance. The trend in green offices is towards more open-plan working, and the use of atria and malls inside buildings to maximise daylight penetration and promote solar-assisted ventilation. There is also the growing intensification of the use of space (especially in call centres) and the concept of 'hot-desking'. Added to this, the speed and flexibility afforded by prefabricated construction have reduced the acoustic and thermal mass of modern buildings, adding to potential noise levels and temperature fluctuations in the workplace. As a consequence, noise and comfort toleration is a growing problem in green buildings. So whereas the natural conditions in green offices are favoured by workers, adding to productivity and reduced absenteeism, there is a risk of high levels of ambient noise and temperature peaks, which can have a detrimental impact on the very people sustainable design is seeking to benefit [8]. Noise is not only a limiting factor in green offices – it has also proved to be a problem with green schools, hospitals and libraries [9].

Procurement of Green Offices

The procurement of innovative sustainable buildings can be a precarious business undertaking despite the productivity advantages which result from higher morale, less staff illness and lower levels of staff turnover. For companies that build for their own staff there is clearly an incentive to invest in green design, but where developers build speculatively there is little motivation to care for an unknown workforce [10]. In the latter case, the arguments in favour of green design lead to developers addressing energy and other utility costs rather than the performance of occupants or the image of tenants. It remains a sobering reflection upon the UK construction industry that 20 per cent of all energy used in buildings is wasted by poor design and inadequate understanding of those who manage the buildings [11]. Guidance from government has moved in the past ten years from design and technology solutions to management and procurement ones. Key industry initiatives such as the Latham Report (1994) [12] and Egan Report (1998) [13] have failed to address how environmentalism is to be integrated with the drive to improve construction-site practices. As a result, better briefing and greater use of component standardisation have been allowed to develop independently of the need to achieve more sustainable construction.

After 2000, however, the two agendas of construction productivity and energy efficiency were joined by an initiative known as M4i (Movement for Innovation),

Benefits and costs of green office design to different stakeholders

Stakeholder		Benefit
Public	Government	Lower healthcare costs
		Improved performance of the national economy
		Greater energy efficiency and lower fossil fuel dependency
	Regulatory bodies	Helps achieve national and international environmental obligations
		Improves regional image
Private	Developer	Enhanced business efficiency
		Reduced long-term costs
		Greater competitiveness through enhanced staff productivity
		Improved company image
	Designer	Enhanced reputation
		Better relationship with regulators
		Improved profile through publications
		Development of 'future' skills
		Ethical compliance
	User	Enhanced levels of productivity
		Improvement in personnel health
		Stimulating working environment and less stress
		More sociable working life

Source: Adapted from (with expansion) *A Developer's Guide to Environmentally Smart Buildings: Good Practice Guide 258*, BRE, 1999

which sought to demonstrate through case studies the benefits of good sustainable design [14]. In effect M4i, with its emphasis on the user, life-cycle costing and legislative compliance, brought the question of sustainability to bear upon issues which had become process-led rather than quality-led. The analysis of buildings such as the MOD office at Abbey Wood, the Bristol and West plc

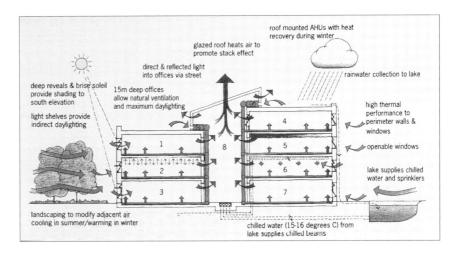

Fig 4.15
Environmental section of the Barclaycard
Building, Northampton, designed by Fitzroy
Robinson and Partners.

Source: Fitzroy Robinson and Partners

headquarters and the BP office at Sunbury confirmed the business advantages of
green offices [15]. Evidence began to be found that there were many formerly
invisible benefits of good environmental design which purely technical
performance indicators failed to identify [16]. As a result, a new set of Design
Quality Indicators (DQIs) have been evolved through an initiative by CABE
(Commission for Architecture and the Built Environment) which put sustainable
design into the procurement process.

PROBE Studies [17]

In parallel with the research conducted through M4i, a group of researchers
undertook an initiative known as PROBE (Post-occupancy Review of Buildings
and their Engineering). PROBE (and the more recent work undertaken in the
USA by G. H. Kats [18]) was keen to compare the energy performance of green
buildings in use with the predictions made at the design stage, and to correlate
these findings with user and management consequences. What was discovered
was that green buildings often failed to achieve energy saving expectations, not
through design shortcomings but as a result of poor construction or building
operation [19]. The weak link appeared to be the user, and specifically how
occupants sought to modify the internal working environment to meet their own
personal needs, often at the expense of the performance of the building as a
whole [20]. The main conclusions were:

- buildings are not as air-tight as expected, resulting in draughts, poor energy performance and user modification;
- window blinds do not work as planned (especially at corners of buildings);
- users complain of the lack of control over their working environment;
- noise is a problem, especially in open-plan buildings;
- management can be slow to adjust environmental systems;
- maintenance of building plant is difficult, and the energy systems are not always understood by managers.

In drawing attention to the interrelationships between design, construction, occupant comfort and management issues, the PROBE studies have provided useful insights into green buildings [21].

What users like

Users prefer:

- shallow building plans which provide an interface between inside and outside;
- high thermal mass for stable temperatures;
- windows that they can open and blinds they can control;
- clearly defined occupancy zones (cellular offices rather than open plan) with social as well as functional spaces;
- personal interface between PC keyboard and control of the working environment;
- building management which responds quickly to internal environmental problems;
- natural materials and planting in the workplace.

The list highlights not only the necessary overlap between design and management but also the importance of placing the needs of the user to the fore at the briefing stage [22]. PROBE also highlighted the gap which often exists between concept and execution, with poor workmanship (rather than design) being responsible for the bulk of energy problems. The studies also showed that management was often indifferent or under-informed about the technical operation of the building, a problem which increases with time. The more innovative the office building, the greater the need for shared environmental values between client, designer, building manager and user. As PROBE notes, good performance normally stems from 'relatively simple, thoughtful solutions,

Fig 4.16
Project ZED, a low-energy office in Toulouse
designed by Future Systems.
Source: Future Systems

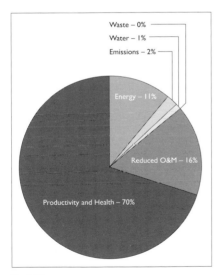

Fig 4.17
Financial benefits of green offices in USA over a
20 year period, according to research
undertaken by Capital-E.
Source: Capital-E

implemented … with attention to detail' [23]. However, unless the user is taken on board and management acts as an effective bridge between concept and reality, the benefits of sustainable design can be undermined by a revengeful workforce [24]. Two main conclusions can be drawn. First, sustainable design principles should be in the brief and understood by all. Second, the benefit to users of a healthy and stimulating working environment should be recognised in economic and cultural terms.

The Economic Case

It is now increasingly recognised that green office buildings – which give staff some perceptual contact with the outside world of wind, rain and sun as well as with sunlit internal spaces – lead to enhanced levels of staff satisfaction and performance. This in turn leads to lower turnover of staff through greater job satisfaction. Research suggests that the naturally lit and ventilated office generates less absenteeism through sickness or poor morale than air-conditioned offices – in other words, green buildings not only conserve energy, they also help reduce company staff costs by stimulating better staff motivation. In fact, the 2–6 per cent increase in worker productivity recorded by studies of green offices nearly pays for all the annual energy costs of a typical big company building [25]. Studies in the USA of office buildings accredited by LEED (Leadership in Energy and Environmental Design) – the American equivalent to BREEAM – suggest that over a 20 year period, the productivity benefits of green design outweigh the energy benefits by a factor of six [26]. In life-cycle costing terms, although sustainable approaches may add 1–3 per cent to building costs, the financial benefits are accrued in 5–8 years, mainly as a result of improved productivity. For organisations in the UK such as Boots, BA and the Barclay Group, the procurement of green buildings is as much a question of good management and sound investment in people as it is an exercise in saving energy. In this sense, the current government's emphasis on energy efficiency is too narrow a focus for the business sector. For many companies the motive for sustainable design stems from a genuine concern to invest in people – to give the workforce an environment which promotes health, commitment and productivity. In this sense, sustainability has come of age in the design of office buildings: the tripartite agenda of social, economic and environmental sustainability has begun to replace energy conservation for its own sake.

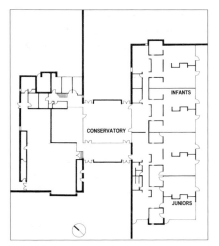

Fig 4.18
The conservatory at Newlands School, Hampshire, acts as a link and environmental space.
Source: Hampshire County Council

Green Schools [27]

Guides are available to help architects and engineers develop school designs that are both effective as learning environments and help achieve sustainable solutions. Many architects aspire to create stimulating, light, spacious and airy schools which exploit solar energy for heat gain and ventilation. The most useful guides for the UK are the Department for Education and Skills' (DfES) *Building Bulletin 87: Guidelines for Environmental Design in Schools* (second edition 2003) and the Building Research Energy Conservation Support Unit's (BRECSU) *Good Practice Guide 173: Energy Efficient Design of New Buildings and Extensions – For Schools and Colleges*. Both provide valuable guidance on topics such as orientation, materials, finishes, daylight, ventilation, acoustics and thermal performance. Guidance is also provided on plan type and to a degree on the sectional profile of school buildings in order to support low-energy solutions. As a consequence, school design in the UK is relatively well prescribed, leading to recognisable layouts for different types of school (rural or urban) and schools at different levels (primary or secondary).

In 2004–5, the UK government has also been testing new approaches to school design via the Exemplar Schools programme. This has focused on the classroom as the prime learning space in the school and hence the area where environmental conditions most impact upon learning.

Five main plan typologies [28] are commonly adopted for schools:
- compact plan;
- courtyard plan;
- radial plan;
- linear plan;
- organic plan.

The most commonly used roof profiles are:
- flat roof with central atria, glazed mall and classroom roof-lights;
- pitched roof with glazed perimeter buffer or solar spaces, sometimes with central mall;
- wave or stepped roof to provide cross-ventilation at different levels, often solar assisted.

These plan and sectional typologies are used in simple or hybrid form according to site characteristics, design brief, sustainability aspiration and orientation. Passive solar design schools are usually single storey with extensive south-facing classroom glazing, conservatories and high-level ventilation on the north side. Some green schools adopt a more pluralistic approach and employ central wind-tower ventilation systems (based on windcatcher technology), while others use wood-chip heating systems and occasionally PV panels for electricity production. Some of the Exemplar Schools designs have organic shapes dictated by ecological factors or site features.

Many schools commonly employ central glazed malls which provide central solar-heated buffer zones, which in turn provide exhibition-cum-social space. In all configurations, the objective is to meet the educational needs at reduced energy and resource costs. In the process, the school can be employed to help reinforce the message of environmentalism through the approach to design. In this sense the school becomes part of the curriculum in the manner promoted by the Eco Schools movement [29].

Whatever plan form is adopted it is vital that there is ample and well-distributed daylight and sufficient ventilation to exhaust internal pollutants, particularly carbon dioxide. It is also vital to consider the acoustic needs of learners and teachers in the classroom, since with open plan solar schools there can be excess noise transmission from one classroom to another. Here, the use of carpet finishes employed for comfort and sound insulation may run counter to the need for exposed thermal mass (to moderate peaks in temperature, especially with passive solar schools) and the reflectivity of floor finishes (essential for daylight penetration into deep classrooms). Since electricity has a high CO_2 rating per unit of power, there needs to be particular attention paid to both artificial lighting and fan-assisted mechanical ventilation. By exploiting wind and sun as a source of energy in the school it may be possible to generate electricity (using PV panels or wind generators), thereby driving down running costs and preparing pupils for a life without cheap fossil fuels.

Atria, glazed malls and attached conservatories are a common feature of school design. They provide a valuable unheated amenity-cum-classroom space. Glazed malls bisecting deep school buildings, as employed for example at Swanlea School in Whitechapel in London, provide a chance for pupils to socialise under teacher surveillance during school breaks. Unlike playgrounds, where socialising is commonly not supervised (and hence where bullying tends to occur), these

Fig 4.19
Inner-city London: Swanlea School,
Whitechapel, with glazed mall *(right)*.
Source: *Percy Thomas Architects and Edward Cullinan and Partners*

Fig 4.20
Environmental control at the edge of a
classroom *(far right)*.
Source: *ECD Architects*

amenity spaces which are justified on low-energy grounds also provide useful support for the life and welfare of the school. However, such spaces can prove so attractive that teachers are tempted to heat them using mobile fan heaters. This tends to undermine the energy strategy for the school as a whole, disrupting the balance between solar heating and natural ventilation established at the design stage. Also, because such spaces are uninsulated, heating adds considerably to energy costs (and CO_2). As with office buildings, the ethos of the school and the environmental strategies need to be understood by teachers, janitors and pupils alike.

Usually, the glazed malls and atria that divide blocks of classrooms are separated from the teaching areas by walls which have opening windows or large double doors. These openings can act as flexible links between classrooms and sun-spaces. The flow of warmed air should be encouraged from the sun-space on sunny days and discouraged on overcast days. The obvious benefit of glazed malls is that of modification of the internal climate of the school by allowing the interior and exterior worlds to be connected climatically. It also allows the exterior

environment of the school to perceptually enter the classroom, to the benefit of
pupil well-being. As a teaching aid, the temperature gradients can be mapped,
encouraging the pupils to understand the laws of physics without resorting to
textbooks.

To achieve maximum benefit from low-energy design in the classroom there
needs to be:
- adequate window and door control between teaching and sun-spaces;
- adequate acoustic protection of the classroom from both interior ambient
  noise and external disturbance;
- recognition that sun-spaces reduce the daylight and ventilation of the teaching
  areas to which they are attached;
- a responsive system of blinds and solar shading to prevent overheating in the
  summer and heat loss in winter;
- finishes which maximise daylight penetration;
- ventilation which is solar or wind assisted via low-level and high-level windows,
  perhaps supported by sloping classroom ceilings;
- an understanding by teachers and janitors of the energy design strategy.

Advantages of Different Plan Types [30]
The **compact plan** is commonly adopted in school design, especially for primary
schools (ages 5–11) in urban areas. It consists roughly of a square with classrooms
on two or three sides and the school hall, offices and library on another. It is
sometimes left open on one side to allow for solar penetration or external views.
The compact plan is relatively energy efficient as long as the classrooms face
mainly to the south and advantage is taken of using the roof for lighting and
ventilation. The plan works well in single-storey or multi-storey form, although the
angle of roofs should be kept low (but not flat) to allow for solar penetration.

In the compact plan, particular attention needs to be paid to the shape of the
roof. Classrooms should have monopitch roofs tilted downwards to the south
and ending in generous eaves overhangs (to prevent summertime overheating).
At the higher, north side clerestorey lighting should be provided along with high-
level vents or opening windows. Lighting the classroom from both sides gives an
even distribution of daylight and facilitates natural cross-ventilation. The
disadvantage is that mechanical ventilation and cooling may be necessary as
schools expand their use of IT. High levels of computer use add to incidental heat

Fig 4.21
Sections through classrooms at John Cabot
School, Bristol designed by Feilden Clegg
Bradley showing the ventilation strategy at
different seasons.
Source: Feilden Clegg Bradley

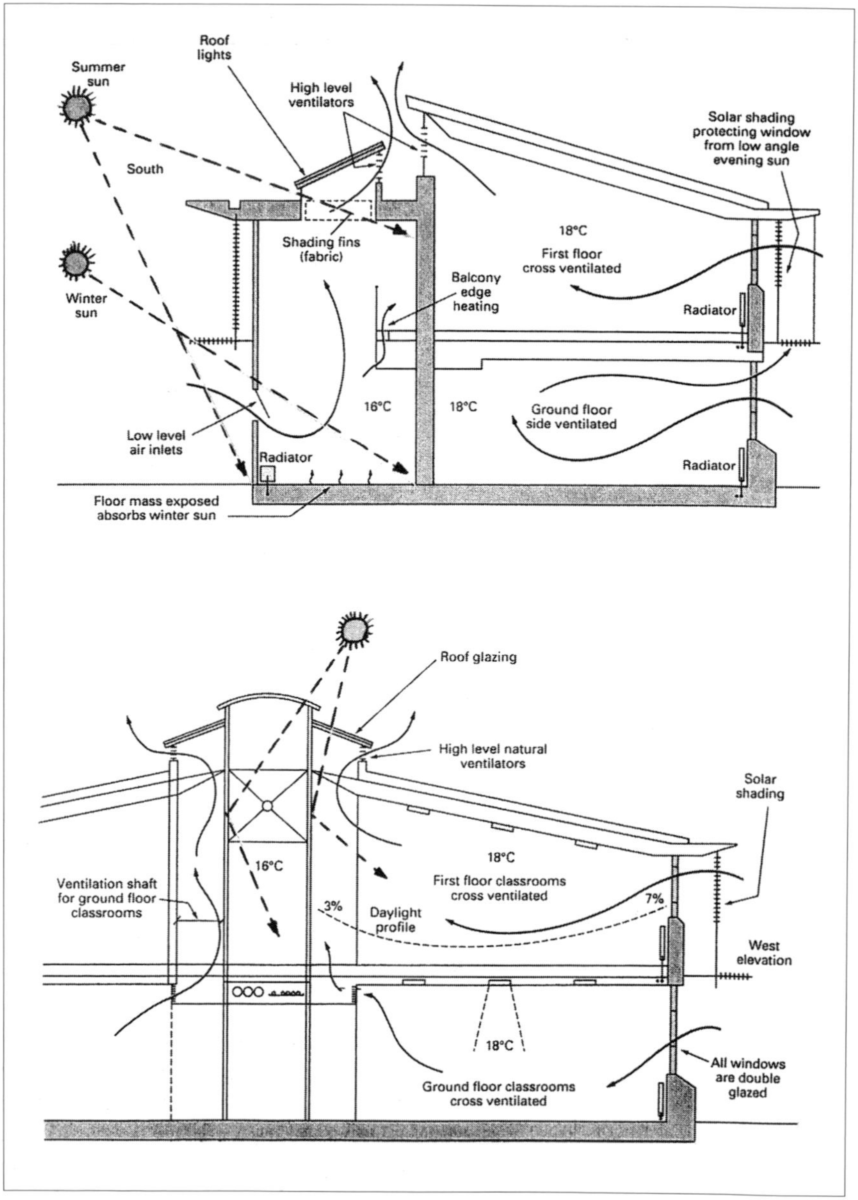

gains, which in turn may necessitate mechanical cooling – which can increase noise levels in the school. Since for many pupils English is not a first language, the spoken word must be heard clearly in all corners of the classroom.

The **courtyard plan** shares similarities with the compact plan except that there is an open and unroofed square in the centre. Normally, the entrance, library and school hall are placed to the north and the classrooms wrap around on the other sides. Since the number of classrooms does not normally fill three sides of the courtyard it is more common for the classrooms to occupy two wings (orientated south-east and south-west) with offices, library, etc., placed on the third side. This allows the school to address both the internal and external worlds.

With the courtyard plan the sectional profile of classrooms is similar to that in compact layouts (southerly roof overhangs and high-level north-facing windows). One advantage of the courtyard plan is that the central corridor provides views into both the courtyard and the classrooms – providing good surveillance for teachers and a welcoming atmosphere for visitors. One disadvantage is the high ratio between perimeter wall area and internal volume, which can add to construction costs. However, the courtyard form readily adapts to irregularly shaped sites, providing an informal architecture which suits the character of many village locations. Like the traditional courtyard house, the courtyard school plan provides a high level of security, good environmental performance and the potential benefit of standardised units of construction.

The **radiant plan** is arranged so that the classrooms occupy linear projections from a central communal area. The plan allows the wings to radiate out to take advantage of climatic and environmental features. As in other layouts, it is important that the classrooms face generally to the south, but the detailed design needs to overcome summertime overheating by employing external sunshades, internal blinds or special glass. With this configuration there is also the need to ensure that classroom spacing allows for adequate daylight penetration in the winter. Ideally, south-east to south orientation should be sought for classrooms rather than west since winter solar gain can be beneficial in reducing heating loads. In this layout, larger specialist spaces in the school (such as a hall and a library) can benefit from the northern light. Another advantage of the layout is the way that wings can be aligned to protect the school from adverse climatic conditions, creating sheltered spaces in the gaps between classrooms.

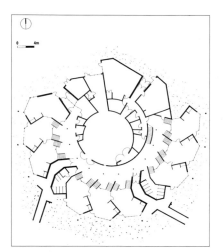

Fig 4.22
Organic plan – Stoke Park School, Hampshire.
Source: Hampshire County Council

Fig 4.23
Example of atrium-based urban school in
Hampden Gurney, London, designed by BDP:
final section.
Source: BDP

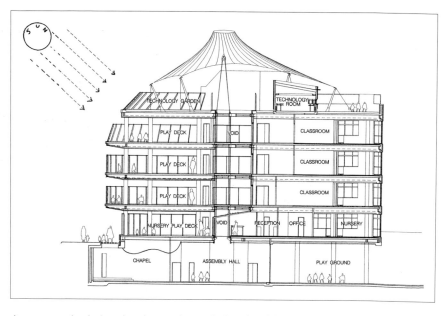

As a general rule in schools, southern glazing should be around 60 per cent of the wall area and northern glazing about 30 per cent. This allows for an optimum balance to be struck between winter solar gain and daylight penetration while also avoiding fabric heat loss and summer overheating. However, overshadowing by adjacent buildings and trees may affect these ratios, and local variations in climate must also to be accommodated. Hence an ideal solution for a school in northern Scotland will be quite different to one for a school in southern England.

The **linear plan** is arguably the most common plan type for schools in the UK and is much adopted in the Exemplar Schools programme, supported by the DfES. This plan offers many organisational, social and environmental benefits. The classrooms usually face south with the other accommodation to the north, separated by a spine corridor or glazed street. The building section is arranged so that the classrooms take advantage of high-level windows facing north, alongside the spine corridor. The accommodation to the north also benefits from roof-lights facing south, sometimes looking into the glazed street. The section not only allows daylight to penetrate deep into the plan but also facilitates cross-ventilation without mechanical backup.

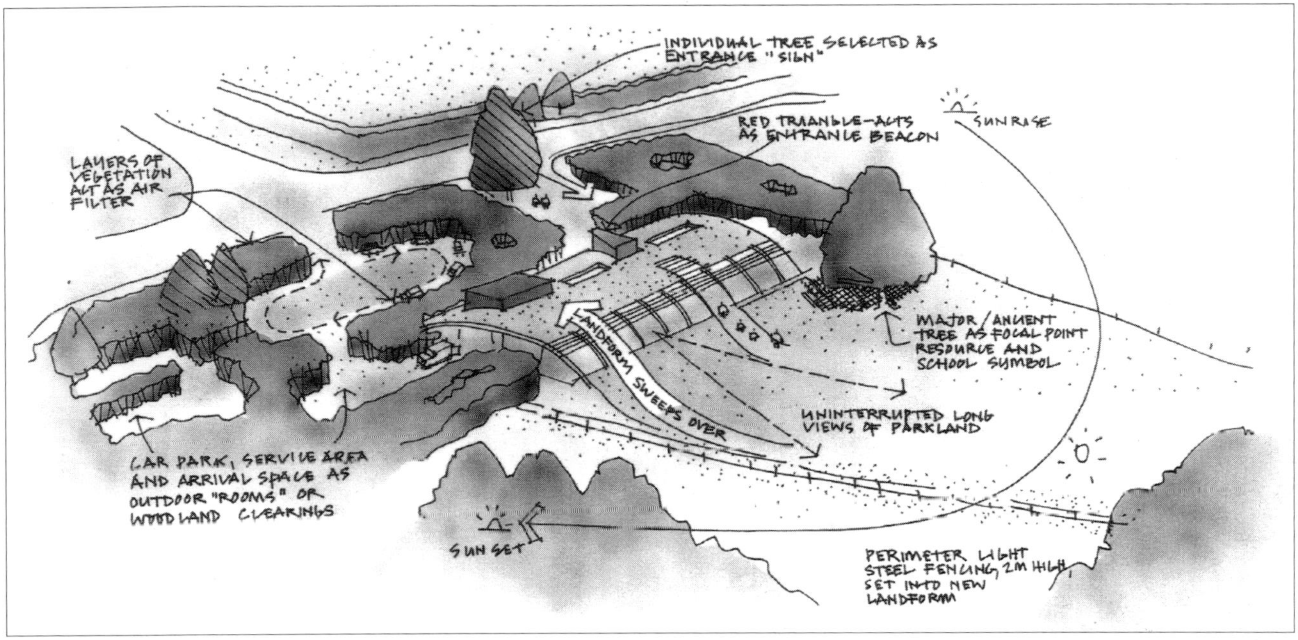
INDIVIDUAL TREE SELECTED AS ENTRANCE "SIGN"
RED TRIANGLE-ACTS AS ENTRANCE BEACON
SUNRISE
LAYERS OF VEGETATION ACT AS AIR FILTER
LANDFORM SWEEPS OVER
MAJOR/ANCIENT TREE AS FOCAL POINT RESOURCE AND SCHOOL SYMBOL
UNINTERRUPTED LONG VIEWS OF PARKLAND
CAR PARK, SERVICE AREA AND ARRIVAL SPACE AS OUTDOOR "ROOMS" OR WOODLAND CLEARINGS
SUN SET
PERIMETER LIGHT STEEL FENCING, 2M HIGH, SET INTO NEW LANDFORM

Fig 4.24
Design for a sustainable school in Sevenoaks, Kent by Architects Design Partnership.
Source: Architects Design Partnership Ltd

However, the linear form requires particular attention to be paid to the shapes and angles of roofs and the heights of walls. Daylight, sunlight and ventilation are encouraged by employing wave-shaped roofs and different heights of rooms. As with other green school plan types, the area of glazing needs to be adjusted according to orientation, local climate and the balance between fossil fuel and renewable energy use at the school. The linear plan is best suited to a site which offers a long east–west axis (i.e. with a long south-facing aspect). If it is employed at right angles to this axis there can be serious problems in the classroom with glare when the sun angle is low, as well as considerable energy inefficiency.

The **organic plan** is often employed as a hybridisation of the other plans and has the advantage that the layout can respond directly to the natural features of the site. Also, where vernacular methods of building are employed (in order to maintain regional building traditions), the resulting design tends to reflect ecological principles rather than low-energy ones. As a result, the school is likely to have randomly oriented classrooms, a footprint which is readily absorbed into the local scene, and materials of construction which are local in origin (such as timber) rather than machine made (such as concrete block). The organic plan generally results in organic elevations since the same principles that shape the plan find expression in the section and construction details (e.g. Stoke Park Infants School at Bishopstoke in Hampshire).

Selecting the Plan Type

The first four plan configurations are remarkably similar in terms of potential energy efficiency. The organic form is unlikely to be as energy efficient; however, it does bring other environmental benefits, and if local construction materials are employed the embodied energy levels will be lower. The organic plan offers a quasi-vernacular solution which may suit semi-rural locations or the use of traditional forms of construction.

The choice of plan type is likely to be the result of site characteristics and the preferences of the local education authority rather than the search for sustainable design *per se*. However, if more clients were to prioritise green aspirations in the brief there would be greater motivation to apply innovative eco-thinking by designers. The plan analysis also suggests that ecological design tends to favour indigenous, organic layouts, inspired perhaps by vernacular practices, while for energy efficiency and economy of construction more rational plan types are preferable (e.g. the courtyard or linear plan).

The choice of layout needs also to address aspects of social sustainability and the interactions between teacher, pupil, parent and community. The school is an important place for the social development of children, and different plan types offer quite distinctive spaces for socialising. The courtyard form, for instance, provides an inner world which is easily supervised, while the linear form offers a long central space whose characteristics are not unlike a shopping mall. The radiant plan provides spaces which address the external world of playgrounds and sports fields. Different plan types also take advantage of different degrees of solar access and different levels of climatic exposure. The linear form is well suited to an open southerly aspect, the courtyard form to where shelter is required (from wind and noise), the compact form to where land is at a premium, and the organic to where harmony between buildings and nature is required. Whichever plan arrangement is used it is important that the architect understands that the school must be a learning environment as well as a low-energy one.

Fig 1.25
Compact low-energy social housing at
Beddington, London, designed by Bill Dunster
Source: Bill Dunster

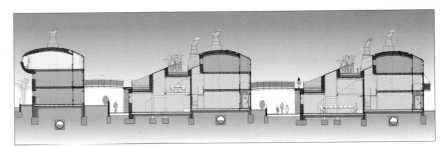

The French philosopher Roland Barthes described the classroom as 'four walls around a future'. Architects have the difficult task of designing those walls and deciding whether walls are needed at all. At Bexley Academy in London, Foster and Partners have created a school which, through its flexible almost wall less classrooms and high levels of IT learning, questions the very fundamental assumptions behind the design of the classroom.

Sustainable Housing

Sustainable housing is often presented purely as an exercise in low-energy design, although it is as much a question of creating sustainable communities. Social inclusion and energy efficiency come together most closely in the arena of housing. The efficient use of resources, especially energy, should concur with the spatial dimensions and social parameters needed to create robust communities. Too often, a concentration on technological innovation, high-rise utopianism and low cost have led to housing which has performed badly in terms of social cohesion and sustainable development.

A Definition

Sustainable housing may be defined as 'housing that creates sustainable communities in a resource-efficient manner'. Here, of course, the resources referred to are energy, water, land, materials and human labour. Sustainable housing projects need to be:

- energy efficient;
- efficient in the use of other resources, especially water;
- designed to create robust, self-sustaining mixed-use communities;
- designed for long life;
- designed for flexibility in lifestyle and tenure;
- designed to maximise recycling;

- healthy; and
- designed to embrace ecological principles.

Sustainable housing is more than an exercise in physical attributes. It will be judged a success only if it leads to economic prosperity, stimulates social cohesion, provides security, supports social welfare and is designed to enhance personal, community and global health. All of this, added to the energy considerations, results in housing being one of the most complex of design tasks facing the architect. Sustainable housing brings together physical, social and cultural factors into a single agenda.

Housing and CO_2 Emissions

Housing is responsible for around 27 per cent of the UK's production of CO_2 through the burning of fossil fuels, either in the home or indirectly through the use of electricity. Sixty per cent of domestic CO_2 is produced by heating and 25 per cent by lighting, the other significant culprit being domestic equipment – televisions, cookers, refrigerators, etc. Taking all the fossil fuel energy impacts together (building and domestic activities), housing is responsible for between a quarter and a third of total carbon emissions in the UK, and if transport to homes is included then housing design and layout accounts for 40 per cent of national carbon emissions.

There is a clear correlation between housing density and energy use. Generally speaking, the more compact and dense the housing, the greater the energy efficiency. This greater efficiency comes from a number of sources – domestic heating, transport, and communal energy initiatives such as combined heat and power (CHP). The main constraints on density are access to daylight and sunlight, and social acceptability.

The advantage of compact buildings is that heat loss from one dwelling becomes the heat gain for another. If you mix housing with offices, shops or small workshops, the heat loss from these during the day can make a useful contribution to the heating of the neighbouring housing units during the evening and overnight (when they are most occupied). Hence, a dense mixed-use neighbourhood consumes significantly less primary energy than a dispersed, low-density one. Also, only medium-to-high density development can sustain public transport, with all the energy and community benefits this entails. A relatively high density of about 200 units per hectare, achieved with four-storey buildings, consumes less than a third of the fossil fuel energy that suburban housing constructed at 20 units per hectare consumes. If you take into account transport to shops, schools and work, the energy differential (and hence carbon emission ratio) further benefits compact forms.

So, from an energy efficiency point of view, suburban development is undesirable. Unfortunately, it is the standard 21st-century solution for much of the world – promoted inadvertently on TV series such as *Neighbours* and *The Simpsons*. However, as density rises, so do other problems, such as crime, lack of personal security, alienation and loss of community.

Factors which have significant impact on energy consumption in housing

- **Built form:** the benefits of compact development
- **Building construction:** the use of thermal capacity to absorb solar radiation and delay the night-time temperature falls coupled with high levels of insulation.
- **Orientation:** layout to maximise exposure to sun and minimise exposure to prevailing winds.
- **Microclimate:** use building layout to create shelter, working with planting design.
- **Transport:** site buildings to reduce vehicular movement and increase density at transport nodes and along public transport routes.

Template for sustainable urban housing

- Plan depth limited to 10–12m.
- Solar orientation between south-east and south-west.
- Avoid obstruction angle above 30°.
- Theoretical design density of 200 dwellings per hectare.
- Three- and four-storey buildings preferable.
- Every percentage point increase in obstruction over 30° results in the same percentage point increase in energy use.

Source: Adapted from Koen Steemers, *The Architects' Journal*, 2 November 2000, p. 42

Fig 4.26
Passive solar housing at Norrkoping, Sweden, designed by Krister Wiberg.
Source: Krister Wiberg

A balance is needed between defensible space and sustainability, producing streets that are neither alienating nor energy inefficient. Beyond 80 dwellings per hectare, overshadowing makes it difficult to take advantage of passive solar gain. Solar gain can provide 20 per cent of the primary energy needs of a typical house and, with the enlargement of windows to the south, the use of conservatories and solar water heaters, the total energy savings can approach 40 per cent in southern Britain and 35 per cent in Scotland. These advantages decrease as density increases. However, for dwellings on upper floors these advantages persist. To take advantage of passive solar gain, buildings need to be orientated to the south, with roofs which do not overshadow neighbours. As a result, with anything other than linear forms (e.g. courtyard forms) it is difficult to achieve similar levels of energy efficiency. Here lies another dilemma for sustainable housing: the creation of communities entails shared values, shared space and physical enclosure, whereas the physics of solar gain leads to long antisocial spaces, parallel buildings and private gardens (to protect southern solar apertures). It is a dilemma which is likely to increase as pressure mounts to erect PV panels on roofs and to create sun-spaces for passive solar heating.

Housing and Community

Quality of housing affects quality of life – arguably more so than other forms of built development. It impacts on several areas of government policy – employment, education, transport, health and, most importantly, community well-being. As such, there is a great deal of guidance provided by the UK government on the density and layout of towns in documents such as *Planning Policy Statement 1: Delivering Sustainable Development* (PPS1) and *Planning Policy Guidance 3: Housing* (PPG3). Housing is a fixed long-term capital asset or, depending on how you look at it, liability. The physical building is both a financial investment and a cultural statement. Sustainable housing, therefore, addresses three important areas in parallel:

- energy efficiency, waste minimisation, resources, etc.;
- community and social welfare; and
- economic prosperity, especially employment and education.

The environmental dimension is necessarily balanced by social, cultural and economic factors. Residential design is primarily concerned with creating coherent, high-quality, socially responsive, low-energy neighbourhoods [31]. The performance of existing areas can be assessed using simple measures, such as property values,

A	–	Southampton	(20m)
	–	Leeds	(25m)
	–	Edinburgh	(30m)
	–	Inverness	(35m)

Fig 4.27
Spacing for solar gain varies according to latitude.
Source: Brian Edwards/BRE

Fig 4.28
Solar and earth sheltered housing at Hockerton Energy Village, Nottinghamshire, designed by Robert and Brenda Vale.

Source: Hockerton Energy Village

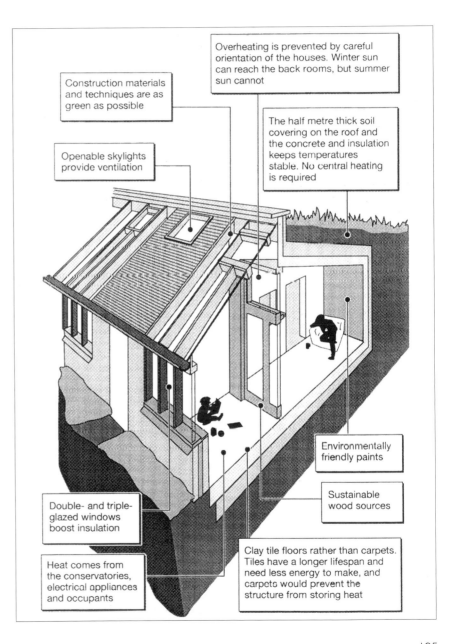

Construction materials and techniques are as green as possible

Openable skylights provide ventilation

Overheating is prevented by careful orientation of the houses. Winter sun can reach the back rooms, but summer sun cannot

The half metre thick soil covering on the roof and the concrete and insulation keeps temperatures stable. No central heating is required

Environmentally friendly paints

Sustainable wood sources

Double- and triple-glazed windows boost insulation

Heat comes from the conservatories, electrical appliances and occupants

Clay tile floors rather than carpets. Tiles have a longer lifespan and need less energy to make, and carpets would prevent the structure from storing heat

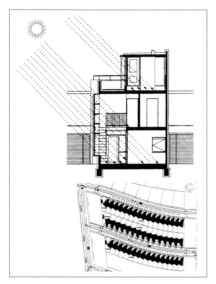

Fig 4.29
Passive solar housing in Almere, Holland, designed by Aldo van Eyck and Partners.
Source: Van Eyck and Partners

public-health statistics, energy consumption per square metre (deduced from utility accounts) and turnover. Neighbourhood sustainability, which underpins building sustainability, depends on many factors, not all of which are within the province of architecture and planning. However, both are valuable in creating or nurturing environments which foster social interaction and economic prosperity.

Neighbourhood or settlement design has, at a macro-level, a big impact upon energy efficiency (especially in transportation) and, at the medium scale, can be addressed through climate-responsive urban design. Energy efficiency should be the overriding discipline behind questions of layout, density and extent of non-residential land uses. CO_2 reduction provides the basis for housing layout in broad physical terms, but social integration across wealth and tenure barriers should inform the detailed design considerations. Community and social harmony are essential if the building resources are to be successful long-term assets. Simple measures are often the most cost-effective, such as the use of shallow roof pitches to allow for sun penetration between buildings and the inclusion of upper stories within roof spaces. As with all building types, sustainable design is best met when green issues are introduced at the briefing stage rather than once the building design has begun to take shape.

Policies for sustainable housing

- Ensure social integration through mixed tenure housing types
- Integrate residential and non-residential land uses
- Use energy efficiency to dictate settlement design
- Maintain density to support public transport
- Use urban design to modify climate
- Ensure access for all
- Limit car parking by setting maximum, not minimum, standards
- Place garages and tall buildings to the north of developments
- Exploit existing infrastructure to the full
- Reuse urban land and buildings
- Create car-free developments
- Exploit renewable energy sources
- Source materials and labour locally

Source: Adapted from DETR, *Scottish Office and Urban Task Force guidelines*

Fig 4.30
Low-energy community-based car-free housing
in Edinburgh, designed by Hackland Dore.
Source: Hackland Dore

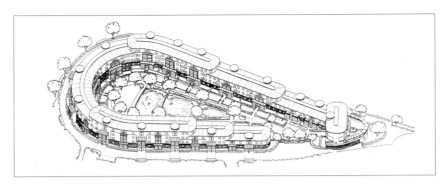

Housing and Transportation

The greater the density of housing and the greater the diversity of land uses the more viable becomes public transport. Above about 160 persons per hectare and two land uses per hectare (housing and shopping) it becomes viable to provide a bus service. Above 240 persons per hectare and three land uses (housing, shopping, offices) within a ten minute walking distance of the transport corridor it is possible to run a viable tram service [32]. With 300–500 persons per hectare and a further land use (say, college) within a 10–15 minute walking corridor, the case can be made for suburban rail services. However, much depends on car constraint or fuel pricing policy and also upon the nature of the community. Where there is social and employment diversity there is more likely to be public transport. Hence the design of the neighbourhood (and not just in terms of densities) has a bearing on the viability of public transport.

Density and the Benefits of Mixed-Use Neighbourhoods

Only by achieving housing densities above 80 units per hectare can a diversified pattern of public transport be sustained. According to the Urban Task Force Report, increased density is important because it progressively reduces the need to use private cars. Above 80 units per hectare, development readily supports local shops, employment, schools, etc., and encourages walking, riding bicycles and taking longer journeys by bus, tram or train. Density is crucial to reducing CO_2 reduction and other transport-related pollution, and leads to an urban layout that creates sheltered streets and convivial spaces. As housing density increases yet further potential is unleashed, such as community-power initiatives and the economic viability of facilities such as art centres and branch libraries, which often bring redundant buildings back into use.

Fig 4.31
Low-energy community-based housing in Leeds,
designed by Levitt Bernstein.
Source: Levitt Bernstein

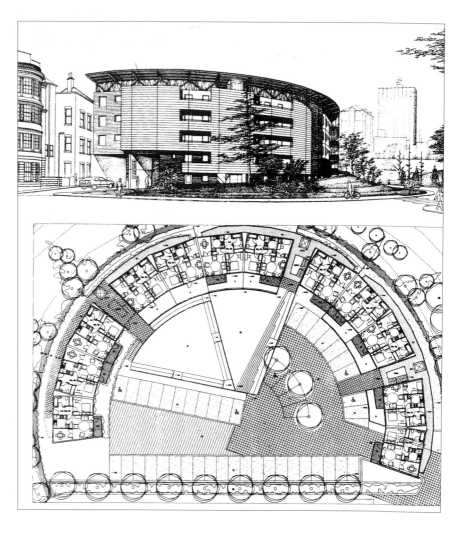

High density should, however, be accompanied by a clear strategy for open space,
landscape and urban design, and the promotion of mixed-use residential
neighbourhoods. Mixed uses also improve personal security and security of
premises and engender a feeling of respect and safety which elderly people in
particular value. Mixed-use neighbourhoods are more likely to offer employment

Fig 4.32
Low-energy community-based housing in
London, designed by Cartwright Pickard.
Source: Cartwright Pickard

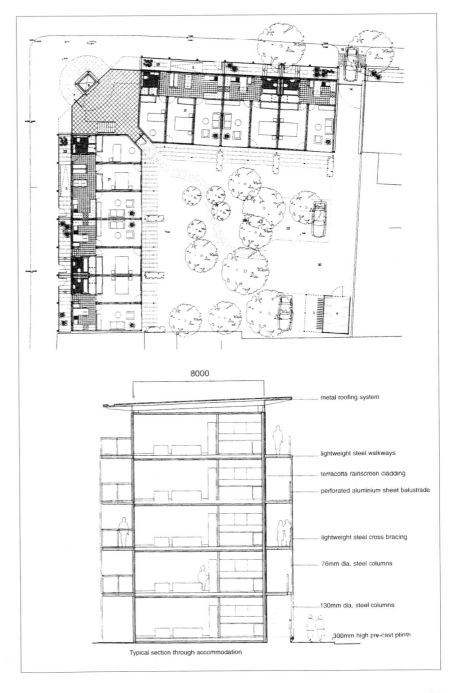

8000

metal roofing system

lightweight steel walkways

terracotta rainscreen cladding

perforated aluminium sheet balustrade

lightweight steel cross bracing

76mm dia. steel columns

130mm dia. steel columns

300mm high pre-cast plinth

Typical section through accommodation

locally and encourage links between colleges and workplace, enhancing training opportunities. High-density, mixed-use neighbourhoods give back the sense of place that 20th-century planning policies undermined.

Architects, in parallel with developers, should seek to reuse 'brownfield' sites. These are normally well serviced by infrastructure of various kinds (electricity, water, sewerage, public transport, etc.), although they may be contaminated or suffer from pollution from roads or industry. Not only does redevelopment of brownfield sites reduce pressure on green-belt land, it also provides the opportunity to create new, integrated communities close to work, leisure and education. Significantly, it also provides sites that require a designer solution rather than a developer one, enabling architects to innovate in environmental issues as they relate to building design. Brownfield site redevelopments, such as those at Salford in Manchester and the Gorbals in Glasgow, can do much to regenerate city pride, providing a platform to rebrand the city, an increasingly important aspect of post-industrial reconstruction.

Brownfield site use is central to government policy. According to the UK Deputy Prime Minister John Prescott, 60 per cent of the new homes required to accommodate an expected 4.1 million new households between 2002 and 2016 are to be built on brownfield sites [33]. As the Urban Task Force, under the guidance of Richard Rogers (Lord Rogers of Riverside), reminded us in its report, [34] reusing brownfield land assists in social and economic regeneration as well as enhancing the appearance of towns. However, density is critical not just to effective land utilisation but also to the support of public services on which quality of life increasingly depends. Without schools, health centres, local libraries and public transport, many people, especially the elderly and poor, are disadvantaged despite being centrally located.

Microclimate Design

As density and complexity of land use and tenure increase, so too does the need for integrated measures across the frontiers of urban, landscape, transport and building design. In the past, urban design was neglected and overtaken by mechanistic measures of performance (leading to high-rise and monotonous system-built blocks). Without a structure of spatial urban patterns based on design guidelines, the benefits of high density are negated. Urban design for housing needs to respond to four imperatives:

- the forging of social space;
- the enhancement of the urban microclimate;
- the creation of place not placelessness; and
- the provision of solar penetration without windy conditions.

Urban design can engineer social space by developing a clear framework of enclosed volumes (small and large) and by the provision of various forms of linkage (streets, alleys and footpaths). Human interaction often takes place in sheltered, sunny, overlooked spaces, often near to the thresholds of dwellings. Plants, seats and attractive paved finishes give such areas their quality and their sense of purpose.

Comfortable microclimates are created by forming protected external volumes adjacent to south-facing (or at least sunny) dwellings. Groups of houses, either terraced or, more appropriately, built as apartments, should be placed to break down large areas into sheltered parcels. Planting around the edge can deflect or reduce wind speeds and, in the centre, can provide local shelter and summer shade. Surface roughness, achieved through a combination of dense planting and buildings, helps provide an urban texture which enhances the microclimate, especially when sensitively orientated.

Sense of place is an elusive concept: it is formed partly by attitude, partly by use and partly by physical attributes. Whereas space is abstract and measurable, a sense of place is shaped by social perception. Good urban design can help build a sense of place by providing lively areas and focal points and by articulating the public realm through exciting architectural design for key buildings (such as a school or doctors' surgery), public art, the use of water and perhaps a small amphitheatre for community use. Most of all, place requires a critical mass of people, landscape and activity.

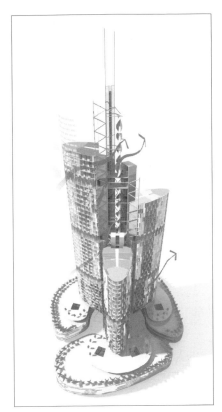

Fig 4.33
Skyhouse Project a fresh approach to sustainable urban living designed by Marks Barfield Ltd.
Source: Marks Barfield Ltd

Fig 4.34
Two examples of dense inner-city housing on brownfield sites: Greenwich Millennium Village *(right)*; Maryhill, Glasgow *(far right)*.
Source: Brian Edwards and MLDO

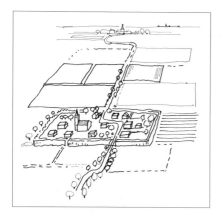

Fig 4.35
Planting to improve microclimate in a Lincolnshire village.

Fig 4.36
Planting in the gaps between buildings can do much to improve the microclimate and hence energy efficiency.

Fig 4.37
The heat island effect. Isolated tall buildings damage the heating island, leading to greater energy use elsewhere.

Sustainability Assessment Methods for Housing

Various assessment tools are available to guide the designer, with regard both to the design of new housing and to the upgrading of existing buildings. Two are commonly used in the UK: the Building Research Establishment Domestic Energy Model (BREDEM) [35] and the Standard Assessment Procedure for Energy Rating of Dwellings (SAP) [36]. BREDEM can be used for:

- estimating energy requirements in different dwelling types;
- estimating heating running costs in a property;
- ensuring that the most appropriate measures are taken when upgrading property;
- estimating the savings arising from different energy measures; and
- estimating internal temperature and comfort conditions.

In other words, BREDEM is an energy modelling tool. Its weakness is that it does not consider other factors (such as water use) or related matters (such as life-cycle costing of different energy upgrading solutions). It remains, however, a useful

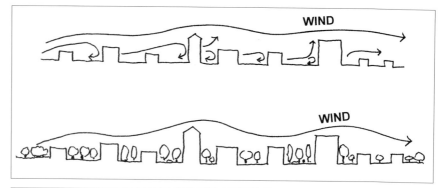

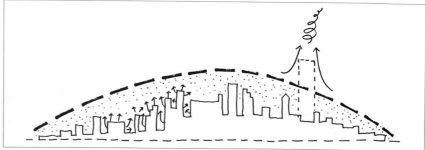

measure of the interaction between physical characteristics, heating, insulation, orientation and level of occupancy. Subsequent testing confirms that the BREDEM model is reasonably accurate, its predictions normally being within 10 per cent of actual energy use. There is also EcoHomes, the homes version of BREEAM, sponsored by the NHBC, which helps address environmental performance under seven headings: energy, water, pollution, materials transport, ecology and land use, and health and well-being.

A more simple measure is SAP, which provides energy ratings for dwellings without taking account of occupancy differences. SAP assumes a standard occupancy pattern and consistent heating regimes between regions, building types and floor areas. The SAP rating is a score out of 100 – the higher the score the better the energy performance. Like BREDEM, the SAP rating is based on physical design characteristics (solar gain, ventilation rates, insulation levels, etc.) and also on the efficiency of and ability to control the heating and hot-water systems. SAP is a useful guide not only to the efficiency of different heating strategies but also to the likely energy bills for a given type of fuel. As such, it is a welcome addition to our knowledge of wider environmental issues (such as CO_2 emissions) and of the relationship between fuel poverty and multiple deprivation (especially of council housing estates). Evidence suggests that poorly insulated properties with inefficient boilers aggravate deprivation, leading to further social exclusion [37]. This is one reason why all new housing built after 2005 has to display its SAP rating to potential buyers under revisions to the Building Regulations. It is expected that after 2006 the same will apply to refurbished properties (see Chapter 2).

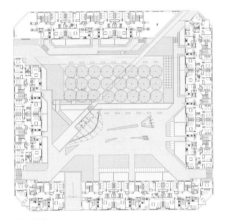

Fig 4.38
Social housing project in Madrid, designed by Feilden Clegg Bradley: site plan *(above)*, perspective *(below)*, section *(below right)*.
Source: Feilden Clegg Bradley

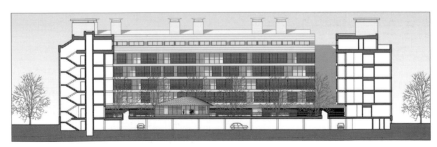

Fig 4.39
Three examples of housing design for energy efficiency: House of the Future designed by Jestico and Whiles *(opposite)*; MacRae House, Bristol, designed by Michael MacRae, and Apartment Building, Greenwich, designed by Andrew Wright *(on following pages)*.
Source: Jestico and Whiles, Michael MacRae, Andrew Wright

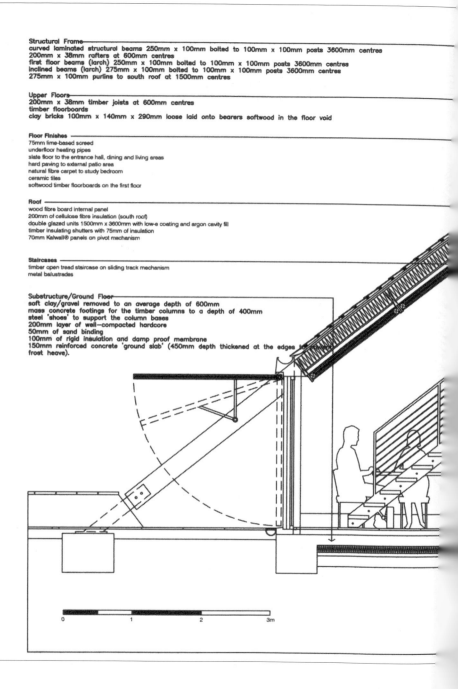

Structural Frame
curved laminated structural beams 250mm x 100mm bolted to 100mm x 100mm posts 3600mm centres
200mm x 38mm rafters at 600mm centres
first floor beams (larch) 250mm x 100mm bolted to 100mm x 100mm posts 3600mm centres
inclined beams (larch) 275mm x 100mm bolted to 100mm x 100mm posts 3600mm centres
275mm x 100mm purlins to south roof at 1500mm centres

Upper Floors
200mm x 38mm timber joists at 600mm centres
timber floorboards
clay bricks 100mm x 140mm x 290mm loose laid onto bearers softwood in the floor void

Floor Finishes
75mm lime-based screed
underfloor heating pipes
slate floor to the entrance hall, dining and living areas
hard paving to external patio area
natural fibre carpet to study bedroom
ceramic tiles
softwood timber floorboards on the first floor

Roof
wood fibre board internal panel
200mm of cellulose fibre insulation (south roof)
double glazed units 1500mm x 3600mm with low-e coating and argon cavity fill
timber insulating shutters with 75mm of insulation
70mm Kalwall® panels on pivot mechanism

Staircases
timber open tread staircase on sliding track mechanism
metal balustrades

Substructure/Ground Floor
soft clay/gravel removed to an average depth of 600mm
mass concrete footings for the timber columns to a depth of 400mm
steel 'shoes' to support the column bases
200mm layer of well-compacted hardcore
50mm of sand binding
100mm of rigid insulation and damp proof membrane
150mm reinforced concrete 'ground slab' (450mm depth thickened at the edges to [...] frost heave).

0   1   2   3m

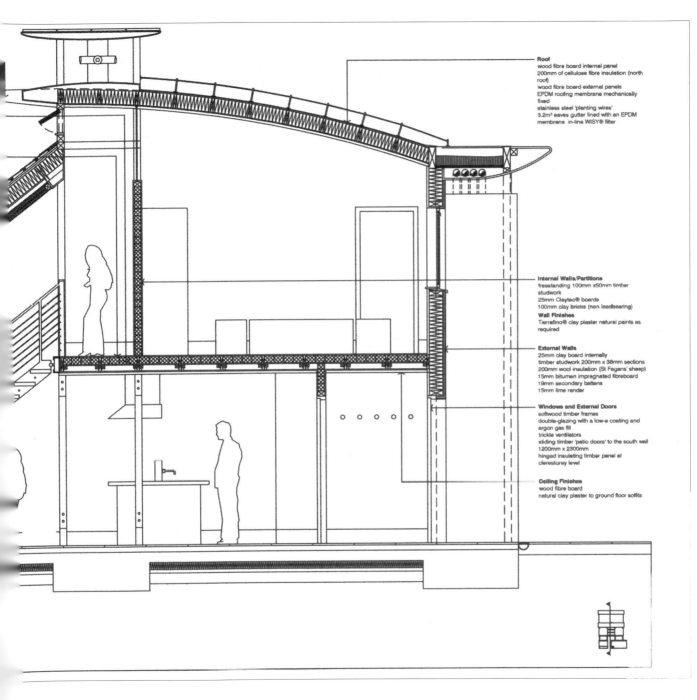

Roof
wood fibre board internal panel
200mm of cellulose fibre insulation (north roof)
wood fibre board external panels
EPDM roofing membrane mechanically fixed
stainless steel 'planting wires'
3.2m³ eaves gutter lined with an EPDM membrane in-line WISY® filter

Internal Walls/Partitions
freestanding 100mm x50mm timber studwork
25mm Claytec® boards
100mm clay bricks (non loadbearing)
Wall Finishes
Tierrafino® clay plaster natural paints as required

External Walls
25mm clay board internally
timber studwork 200mm x 38mm sections
200mm wool insulation (St Fagans' sheep)
15mm bitumen impregnated fibreboard
19mm secondary battens
15mm lime render

Windows and External Doors
softwood timber frames
double-glazing with a low-e coating and argon gas fill
trickle ventilators
sliding timber 'patio doors' to the south wall 1200mm x 2300mm
hinged insulating timber panel at clerestorey level

Ceiling Finishes
wood fibre board
natural clay plaster to ground floor soffits

205

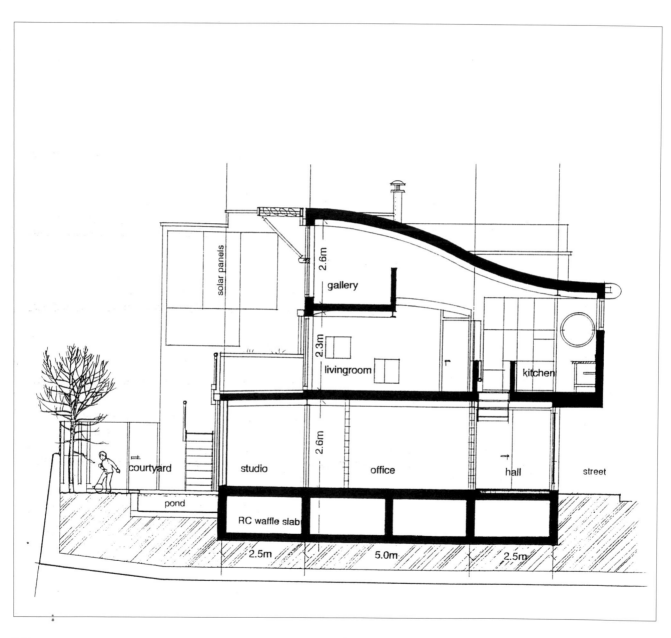

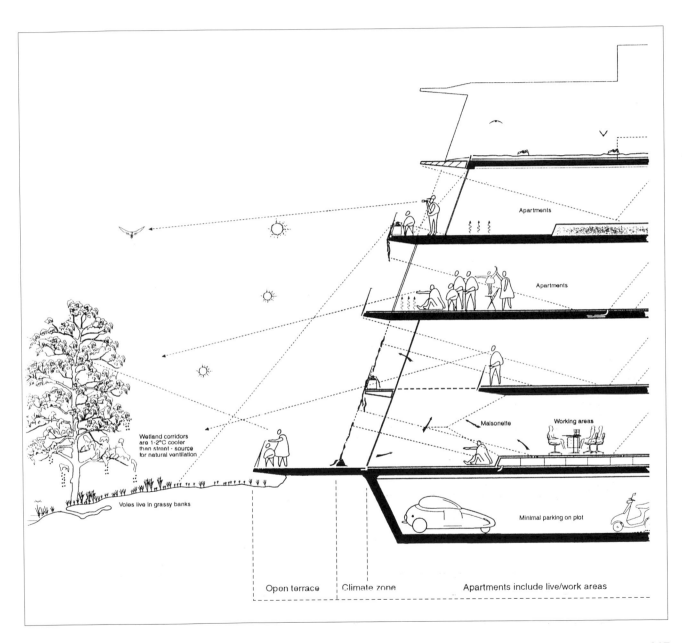

Wetland corridors
are 1-2°C cooler
than street - source
for natural ventilation

Voles live in grassy banks

Apartments

Apartments

Maisonette

Working areas

Minimal parking on plot

Open terrace | Climate zone | Apartments include live/work areas

Measures to Improve Energy Efficiency in the Existing Housing Stock

Existing buildings are central to any strategy for carbon-emission reduction, seeing as we add to our housing stock at a rate of only 2 per cent per year. According to the Energy Savings Trust (EST), 79 per cent of British people claim they have an 'environmental conscience'; however, only 8 per cent consider energy efficiency when they buy a home or appliance [38]. The government target of achieving a 20 per cent reduction in CO_2 emissions by 2010 can be met only by having a better educated public and better informed and motivated construction industry. The EST advocates the following relatively easy measures for people to take with regard to their homes:

- **Lighting:** Use energy-efficient light bulbs. They consume only 25 per cent of the electricity of conventional ones and last up to ten times longer. If all the UK moved to them, the energy saving would pay for all of the country's street lighting.
- **Heating:** Replacing old boilers with modern condensing boilers can save 45 per cent of energy use. Simply maintaining old boilers properly can save 10–15 per cent.
- **Insulation:** Cavity fill insulation to existing buildings can reduce energy loads by 60 per cent. Increasing loft insulation to 50 mm can save 20 per cent on heating bills. Taking all the insulation measures together – cavity fill, loft super-insulation, double glazing using low-E glass (glass with insulating properties) and draught proofing – can avoid the need for conventional heating boilers altogether.
- **Controls:** Adding modern controls to old central heating systems can be highly cost (and energy) efficient. The new controls need to be at both the radiator and the boiler to be most effective.

Energy use per person has grown nearly fourfold over the past 100 years. As a global average, each person in 2000 used energy at a rate of 2.3 kW, compared with 0.6 kW in 1900 [39]. Much of this increase is the result of energy used in existing homes, and so this is where the most effort should be concentrated.

Fig 4.40
Relationship between high-density urban nodes
and railway system in Tokyo.

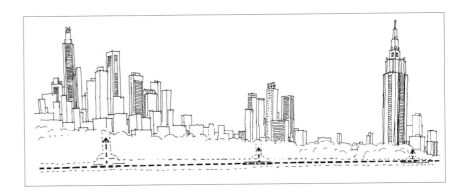

City Form for the 21st Century

Increasing, the density of development in urban areas brings the following advantages:

- it supports public transport better;
- it creates the opportunity to form cohesive neighbourhoods;
- it enhances the urban microclimate; and
- it improves the energy efficiency of buildings.

As density rises, so does physical compaction, which allows heat loss from one building to become the heat gain for another. Greater physical proximity also encourages walking, cycling and the use of public transport.

Fig 4.41
Private transport of the future: the electric car.
Source: Richard Parnaby

The compact, mixed-use city is the only sustainable urban model. However, there are limits to how far things can be improved. For example, commercial buildings need space for cooling and ventilation – over-compaction can lead to an increase in energy use and not the reduction that we see in residential neighbourhoods. As densities increase there is a corresponding reduction in access to renewable energy – sun and wind. Too much physical closeness can reduce daylight in buildings and limit access to solar energy. Over-compact cities can also suffer from air pollution, which has the effect of damaging the health of people and reducing the energy performance of buildings. So, although there are benefits to increased density, these benefits are limited and vary according to climate, land use type, culture and latitude.

From a sustainable development perspective, the ideal city is compact, with well-defined edges and medium-rise buildings that are neither too high nor too low. This is because tall buildings require energy for lifts, they are expensive and difficult to maintain, they cast shadows over the surrounding cityscape, they generate damaging microclimates at their bases, and they puncture the 'heat island bubble'. The best configuration is a high-density, mixed-use, medium-rise urbanism based upon development four to ten storeys high. Taller buildings are best centred on the railway stations and other transport nodes where commercial and retail activities will be concentrated.

Of course, the ideal city will also contain leafy squares and tree-lined streets to bring nature into the heart of the city, purifying the air and uplifting the spirit. The different districts will have their own parks or other green spaces, which will help to stitch together the urban fabric, civilising neighbourhoods. This type of urbanism, once common across Europe from Copenhagen to Barcelona, is the opposite of the typical Western city of the 20th century. Here, buildings are massive and often competitive in form and spirit, and exist in an ill-defined landscape of car parks and low-rise burger bars. The sustainability movement questions the validity of this dispersed city form with its consequent derelict, contaminated, neglected and dangerous urban spaces.

Given that the city for a sustainable future is based on public transport, planning for density of occupation and complexity of movement types will be prerequisites for urban development. People will need to be able to move through the city day and night for purposes as diverse as shopping, leisure, commuting to work and education. The future city will also need inter-modal transport connections – stations which provide smooth access to buses, light railways, taxis and bicycles and which cater for all pedestrians (including disabled people). Such stations will be the urban nodes, and will act as powerful magnets for commerce, recreation, education and culture, all supported by nearby or connected residential areas, giving shape and legibility to the area.

Urban form in the 21st century will consist of a number of such urban nodes dispersed throughout the city. There will in all probability be a single main centre, but sub-centres will exist and compete with it for investment and attention. London is already growing into this form, with Docklands, Hammersmith, Croydon and other areas challenging the centre. Other UK cities are developing

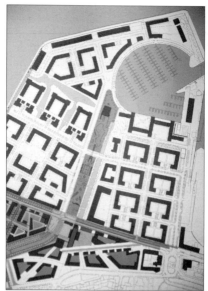

Fig 4.42
Masterplan for the regeneration of the Granton area of Edinburgh by Llewelyn Davies. Notice how the urban blocks open to the south for solar aperture.
Source: Llewelyn Davies

Fig 4.43
Redevelopment of Greenland Dock in London integrates well the old and new neighbourhoods.
Source: Conran Roche

Fig 4.44
Orderly relationship of landscape and city block in San Francisco.

in similar form – Manchester has powerful sub-centres in places such as Salford Quays, and in Edinburgh, Granton is a growth point just outside the traditional commercial core. Each of the new centres is helping to diversify the city while adding to the overall compaction of urban areas. Brownfield sites are exploited and existing buildings recycled. Historic buildings and structures can help enhance a neighbourhood's identity, and where large industrial structures exist, they should be converted to commercial, cultural or residential use.

A city of sub-centres requires a web of connecting tissue. Besides public transport links, there also needs to be linking streets of special quality (not merely roads). These provide both physical connection and psychological linkage; they are the means by which social exchange takes place, and as such they should be seen as exercises in urban design (not traffic engineering), with the major neighbourhood buildings positioned along their length. These memorable streets (such as The Headrow in Leeds or Buchanan Street in Glasgow) link together neighbourhoods of commerce and people.

UK Cabinet Office policies for urban design to create conditions for sustainable living

- Improve the 'liveability' of urban areas
- Promote urban regeneration
- Promote mixed-use, compact development
- Improve access for pedestrians and cyclists
- Concentrate development around public transport nodes

The cities of the UK and the USA are in urgent need of repair (mainland Europe has nurtured its towns better). Urban repair follows naturally from a philosophy of sustainable development since it integrates environmental concerns with social and economic ones. Energy is clearly the overriding environmental concern, especially for building designers, but concern for the human and natural ecology of the city is also important. Rivers, canals, parks, gardens and planted roofs all offer the opportunity to bring nature back into our cities.

As brownfield sites are developed, the city will again achieve its former vibrancy. The trend in places such as Liverpool and the east end of Glasgow has been to

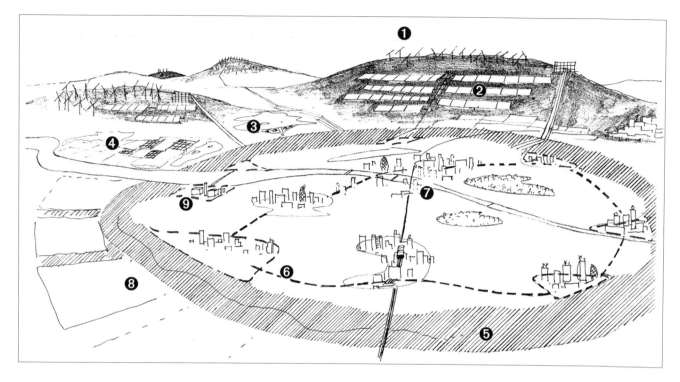

Fig 4.45
The author's vision for Glasgow in 2040:
(1) wind farms, (2) solar power,
(3) hydropower, (4) ecological drainage
systems, (5) urban fringe biomass planting,
(6) tram system, (7) mixed-use dense urban
centre, (8) urban fringe farming and allotments,
(9) combined heat and power.

suburbanise older residential areas. Semi-detached houses have replaced compact terraces or tenements, reducing density from 400 habitable rooms per hectare (HR/H) to about 150. The sustainable ideal is for densities of 500 HR/H, with up to 1,000 HR/H around railway stations or in city centres. These central buildings will need to rise to 10 or 12 storeys before the compact, self-sustaining (in terms of jobs, health care, education, leisure and living) city can emerge.

As densities rise, the concept of a 'collage city', proposed by theorists such as Colin Rowe and Fred Koetter, [40] will become a reality. Rowe and Koetter argue that the complex layering of different compact urban forms over centuries creates not disorder but satisfying convivial cities. Changing aspirations give texture and identity to towns, providing those things which civilisation requires in terms of the art and culture of cities. Sustainable development, with its requirement of density, mixed land use and compaction, could provide another layer to older cities such

Sustainable development design principles

At city level
- Compaction
- Streets reclaimed from traffic
- Increased density in suburban areas
- Intensification of use where areas are well serviced by public transport (nodes and sub-nodes)
- Four-storey housing
- Legibility

At neighbourhood level
- Diverse pattern of land uses
- Safe and friendly streets
- Keep historic buildings
- Cycle routes
- Tram routes/corridors
- Use local energy sources

At local level
- Design with nature (parks, streets, etc.), biodiversity
- Use derelict land/buildings first
- Strengthen green belts and green corridors

At building level
- Design for low environmental impact (locally, regionally, globally)
- Design for durability
- Design for reuse
- Maximise renewable energy use
- Self-sheltering layouts
- Energy management under users' control
- Design with climate
- Design for health
- Learn from vernacular practices

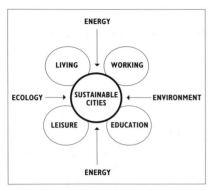

Fig 4.46
Key interactions in sustainable cities.

The challenge today is to resurrect our cities from urban decay by creating a desirable, sustainable, safe and attractive urbanism without discarding the as Rome, Paris or London. For new cities such as Milton Keynes it needs to be the basis, not for the founding layer, but for the structures which colonise it. The imperatives of sustainable design can provide a rich new layer even to new towns that were designed on the assumption of endless supplies of cheap energy. What Rowe and Koetter argue in their influential book, *Collage City*, [41] and which Richard Rogers and Anne Power also acknowledge in *Cities for a Small Country*, [42] is the role that urban typologies play in providing the raw material for civilised cities. The street, terrace, apartment block, square, park, monument and so on are each reinterpreted by successive generations. What makes the concept of sustainable cities different is the way that climate and energy conservation in particular will refashion these urban building blocks. traditional elements of city making. This can be achieved only by recognising that existing buildings are a valuable resource. The key to a more sustainable future lies in transplanting new low-energy systems into existing structures, and designing new buildings with environmental and ecological imperatives to the fore. Walls, windows and roofs already exist in countless buildings; now we need to modify them using green technology developed in new construction. We need to transfer design approaches from the innovative green offices, schools and houses discussed earlier into the inefficient buildings inherited from the past, the so-called eco-retrofit. Without attention being paid to the performance, especially the energy performance, of the existing building stock, the new urbanism promulgated by Rogers and others will fail to bring about an urban renaissance.

Notes

[1] Sunand Prasad, 'Inclusive Maps', in Sebastian Macmillan (ed.), *Designing Better Buildings*, Spon Press, London, 2004, p. 179.

[2] Bill Bordass, 'Cost and value: fact or fiction', *Building Research and Information*, Vol. 28 No. 5/6, pp. 338–52.

[3] *The Architects' Journal*, 26 February 2004, p. 4.

[4] Brian Edwards, *Green Buildings Pay*, 2nd edn, Spon Press, London, 2003, pp. 114–21.

[5] This section adapted from Brian Edwards, 'Benefits of Green Offices in the UK: Analysis from examples built in the 1990s', *Sustainable Development* (13), 2005, pp. 24–40.

[6] G. J. Raw and M. S. Roys, 'Sick Building Syndrome, Productivity and Control', *Property Journal*, August 1993, pp. 17–19. See also 'Healthy Buildings and Their Impact on Productivity', *Indoor Air* '93, Vol. 6, 1993, pp. 41–6, and G. H. Kats, *Green Buildings: Costs and Financial Benefits*, Massachusetts Technology Collaborative, 2003, pp. 5–6.

[7] *op. cit.*, Edwards, *Green Buildings Pay*, 2nd edn, p. 205.

[8] Bill Bordass and Adrian Leaman, 'Building Services in Use: Some Lessons for Briefing, Design and Management', BIFM Annual Conference, London, 17 September 1997.

[9] *op. cit.* Edwards, *Green Buildings Pay*, 2nd edn, pp. 122–57. See also the NHS Estates' *Achieving Excellence: Design Evaluation Toolkit*, Department of Health, London, 2001.

[10] Brian Edwards 'Benefits of Green Offices in the UK: Analysis from examples built in the 1990s'. *Sustainable Development* (13), 2005, p. 29.

[11] Paul Ruyssevelt, 'Design for occupant interaction', Sustainable Architecture Conference, De Montfort University, Leicester, 3 May 2001.

[12] Sir Michael Latham, *Constructing the Team*, HMSO, London, 1994.

[13] Sir John Egan, *Rethinking Construction*, The Construction Task Force, DETR, London, 1998.

[14] Sebastian Macmillan (ed.), *Designing Better Buildings*, Spon Press, London, 2004. p. 3.

[15] *ibid.*, pp. 72–85.

[16] Brian Edwards, *Green Buildings Pay*, 1st edn, Spon Press, London, 1998, pp. 2–23.

[17] Adapted from *op. cit.*, 2nd Edition Edwards, pp. 204–8.

[18] G. H. Kats, *Green Buildings: Costs and Financial Benefits*, Massachusetts Technology Collaborative, 2003, and www.cap-e.com.

[19] Bill Bordass, 'Lessons from post-occupancy surveys', *EcoTech*, Issue 1, March 2000, p. 30.

[20] *ibid.*

[21] *ibid.*, p. 31.

[22] *op.cit.*, Macmillan, pp. 56–8.

[23] *op.cit.* Bordass, p. 31.

[24] *ibid.*

[25] Brian Edwards, 'Institutional Barriers and advantages of designing office buildings to sustainable principles', in *Environmental Policies: Towards Sustainability*, ERP, 1998, pp. 44–8; see also Edwards *Sustainable Development* (13) 2005, p. 30.

[26] *op. cit.*, Kats.

[27] Adapted from *op. cit.*, 2nd Edition Edwards, pp. 149–57.

[28] Sebastian Macmillan, Nick Baker and Michael Buckley, 'Educational Environments', *The Architects' Journal*, 26 February 1998, p. 53. The author has adapted and expanded the list.

[29] www.eco-schools.org.uk

[30] The author is indebted to Macmillan, Baker and Buckley (*op. cit.*) for the analysis of plan types.

[31] Fionn Stevenson and Nick Williams, *Sustainable Housing Design Guide for Scotland*, HMSO, 2000, pp. 9–15. See also for the government view *Sustainable Communities – Delivering Through Planning*, ODPM, 2002.

[32] H. Barton, G. Davis and R. Guise, *Sustainable Settlements: a Guide for Planners, Designers and Developers*, Local Government Management Board, 1995.

[33] *Planning for Sustainable Development: Towards Better Practice* HMSO, 1998. See also Planning Policy Statement 1 (PPS1) and Planning Policy Guidelines (PPG) 3, 6 and 13.

[34] *Towards an Urban Renaissance: Report of the Urban Task Force*, E&FN Spon, 1999.

[35] *General Information Leaflet 31*, Department of the Environment, 1999.

[36] *Standard Assessment Procedure for Energy Rating of Dwellings Practice Note*, DETR, 1998.

[37] Hilary Armstrong, 'Sustainability and Housing: The Government View', in Brian Edwards and David Turrent, *Sustainable Housing*, E&FN Spon, London, 2000, pp. 1–3.

[38] Helen Jones, 'Money for Nothing', *The Guardian*, 26 October 2000, p. 14.

[39] Figures from the Royal Commission on Environmental Pollution, quoted in *The Architects' Journal*, 16 November 2000, p. 16.

[40] Colin Rowe and Fred Koetter, *Collage City*, MIT Press, 1978.

[41] *ibid.*

[42] Richard Rogers and Anne Power, *Cities for a Small Country* (Faber and Faber, 2000). See also Richard Rogers *Design for a Small Planet* (Thames and Hudson, 1995), and *Our Towns and Cities: The Future*, Delivering an Urban Renaissance Urban White Paper, DETR, 2000.

Select Bibliography

- Blewitt, J. and Cullingford, C. (eds), *The Sustainability Curriculum: The Challenge of Higher Education*. Earthscan, 2004.
- Edwards, B. (ed.), *Green Buildings Pay*, 2nd edition, E&FN Spon, 2003.
- Edwards, B. and Turrent, D. (eds), *Sustainable Housing: Principles and Practice*, E&FN Spon, 2000.
- Girardet, H., *The Gaia Atlas of Cities*, Gaia Books, 1992.
- Goulding, J. R. and Lewis, J. O. (eds), *European Directory of Sustainable and Energy-efficient Building*, James and James, 1999.
- Goulding, J. R., Lewis, J. O. and Steemers, T. C. (eds), *Energy Conscious Design: a Primer For Architects*, Commission of the European Communities, 1996.
- Hawken, P., Lovins, A. B. and Lovins, L. H., *Natural Capitalism: the Next Industrial Revolution*, Earthscan, 1999.
- Hawkes, D., *The Environmental Tradition: Studies in the Architecture of Environment*, Spon Press, 1996.
- Rogers, R., *Cities for a Small Planet*, Faber and Faber, 1997.
- Smith, P., *Architecture in a Climate of Change: A Guide to Sustainable Design*. Architectural Press, 2001.
- Smith, P. and Pitts, A. L., *Concepts in Practice: Energy*, Batsford, 1997.
- Stevenson, F. and Williams, N., *Sustainable Housing Design Guide for Scotland*, HMSO, 2000.
- Thomas, R. (ed.), *Environmental Design*, E&FN Spon, 1996.
- Thomas, R. (ed.), *Photovoltaics and Architecture*, Spon Press, 2001.
- *Towards an Urban Renaissance*, Urban Task Force Report, E&FN Spon, 1999.

Index

'Agenda 21', 42, 43
air pollution, 16–17 (*see also* carbon dioxide
     emissions; indoor air quality)
aluminium, 127, 131, 132
Architects Registration Board (ARB), 40, 41, 42,
     45–6, 48
architectural education, 36, 37–51
assessment methods and tools, 94–7, 117–21,
     202–3 (*see also* life-cycle assessment
     (LCA))

Banham, Reyner, 38
bio-mimicry, 13–14
biofuels, 86–9
BRECSU. see Building Research Energy
     Conservation Support Unit
BREDEM. see Building Research Establishment
     Domestic Energy Model
BREEAM. see Building Research Establishment
     Environmental Assessment Method
brick construction, 129, 131
brownfield sites, 138–9, 200
Brundtland Report, 19, 24–5
building density. see density of development
Building Research Energy Conservation Support
     Unit (BRECSU), 182
Building Research Establishment Domestic
     Energy Model (BREDEM), 120, 202–3
Building Research Establishment Environmental
     Assessment Method (BREEAM), 94,
     118, 120–1
building reuse, 22, 135–6
Building Services Research and Information
     Association (BSRIA), 19

'capital', 24–6
carbon conversion, 68, 87
carbon dioxide emissions, 6, 63–4, 66–7, 192
carbon tax, 71
carbon trading, 63, 67, 113
CFCs (chlorofluorocarbons), 144
Citizens' Environment Initiative, 31
climate change, 7–8, 62–7
collage city, 212, 214
combined heat and power (CHP), 89
comfort factors, 141–2, 144–5, 177
concrete, structural, 128, 131, 132, 174

construction materials
     environmental impacts, 121, 123–6
     organic, 149–52
     recycling, 124–5, 136–7
     traditional buildings, 163–4
contaminated land, 138–9
cultural capital, 26
cultural perspectives, 16–18

daylighting, 74, 169
definitions, sustainable development, 19–20
density of development, 192–3, 194, 197–8,
     209–10, 212
Department for Education and Skills (DfES),
     121, 182
design quality indicators (DQIs), 159
Dimbleby, Jonathan, 46–7
district heating, 74, 88
domestic buildings, 120, 191–208

earth products, 149–50
Earth Summit, 90–2, 93
Eco-Management and Audit Schemes (EMAS),
     118
eco-Quantum. see quantum auditing
EcoHomes, 203
ecological accounting, 15
ecological capital, 25
economic benefits, 175–7, 178, 181
economic capital, 24
education for sustainability, 28, 30–2 (*see also*
     architectural education)
Egan Report, 27
embodied energy, 122, 124, 131–2
Emissions Trading Scheme (UK), 71
Emissions Trading System (ETS), 63, 67
energy consumption, 55–7, 166, 169
energy efficiency, 58–62, 89–94, 172, 193–4,
     196, 208
Energy White Paper, 60, 61–2
environmental capital, 25
environmental impacts of buildings, 28, 32–6
     (*see also* resource consumption)
Environmental Management System (EMS),
     118–19

European Union
     Architects' Directive, 41–2
     Energy Performance of Buildings Directive,
       58, 60, 62
     energy policies, 73
     environmental policies and legislation, 43–4,
       71–2
     Landfill Directive, 127
European Window Energy Rating Scheme, 149
Exemplar Schools programme, 182–3

'factor four concept', 6–7
flooding, 34–6
fuel cells, 71–2, 84

geothermal energy, 84–6, 87
glazing, 149, 172
Gordon, Alex, 39
Government Panel on Sustainable
     Development, 31
greenhouse gases, 62–7 (*see also* carbon
     dioxide emissions)
grey water recycling, 106–7

Hague Conference on Climate Change, 21
HCFC (hydrochlorofluorocarbons), 144
health issues, 141–5
housing, 120, 191–208

indicators, 94–7, 159
indoor air quality, 142–4
insulation, organic, 151
international environmental agreements, 8,
     20–1

Johannesburg World Summit on Sustainable
     Development, 20–1, 22

Kyoto Protocol, 63

land reclamation, 138–9
landfill, 126, 127

Layton Report, 40
Leadership in Energy and Environmental Design
    (LEED), 118, 181
'learning from nature', 12–13
LEED. see Leadership in Energy and
    Environmental Design
legislation
    European Union, 41–2, 43–4, 58, 62
    UK, 58, 60–1, 71
Leicester Community CHP Programme, 89
life-cycle assessment (LCA), 113–17, 124, 132
lime mortars, 151
local crafts, 164–5
local materials, 122, 164

M4i (Movement for Innovation), 177–9
materials, construction. see construction
    materials
Matthew, Sir Robert, 41
McHarg, Ian, 12–13
methane emmisions, 66
microclimate design, 200–1
mixed-use development, 197–8

natural capital, 6–7, 26
natural cooling, 174
natural habitats, 33
natural lighting, 74, 169
natural ventilation, 146–9
nature as design guide, 11–15

office buildings, 120–1, 166–81
organic insulation, 151
orientation of buildings, 170, 172
Oxford Conference on Architectural Education,
    38–9

paints, water-based, 152
passive solar design, 72–3, 194
photovoltaics, 74–82
pollution, building-related, 18 (see also air
    pollution)
Post-occupancy Review of Buildings and their
    Engineering (PROBE), 179–81

quantum auditing, 15, 115–16

radon, 144
recycling
    materials, 124–5, 136–7, 165–6
    water, 106–7
renewable energy, 55–7, 68, 69–88
residential buildings, 120, 191–208
resource consumption, 6–7 (see also
    construction materials; energy
    consumption)
    in buildings, 17, 22–3
    reducing, 134
reuse of buildings, 22, 135–6
RIBA
    professional education, 38, 39, 42, 46, 48
    professional standards, 40
    Sustainable Futures Committee, 42
Rocky Mountain Institute, 6–7
Rogers, Richard, 46

SAM. see Sustainability Assessment Model
SAP. see Standard Assessment Procedure for
    Energy Rating of Dwellings (SAP)
school buildings, 121, 182–91
Schools Environmental Assessment Method
    (SEAM), 118, 121, 123
social capital, 24
solar design, 72–4, 170, 172–3, 194
solar power, 56, 72–82
solar water heating, 74
Standard Assessment Procedure for Energy
    Rating of Dwellings (SAP), 203
standards (see also assessment methods and
    tools)
    building, 59, 60–1, 149, 182
    professional, 40, 41, 45–6
steel, structural, 127, 131–3
stone, 151
Sustainability Assessment Model (SAM), 117–18
sustainable development, definitions, 19–20
Sustainable Development Education Panel,
    31–2
Sustainable Futures Committee (RIBA), 42

tall buildings, 210
technological capital, 24–5
timber construction, 128–9, 151
Toyne Report, 44, 50
traditional architecture, 162–6
traditional materials, 149–51
transport issues, 132, 164, 197, 210–11

UK Building Regulations, 59, 60–1, 149
UK government policies
    energy policy, 58, 60–1
    sustainable development, 9, 27, 29, 140,
        160, 211
UN Earth Summit, 42–3
UN Environment Commission, Brundtland
    Report, 19, 24–5
UNESCO, 30
Union of International Architects, 45
upgrading existing buildings, 208
urban design, 137–8, 200–1, 209–14
Urban Task Force, 46
user satisfaction, 145, 179–81

vernacular buildings, 162–6
VOCs (volatile organic compounds), 142

Waste and Emissions Trading Act 2003, 127
waste, construction, 126–7
water conservation, 16–17, 97–108
water recycling, 106–7
wind power, 83–4
windcatchers, 146–8
window design, 149 (see also glazing)
wood construction. see timber construction
wood fuel, 86–8
World Summit on Sustainable Development,
    20–1, 22, 55